RETHINKING
THE PENTATEUCH

RETHINKING THE PENTATEUCH

Prolegomena to the Theology of Ancient Israel

Antony F. Campbell, SJ
and
Mark A. O'Brien, OP

WJK WESTMINSTER
JOHN KNOX PRESS
LOUISVILLE • KENTUCKY

Book design by Sharon Adams
Cover design by Lisa Buckley

First edition
Published by Westminster John Knox Press
Louisville, Kentucky

This book is printed on acid-free paper that meets the American National Standards Institute Z39.48 standard. ♾

PRINTED IN THE UNITED STATES OF AMERICA

05 06 07 08 09 10 11 12 13 14 — 10 9 8 7 6 5 4 3 2 1

Library of Congress Cataloging-in-Publication Data is on file at the Library of Congress, Washington, D.C.

ISBN 0-664-22809-7

*Dedicated to all
whose faith is deepened through exploring
their Scriptures*

"While it [the Bible] is certainly the end product of a long and complex editorial process, the end product needs to be examined in its own right."
Northrop Frye, *The Great Code*, xvii.

"Genesis is no doubt made up of many strands of tradition, but what is important is how these have been blended together."
Gabriel Josipovici, *The Book of God*, 72–73.

"No clear-cut truths are to be found among these pages because they do not, yet, exist. I hope, however, there will be a great deal that is thought-provoking and useful."
Babette Rothschild, *The Body Remembers*, xvi.

"The only certainty is that nothing is certain."
Pliny, *Natural History*.

"As simple as possible, but no simpler."
(from a saying often attributed to Einstein)

Contents

Acknowledgment   ix

Abbreviations   x

Preface   xiii

1   Introduction   1

2   Evidence   11

3   Outcome   25
   Outcome in Genesis A: Nature of Humanity   26
   Outcome in Genesis B: Ancestors of Israel   30
   Outcome in Genesis C: The Joseph Story and Associated Text
     (Genesis 37–50)   60
   Outcome in Exodus–Numbers: Core of Israel's Experience   68
   Outcome in Deuteronomy: Ideal for Israel   97
   Outcome Overall   100

4   Conclusion   103
   Envoi   105

APPENDIXES

Appendix 1   Two Intensive Studies   107
      "P" and Genesis One   107
      "P" and Genesis 1–11   111

Appendix 2   Two Examples   117
      Genesis 12–13   117
      Genesis 18–19   119

Appendix 3   Two Exceptions   123
              Flood Text (Genesis 6–9)   123
              Sea Text (Exodus 14)   124

Appendix 4   Analysis of the Text
              Genesis–Exodus; Numbers 1–24   127

              Bibliography   157

INDEXES

Scripture Index   163

Author Index   173

Subject Index   177

Acknowledgment

This book took a long time finding its shape;
its final form did not come easily.
We would like to thank all those involved,
above all the people at Westminster John Knox,
and especially Stephanie Egnotovich,
without whose patient commitment
it would not be what it is.

Abbreviations

(Appendix 4 is not included.)

AB	Anchor Bible
ABD	*Anchor Bible Dictionary*
BDB	Brown, Driver, Briggs: *A Hebrew and English Lexicon of the Old Testament*
BETL	Bibliotheca ephemeridum theologicarum lovaniensium
BHS	*Biblica Hebraica Stuttgartensia*
BHT	Beiträge zur historischen Theologie
BJS	Brown Judaic Studies
BKAT	Biblischer Kommentar, Altes Testament
BZAW	Beihefte sur Zeitschrift für die alttestamentliche Wissenschaft
CBA	Catholic Biblical Association of America
CBQ	*Catholic Biblical Quarterly*
CBQMS	Catholic Biblical Quarterly Monograph Series
D	basically, the book of Deuteronomy
DBAT	*Dielheimer Blätter zum Alten Testament*
dtn	Deuteronomic = associated with Deuteronomy and the Deuteronomic reform
dtr	Deuteronomistic = associated with the Deuteronomistic History
E	the hypothetical Elohist and text attributed to E
ExN	Exodus Narrative
FOTL	Forms of the Old Testament Literature
FRLANT	Forschungen zur Religion und Literatur des Alten und Neuen Testaments
Heb.	Hebrew = Masoretic Text
Int	Interpretation
J	the hypothetical Yahwist and text attributed to J

JBL	*Journal of Biblical Literature*
JPS	Jewish Publication Society, *The Holy Scriptures* (1955)
JSOT	*Journal for the Study of the Old Testament*
JSOTSup	Journal for the Study of the Old Testament: Supplement Series
KD	Erhard Blum's Deuteronomic/Deuteronomistic composition level in the Pentateuch
MdB	*Le Monde de la Bible*
NCB	New Century Bible
OBO	Orbis biblicus et orientalis
OTL	Old Testament Library
P	the hypothetical Priestly Writer (or group of writers) and text attributed to P
SaN	Sanctuary Narrative
UTB	Uni-Taschenbücher
VT	*Vetus Testamentum*
WBC	Word Biblical Commentary
WMANT	Wissenschaftliche Monographien zum Alten und Neuen Testament
ZAW	*Zeitschrift für die alttestamentliche Wissenschaft*

Preface

The radically new can be upsetting and difficult to absorb; it may upset what we have been used to for generations. If a new insight is simple and solves troubling problems, it may be welcome, although it may still be upsetting, because what we may have taken for granted for so long is suddenly up for rethinking.

In this book, we propose a radically new insight that eliminates the documentary sources from the Pentateuch altogether: it is the possibility that, in ancient Israel, some biblical narrative was created as a base for users to begin from, a base for storytellers to expand and select from, rather than a completed product to be received by readers or others. This insight can radically simplify apparent complexity in the Pentateuch.

"Radically new" is a big claim to make. Continuous sources—such as the Yahwist, Elohist, and Priestly Document, perhaps reconfigured as traditions or editions and so on—have been part of the mainstay of pentateuchal studies for two or three centuries (involved even in the fragmentary and supplementary hypotheses). To claim that the Pentateuch is better understood if such continuous sources are dispensed with is a big claim. It is radically new. It is the claim that this book makes.

The radically new is never easily understood; the inherited structures of the old stand in the way. Biblical text has been understood for a long time as destined for an end-reader; a change of perception is not easy. Continuous sources have been around for a long time; unsatisfactory though they have become, dispensing with them is not easy. We do not believe, however, that the evidence leaves us any choice but to present our proposal as a possibility for evaluation.

Radically new is the acknowledgment that some biblical narrative was created as a base for users to begin from, coupled with the acceptance that the variant versions of traditions and stories—present in the biblical texts—could have been preserved for selection by the users of those texts in ancient times (as well as still being available for today's users to choose among). Hence we propose the designation "text-as-base-for-user" approach ("user-base" for short); many texts are bases for users.

In this area of biblical scholarship, intelligence is not to be confined almost exclusively to nineteenth-century moderns; a modicum of intelligence must be allowed to users in first-millennium Israel. Israel's authors and editors have just as much right to be reckoned intelligent as many modern biblical scholars. The old assumption that unevenness in a text was adequately explained by editorial intervention or editorial clumsiness is no longer as widespread as it used to be. With the approach assumed here, many narrative texts may be understood as possible bases for intelligent use. The result is a radically simpler and more theologically fruitful approach to the Pentateuch than has been possible in recent decades. The presence of variants and the like in the biblical text has long been known; that these should have been at the service of ancient users opens the way to simplicity and new understanding.

In this book we provide, first, in two core chapters, the theoretical underpinning for what is radically new in this approach (ch. 2: Evidence) and the outline of an outcome from the application of this approach to the understanding of the Pentateuch—outline, because it is necessarily brief; only *an* outcome, because others may see the outcome differently (ch. 3: Outcome). Second, in four appendixes, we offer two intensive studies looking at the principal evidence for the absence of any "P" source in Gen 1–11 (appendix 1), two examples illustrating succinctly how this approach can be helpful with difficult aspects of Gen 12–13 and 18–19 (appendix 2), brief comments on the Flood and Reed Sea texts (appendix 3), and, finally, the chapter and verse analysis, with discussion, for understanding the texts in Genesis, Exodus, and the first part of Numbers (appendix 4).

The difficulty involved in grasping the radically new can be seen from the case of the Yahwist Narrative. Julius Wellhausen remarked that when traditions from prehistory are gathered, the ordering of the material has to come from elsewhere; it is not part of the traditions themselves. Quite right. To this, Christoph Levin added—in arguably the best and most thorough and also the most recent major study of the Yahwist—that the emergence of the present text is unimaginable ("nicht vorstellbar") without an initial editing creating the base for the sequence of the Tetrateuch.[1] Quite wrong. Understandable, perhaps, against the background of a widely shared faith stance; but, in the light of deeper critical reflection, it is not so at all—careful plans and designs can be built up over time. In these broad areas, we are dealing at best with the possible; we seldom have the luxury of certainty, of the "unimaginable." The compiling of what is now the biblical text can have begun in what is now the middle (with the Mosaic exodus that constituted Israel as a people) and moved out from there.

Imagine an endangered Israel encouraged by an account of the exodus from Egypt, beginning with Moses; it is certainly possible—but the Yahwist is thought to have begun back in the Garden, not at the beginning of Israel. *Imagine* com-

---

1. C. Levin, *Der Jahwist*, FRLANT 157 (Göttingen: Vandenhoeck & Ruprecht, 1993), 9.

bining this account with a priestly version of the exodus tradition, again beginning with Moses but ending at Sinai with the sanctuary story; it is certainly possible—but Yahwist and Priestly traditions are not supposed to have been united
until a late compilation. *Imagine* combining the ancestral traditions of north
(Jacob) and south (Abraham) to provide a background for the Moses traditions;
it is certainly possible—but the Yahwist Narrative is not thought of that way.
Imagine using a Joseph story for a late link between ancestors and Egypt; it is certainly possible—but in the Yahwist the Joseph story is not thought of as Diaspora literature. *Imagine* placing stories about humanity at the beginning of
Genesis as a context for it all; it is certainly possible—but these stories are thought
of as the beginning of the Yahwist, not a late stage in the compilation. The possibilities are many; the certainties are few. The weight of the patterns of thought
associated with the idea of the Yahwist or of continuous sources gets in the way
constantly; a change of perception is not easy.[2]

In large part, we cannot be sure how in ancient Israel much of the biblical narrative text was understood. Ben Sirach's praise of the famous begins with Enoch,
not Adam (Sir 44:16; and see 49:16 ["the splendor of Adam"!—Hebrew]).
David's supporters understood the Davidic narratives quite differently from
Saul's (e.g., Shimei ben Gera [2 Sam 16:5–8]). We can be sure, however, that the
final text of a major section such as the Pentateuch could have been the end product of more than one process of growth and compilation. Stages along the way
may have reflected only parts of what became the final product, the present biblical text. Passages may not have been understood in the same way in a different
context. As we noted above, "in these broad areas, we are dealing at best with the
possible; we seldom have the luxury of certainty, of the 'unimaginable.'" In this
domain, the final product is a clamp for many on their freedom of imagination.

---

2. As Rolf Knierim commented when shown a draft of this book, "Ja, Tony, in my day it was
possible for us to learn about the structures (J, E, D, P) *before* we were introduced to the method of
exegesis."

Chapter 1

Introduction

"If it ain't broke, don't fix it" is good advice. But if it is broke, something needs to be done about it. The "it" here is the Documentary Hypothesis as a solution to problems in the Pentateuch. The problems are still there; the Documentary Hypothesis is no longer solving them. A fix is needed.[1]

The Documentary Hypothesis is a catchall name covering the many proposals that emerged to cope with the belief that the positing of two or more sources could perhaps explain puzzling features of the Pentateuch. It began with the realization that coherent narratives emerged when the text of the Pentateuch was divided along the lines of the two names for God present in it—*elohim* and *yhwh*. Explorers looked for truth; traditionalists feared for faith.

---

1. A sensitive treatment of the collapse and some of its implications is given by Jon D. Levenson, "The Hebrew Bible, the Old Testament, and Historical Criticism," in *The Future of Biblical Studies: The Hebrew Scriptures*, ed. R. E. Friedman and H. G. M. Williamson (Atlanta: Scholars Press, 1987), 19–59. In North America, the failure has been increasingly recognized for some time. For Europe, see the remarkably honest and revealing opening paragraph of Reinhard Kratz's *Die Komposition der erzählenden Bücher des Alten Testaments*, UTB 2157 (Göttingen: Vandenhoeck & Ruprecht, 2000)—a move at the perception or paradigm level is needed.

Duality was easy to find: for example, two different passages on creation (Gen 1:1–2:4a and 2:4b–25), at least two sets of data on the flood (within Gen 6:5–9:17), two covenants with Abraham (Gen 15 and 17), two dismissals for Hagar (Gen 16 and 21), and so much more, especially in the detail. The reflectively repetitive nature of Hebrew expression made finding duality relatively simple. Closer attention to the results revealed problems in this sort of distribution. Material attributed to one source, using the term *elohim*, needed to be spread over two sources (one early, the Elohist; the other late, the Priestly Document). The problems multiplied; so did the proposals to resolve them. What had seemed simple became complex. Some of the explorers began to doubt some of the discoveries.

The growth of doubt and dissatisfaction with the various forms of the Documentary Hypothesis covers a long period of time and a number of scholars.[2] At least three factors played a role. First, instead of providing hoped-for certainty about the past, proposals were seen to be no more than possible and hypothetical; fragmentary and supplementary hypotheses were developed, along with older and newer source hypotheses. Second, the lists of features identifying sources were found to apply in limited contexts but not for entire sources. Third, the desire to maintain continuity demanded unnecessary fragmentation of text; acceptable repetition was distributed across sources to provide continuity. Further precision led to further fragmentation (cf., for example, Gen 21; 28; Exod 16; 19).

When individual texts are seen as bases for reflection or storytelling, preserving variant views and traditions, the issue of source continuity is no longer a problem—it is not needed. Attention can be given to the meaning of the text rather than the hypothetical proposal, to the expression of the text rather than the listed features, to the potential power of stylistic unity rather than the disunity needed for continuous sources (i.e., in order to provide the material for separate sources). Emphasis shifts from the later combination of these sources (probably to preserve both past and people) to the initial creation of individual texts, often including varying views and traditions, to serve as bases for users to operate from (whether then or now).

The year 1678 saw the publication of Richard Simon's *Histoire critique du Vieux Testament* (*Critical History of the OT*). An Oratorian, he paid through loss of the membership of his congregation. Hennig Bernhard Witter, in 1711, moved beyond Simon. In 1753 came the (wisely) anonymous publication by Jean Astruc, physician at the French court, entitled *Conjectures sur les mémoires originaux dont il paroit que Moyse s'est servi, pour composer le livre de la Genèse* (*Conjectures on the original documents [more literally: memoirs] that Moses seems to have used to compose the book of Genesis*). Astruc used the names *elohim* and *yhwh* to identify his sources A and B; the complexity is visible already in that Astruc

2. For a summary presentation, see Antony F. Campbell and Mark A. O'Brien, *Sources of the Pentateuch: Texts, Introductions, Annotations* (Minneapolis: Fortress, 1993), 1–20. For more extensive and detailed histories, see below.

needed a further source C, with eight subunits.[3] Specialist histories adequately detail the past; there is no need to rehearse it again here.[4]

Ultimately, these efforts identified Yahwist, Elohist, and Priestly sources, along with Deuteronomy. A little less than a century and a half after Astruc, Julius Wellhausen put his authoritative stamp on the sequence Yahwist (J), Elohist (E), Deuteronomy (D), and Priestly (P). Although this general theory is now largely seen as unhelpful, the sequence and associated habits (such as speaking of a Yahwist or a Priestly Writer) tend to remain. Wellhausen spoke mostly of JE, the combination of Yahwist and Elohist (the Jehovist), rather than of a Yahwist and Elohist, and later trends of research have borne him out. On another level, Wellhausen's predilections were clear and unfortunate: The "Jehovistic history-book . . . is essentially of a narrative character, and sets forth with full sympathy and enjoyment the materials handed down by tradition."[5] The Priestly Document, on the other hand, he argued "is distinguished by its liking for number, and measure, and formula generally, by its stiff-pedantic style."[6] Later in the book Wellhausen is much more contemptuous and scathing—insensitively and injudiciously so. Among the characteristics of P, Wellhausen perceives a taste for barren names and numbers and technical descriptions, an indescribable pedantry, a very passion for classifying and drawing plans; P selects a long-drawn expression wherever he can; he does not weary of repeating for the hundredth time what is a matter of course; what is interesting is passed over, what is of no importance is described with minuteness; his exhaustive clearness with its numerous details confuses our apprehension of what is in itself perfectly clear. This puts the Priestly Code "on the same line with the Chronicles and the other literature of Judaism which labors at an artificial revival of the older tradition."[7] Other scholars from around the time can be just as appalling. Empathy for the priestly undertaking is eminently absent.

Many of those who have brought to the surface the latent dissatisfaction with the documentary hypothesis are by nature not well disposed toward the traditional idea

3. See H. J. Kraus, *Geschichte der historisch-kritischen Erforschung des Alten Testaments*, 2nd ed. (Neukirchen-Vluyn: Neukirchener Verlag, 1956/69), 65–70 (Simon) and 96–97 (Astruc). See also Joseph Blenkinsopp, *The Pentateuch: An Introduction to the First Five Books of the Bible* (London: SCM, 1992), 3. Simon's book is available in a 1685 edition from Rotterdam; Astruc's work fortunately survived, under the (false) imprint Brussels: Fricx, 1753. For details, see the bibliography.

4. In English, see for example: Blenkinsopp, *Pentateuch*, 1–30; Douglas A. Knight, "The Pentateuch," in *The Hebrew Bible and Its Modern Interpreters*, ed. D. A. Knight and G. M. Tucker (Philadelphia: Fortress, 1985), 263–96; Herbert F. Hahn, *The Old Testament in Modern Research*, with a survey of recent literature by H. D. Hummel (Philadelphia: Fortress, 1966); Ernest W. Nicholson, *The Pentateuch in the Twentieth Century: The Legacy of Julius Wellhausen* (Oxford: Clarendon Press, 1998); John Rogerson, *Old Testament Criticism in the Nineteenth Century: England and Germany* (London: SPCK, 1984); John Van Seters, *The Pentateuch: A Social-Science Commentary* (Sheffield: Sheffield Academic Press, 1999), 30–86; R. N. Whybray, *The Making of the Pentateuch: A Methodological Study*, JSOTSup 53 (Sheffield: Sheffield Academic Press, 1987), 17–219. In German, above all, Kraus, *Geschichte der historisch-kritischen Erforschung.*

5. J. Wellhausen, *Prolegomena to the History of Ancient Israel*, Meridian Books (Cleveland: World Publishing, 1957, 7. German original, 1883).

6. Wellhausen, *Prolegomena*, 6. In what follows, the language is taken from Wellhausen.

7. Wellhausen, *Prolegomena*, 350–51.

of sources. They have done a major service to modern biblical scholarship; as Rolf Rendtorff remarked once in conversation: "I put the cat among the pigeons; should I do more?" Put the cat among the pigeons he certainly did, aided and abetted by many others; pigeon fanciers now need to learn from cat lovers. The latter, however, are not always constitutionally suited to navigate some of the issues. Outcomes may differ radically when the focus shifts from the older source critics' question, "What are the possibilities for disunity here?" to explore more recent insights—such as the role of literary style in apparently repetitive text, the probability of intelligent users and editors, the focus on narrative unity rather than division and fragmentation.

Interpretation never comes out of a vacuum. It is helpful to look back over the generations of scholars for some sense of the energies that drove their exploration of biblical text. As the views of writers like Simon and Astruc became more widely known, there had to be a genuine excitement that, when lined up with the divine names (*elohim* and *yhwh*), the various repetitions and overlapping in the Pentateuch fell into something akin to source documents. Most moderns take for granted that P, with its meticulous legislation, dates around the time of exile when a sense of stability was desperately needed. At the start of modern pentateuchal research, however, this was not taken for granted; instead, P was seen at the beginning of it all, deriving from God on Mount Sinai. The names of Graf and Wellhausen are associated with the final stages that located P at the end of the list rather than at its beginning.

Factors beyond the purely exegetical are harder to pin down. Occasional comments in contemporary correspondence of nineteenth-century scholars hint at resistance to the stultifying effect of political and social piety. Probably present, given the age's surge of scientific discovery, but for now undocumented, would have been a felt need for scientific stringency in biblical studies in reaction to the unscientific naivety often perceived in biblical text and its believers.

The increasingly stringent march of biblical research advanced relentlessly, exploiting every possibility, seldom asking whether what was possible was also necessary (i.e., whether what literary analysis identified as possible had ever actually happened in the real realm). Criticism of this "stringent march" came to be expressed on at least two levels. First, at the level of theory, homogeneity and continuity are required of a pentateuchal source; these were not found to be satisfactorily assured. Other theoretical issues were raised. Second, in more practical terms, complaints were leveled at the unnecessary fragmentation of otherwise unified text. In too many cases, it seemed that the major justification for such fragmentation was the need to reconstruct earlier sources. Similarly, critics complained that, when it came down to detailed analysis, objective results were unobtainable, and scholars differed widely in the outcomes of their work.

One of the epigraphs at the head of this book remarks: "While it [the Bible] is certainly the end product of a long and complex editorial process, the end product needs to be examined in its own right."[8] For a long time, biblical scholarship

---

8. Northrop Frye, *The Great Code: The Bible and Literature* (New York: Harcourt Brace Jovanovich, 1982), xvii.

was imprisoned in an iron mask of its own donning—the quest for history. The "long and complex editorial process," becoming evident only slowly, generated an intense scholarly excitement that may have veiled flaws in the historical-critical process. In turn, evidence of the flaws has come only slowly. Habits of mind formed over many years do not disappear overnight, no matter how strong the impact of the recent deconstruction of modernity evident, not quite simultaneously, in art, music, and literature (i.e., modernity with its myths of inevitable progress and perfectibility).

In recent years, complaints about the Documentary Hypothesis have been many; alternative proposals have been few. Our move toward an alternative proposal for understanding the signals in the text benefits from three new understandings: (1) the composite priestly materials themselves are unlikely to have been shaped by a single hand (the shift from "he" to "they");[9] (2) the Bible's narrative texts do not record the performance of a story but prepare for it and preserve alternative versions, from which storytellers could choose. The alternatives preserved (doublets, repetitions, etc.), therefore, need not reflect continuous sources; (3) the alternation of the divine names *elohim* and *yhwh* can be accounted for better and more flexibly than by identifying with putative sources.

What we propose here is a complementary alternative, not an obligatory replacement. The classical documentary hypothesis may be "broke"; whether it is beyond repair is a question we do not try to answer. Unquestionably the pentateuchal text is "the end product of a long and complex editorial process"; it is highly likely that there is more than one way of understanding the process that produced it, as well as more than one way of responding to the text that it has produced. We seek responsibly to propose one possibility, but not to exclude others. We do assert that the understanding proposed here is responsible; we do not assert that it is exclusive.

To take this "responsible possibility" seriously, it is helpful to look at the possibilities on the horizon at present:

1. New insights may rescue and revive the basics of the Documentary Hypothesis.
2. Users may continue to abandon the quest for the past to focus exclusively on the final or present text (i.e., the biblical text we have today). If so, however, it is important to restrict observations to the phenomena in the text and refrain from importing matters such as authorship within the wider text, authorial intention within specific passages, and so on.
3. The proposal we advance here in *Rethinking the Pentateuch*.
4. Other possibilities yet to be put forward.

---

9. It is one thing to agree, as many do, that the Priestly Document is a composite work, for example, J. P. Hyatt: "many scholars have recognized inconsistencies and other evidences of its composite nature" (*Exodus*, NCB [London: Oliphants, 1971], 21–22); unfortunately, many scholars have not recognized that it is something quite different to avoid treating P as though dealing with a single theological mind or attitude.

Properly understood as a "possibility," this proposal is not merely a hypothesis as to what was once in the past, but a possibility for what might have been and still is a legitimate understanding and use of the text.

Three presuppositions are involved in this proposal. While we discuss them in detail below, they should be noted briefly here. First, texts were written for users, as a base for operations, and allowed for variants and a role for storytellers (and other users).[10] Second, characteristics attributed to P (reflecting the author) might instead be attributable to the subject matter (reflecting the topic). Third, the variation of divine names (*elohim* and *yhwh*) can be accounted for in more than one way.

The first presupposition (that texts were written for users, as a base for operations, and allowed for variants) is important enough to be developed a little further here. It involves a paradigm shift that is discussed below. Writers with their contemporary users in mind—users in ancient times who mediated the texts to others—might have given great importance to providing variant versions of a story, or offering options for its telling, or even noting the presence of contradictory views on issues significant to the ancient community. Many readers today tend not to look to the Bible for entertainment or diversion. For a long time, such readers and users have expected biblical texts to inform them about reality; variants, therefore, had little place. However, for users in ancient times, who might mediate texts to others, variants may have been essential for truth. When more than one story has been told, when more than one view has been held, truth may require that these variants be preserved in some way. A change in our attitudes may be required today.

In the main, we are used to text being written for readers. In the days before printing, that was not so; text was composed for users. For most of today's readers, it is quite an adjustment to imagine text being composed as a base for users to operate from. Analogies may help. Part of the way down the track are scriptwriters who write for actors. The dramatist may write the words; a great deal is contributed to them in performance by the actor. Actors, or their directors, will adjust, abbreviate, or extend texts as they believe the occasion demands. Further down the track are composers who write music for performance. The notes of a score give a base and guidelines for performers. The music is then created as the performance. "Music making" is not an empty phrase.

Such a change of attitude requires us to allow for and imagine a particular stage in the process between experience and final text. The writer creates a text where the relevant traditions are presented to the ancient user for selection and articulation. At that point, the text is a *base* from which the early user may begin

---

10. See Antony F. Campbell, SJ, "The Storyteller's Role: Reported Story and Biblical Text," *CBQ* 64 (2002): 427–41. "Users" is intended to embrace the wide range of people who use a text for storytelling, reading, study, prayer, liturgy, preaching, theological reflection, elaborating church or state policies, advising kings, advocating reforms, and so on. Preaching is a major recent use of shorter narrative texts; before the emergence of the synagogue, no appropriate institutional infrastructure in early Israel is known to us.

the process of articulating a particular telling of Israel's traditions, in a given situation. Of course, such a base draws on past traditions and past tellings; but precisely as base—rather than a record of performance—it is the launching platform for a fresh version of the telling. At a much later point, as the text has become canonical, it is turned over to the end-user for understanding and interpretation as well as other uses. At the earlier stage, the text is not the end product of a process but the base for the beginning of a process.

It seems apparent that Older Testament texts were created in the service of a number of functions. We may note some examples, without attempting to be exhaustive: (a) A storyteller might select one option from a text that offered several and then tell the story at some length according to the selected option. We may assume storytellers developed a repertoire, collections of stories and variants. (b) A royal counselor or policymaker might reflect on the actions narrated and their consequences and give wise advice on a course of action to be taken. (c) A theologian might note the options preserved in a text and discuss what each implied or what the preservation of contrasting views meant.[11] (d) A teacher might use texts in a variety of situations. Further examples could be adduced.

The Documentary Hypothesis provided a model within which past generations could account for elements of the pentateuchal text perceived as intractable. Many speculative proposals were advanced, but the framework of the model was considered solid. Now, however, we can recognize that extensive pentateuchal sources are not needed, that smaller sections of text can be interpreted in their own right, for their own meaning, and we provide an alternative model within which the development of the Pentateuch can be envisaged.

In this alternative model we propose: first, an understanding of Genesis grouped around four points ([1] stories of humanity, perhaps of late origin; [2] an Abraham cycle; [3] a Jacob cycle; [4] a Joseph story); second, an analysis of Exodus and Numbers that is grouped around two narratives of the exodus from Egypt (both beginning with a call of Moses; one ending after the Reed Sea, and the other ending with the construction of the sanctuary in Exod 40); third, an understanding of Deuteronomy as an exhortation to the ideal of human living (congruent with the ideal world outlined in Genesis One). These developments are discussed below. The identification of the full text is laid out in appendix 4— that is, Gen 1–Exod 40 and Num 1–24.

It is important to keep an open mind about the manner of Israel's knowledge of its past. We use formulas like "Abraham family traditions," "tradition pool" (the wealth of traditions shaping Israel's perceptions of its past), and so on. Whether any of these were written documents, fixed traditions, or fluctuating memories are questions that here we prescind from. In some cases, it is possible

---

11. This would provide revered ancestry for Jon Levenson's observation that midrash collections, the Rabbinic Bible, and most of the Talmud, one way or another, have "majority and minority positions both preserved and often unmarked" ("Why Jews Are Not Interested in Biblical Theology," in *Judaic Perspectives on Ancient Israel*, ed. J. Neusner, B. A. Levine, and E. S. Frerichs [Philadelphia: Fortress, 1987], 281–307, see p. 300).

to mount arguments for one position or another. Within the limited scope of this book, we have not judged it appropriate to do so.

CONSEQUENCES

The consequences of this alternative model are considerable, among them:

1. Within the pentateuchal text, the focus of this approach on the nature of the text as sometimes a base for operations allows for the recognition of greater unity within the present text, less fragmentation of it, and an improved understanding of its potential function.
2. The Yahwist (J) and Priestly Writer (P), and indeed the Elohist (E— if still given credence), disappear from the scene.
3. Behind the present text of Genesis, the focus on ancestral unity coexists with traces of the diversity of the ancestral traditions.
4. The blending of these ancestral traditions into an affirmed unity is seen to have come quite late. This has implications in relation to the Rebekah material. A similar late dating is assumed for the Joseph story.
5. The difference of structures in the narrative of the plagues allows for the identification of two sources. The Exodus Narrative (beginning with the Exod 3 call of Moses) extends no further than the Song of Moses after the experience at the Sea (Exod 15). The Sanctuary Narrative (beginning with the Exod 6 call of Moses) ends with the completion of the sanctuary (Exod 40).
6. What is now associated with Sinai, in terms of a preceding narrative, is a relatively late creation, focused on the sanctuary constructed there. The Decalogue complex (Exod 19–24) appears to be an independent unit, not evidently attached to any early narrative thread.
7. The understanding of Genesis One (Gen 1:1–2:4a) as an image of an ideal world is appropriately balanced by Deuteronomy as an exhortation to living ideally.
8. With Genesis One understood as an image of the ideal, a source-free approach allows for three blocks of text (Gen 2–4; 5–10; 11:1–9) that, rather than recording traditions of a distant beginning, explore aspects of what is experienced as the human condition. The stories are, therefore, appropriately placed at humanity's beginning.[12]
9. The tracing of the history of Israel, as best it could be done in the hypothetical documents of J and P extending from creation to the eve of conquest, is replaced by the crisper focus of a variety of shorter collections and documents. A more intense focus on theology (the

---

12. For the philosophical underpinning of such interpretation, see, e.g., Paul Ricoeur, *The Symbolism of Evil* (Boston: Beacon Press, 1967).

importance of self-understanding before God) allows release from the task of extracting history out of texts where it does not belong.

10. The complex development of the text is attended to and not glossed over. The reality of present text is appropriately valued.

A minimal reaction to this proposal might be to conclude that once upon a time something like pentateuchal sources probably did exist, and quite possibly more of them than have been identified. But, contrary to some past understandings, the present biblical text *does not preserve* these sources. Among other things, what the present biblical text *does preserve* is many of the traditions, in much of their variety, that once were in these sources.

Note

As is our wont, this book is the joint responsibility of both authors. Over the years, we have sat together at one computer and hammered it out, sentence by sentence.

We are both happy to acknowledge a debt of gratitude to Accordance 5.7 (OakTree Software) for its great help in the swift evaluation of data.

Throughout the book, the letters "a" and "b" indicate the two major divisions of a verse, marked by punctuation in Hebrew (following the sense); as little as possible, but when necessary for clarity, Greek symbols (α, β, γ = alpha, beta, gamma) indicate subdivisions within these two, again marked by punctuation in Hebrew (following the sense). Where it seems simpler and sufficient, the asterisk (*) is used to denote part of a verse.

Two other terms are used often in this book:

> *Enhancement* or *enrichment* designates text that offers an option to the user or is an advance on what was already in place.

> *Present text* or *final text* designates the final biblical text that at present is found in the Bible, which for the purposes of this book is based on the Hebrew or Masoretic Text.

As this book was readied for the press, we became aware that in fact two paradigm shifts are involved in it, rather than one. The first shift, named in ch. 2, is from a "reader-centered" to a "user-centered" focus in understanding the production of much narrative text in ancient Israel (users *expanded* such texts and *selected* from options that were sometimes preserved within such texts; readers do not). The second shift, emerging in ch. 3, is the shift from the Pentateuch as a record of Israel's *remembering its past* to the Pentateuch as a record of Israel's *pondering its present*. The first paradigm shift affects theory; the second affects interpretation. The first has implications for pentateuchal sources; the second has implications for an understanding of the Pentateuch itself.

By way of conclusion here, we may turn to the subtitle at the beginning of this volume. "Prolegomena" was chosen as a deliberate echo of the title of Wellhausen's famous book, *Prolegomena to the History of Ancient Israel*. The echo

acknowledges the incalculable debt we owe to those generations of biblical scholars. The echo of the past may suggest that it is time we moved on and moved
beyond the contributions of that time. Our subtitle heralds a change from the
study of "the History" to the study of "the Theology" of ancient Israel. The change
matters. The activity that generated much biblical literature was primarily theological—trying to understand life. Such literature was composed above all as the
outcome of thought, to be thought about and studied; it was not a record opening the way to the recovery of Israel's history. Finally, "Prolegomena"—with its
meaning of a critical discussion of an introductory nature—is an important statement about this volume. As we have worked closely with these pentateuchal texts,
we have become increasingly aware of just how many avenues are open to exploration. What we can do here is limited by the realities of what the market expects
of one book and what two finite scholars can produce in one book. We hope to
have demolished old shibboleths and opened up new possibilities. We believe that
this book, *Rethinking the Pentateuch*, is rightly no more than Prolegomena.

Chapter 2

Evidence

Overview

The task of this chapter is to provide the evidence for the approach underpinning the rest of the book. It falls into two distinct parts. First is the argument against the presence of P text in Gen 1–11, and indeed in Genesis as a whole. Second is the argument for seeing parts of the biblical text as a base for users, a base to be expanded, and a base with options and variants to be selected.

The first inquiry is straightforward and traditional: an analysis of vocabulary and the patterns of conceptualization. It is not so surprising that Genesis One (Gen 1:1–2:4) is *neutral*, although this conclusion is contrary to the automatic assumption of almost all modern scholarship. Genesis 5:1–2 is *unlikely* as a continuation of Genesis One. More than "not so surprising," it is shocking to find that the so-called P creation account and P flood account are *highly unlikely* to have come from the same origin. When genealogies, ages, and dates are looked at closely, the probability of any significant P traditions in Genesis reduces rapidly toward nil. This is an unquestioned shock to source theory.

The second inquiry begins with two long-recognized factual observations: (1) most biblical story texts are short, too short to record the performance of telling a story; (2) many biblical story texts contain options and variants (the so-called repetitions of source theory). If the focus of attention is moved from the modern scholar to the ancient storyteller or other user, on the one hand, brevity suggests the need for expansion, and, on the other, options suggest the need for selection. A new paradigm allows the possibility that many biblical story texts were bases to be expanded, containing options to be selected—options available for users to choose from. With this understanding, continuous sources or sustained editing become totally unnecessary.

The proposals advanced in this book rest on the absence of evidence for the so-called P text in Genesis and the evident possibility of a "text-as-base-for-user" approach to parts of the text, accounting for its brevity and the options it contains. By "text-as-base-for-user," we mean that parts of the narrative text served as a base for its users: a base to be expanded by storytellers and other users; a base containing options and variants for users to choose from.

The So-Called P Text

No P Text in Genesis 1–11

Two specific and thoroughly traditional factors played a key role in triggering this book. First, close study of Genesis One (Gen 1:1–2:4a) itself, coupled with a close comparison of Genesis One with the traditional P material in the flood narrative, led to the conclusion that there was probably no basis for P in Gen 1–11. If the ground is taken away from beneath one end of a bridge, the bridge collapses. Given the admittedly scanty nature of P narrative in Gen 12–50, the absence of a basis for P in Gen 1–11 suggested the collapse of P in Genesis. Second, close attention to features frequently claimed as evidence for the identification of P text (above all, genealogies, ages, and dates) suggested that they may have belonged to the nature of the topic rather than the nature of the narrator. (Wellhausen's contemptuous view of P, see above, does not contribute to confidence in this regard; to caricature a view found in writings of that time, "if it is boring, it must be P.")

Our detailed and painstaking work on Genesis One and the P flood text (also Gen 5:1–2) is given in full in appendix 1. Here, we may simply note its conclusions. The study of the vocabulary used in Genesis One proved to be *neutral*: that is, the passage might perfectly well have originated from a P source, but equally it might perfectly well have originated from some other sources. It could be P, but it did not have to be P. The comparison of Genesis One with the P text in the flood narrative provided a surprising outcome: it proved *unlikely* that the two texts had the same origin.

No P Text in Genesis at All

A pillar of P in Gen 1–11—the identification as P of the opening account of creation (Genesis One) and the association of the P accounts of creation and flood—proved shaky; naturally, the further identification of P came under scrutiny. Two stages in the investigation are to be kept separate; one is recognizing the presence of repetition and the other the attributing some of the repeated material to P. Among others, three criteria have traditionally been invoked for that attribution to P: (1) the use of the divine name *elohim*, (2) the concern for genealogies, and (3) the concern for ages and dates. To our surprise, these criteria proved to be fragile and far from certain.

1. The Use of elohim for the Name of God

Today, at least three elements may come into play to explain the use of this divine name in contrast to *yhwh*—and the presence of continuous sources need not be one of these elements.[1]

Of these three elements involved in the use of *elohim,* the first is a relatively recent awareness that would not have been available to earlier scholars: Accepting that ancient editors were skillful and intelligent, it is reasonable to assume that such ancient editors on occasion may have sought to highlight their activity rather than conceal it. A change of divine name, therefore, could function as a hermeneutic marker to indicate editorial intervention, where some such indication seemed desirable or necessary. For example, an author or editor incorporating an alternative tradition into a text, or indicating an optional variant available to storytellers, might choose to use *elohim* within the alternative or the variant to differentiate it from the main body of the text using *yhwh*. A few decades ago, the idea of such hermeneutic markers was unthinkable; editors were not thought to announce their presence except by occasional gauche incompetence. Different approaches to the factors in the text suggest now that editors then might well have signaled their activity. The use of a different divine name would have served well as such a signal.

The second of these elements is closely related to the first. Material using *elohim* rather than *yhwh*, or vice versa, may well have come from circles with a preference for one divine name over the other. This phenomenon is present in religious circles today; different groups are easily identified by their language. The practice is assumed by those using the criterion of the divine name for the identification of sources. What is new is simply the assertion that such a practice might apply to a story or a tradition without implying attribution to a continuous source. The originating usage may well have been retained, to serve as what we might today call a "hermeneutic marker," indicating options available to users.

The third element has long been advanced by those opposed to the distribution of the biblical text across different sources. It is the perfectly correct observation that *yhwh* is a personal name and *elohim* a common noun for god. For most scholars, although this observation accounts for a few of the cases of difference, it is far from giving a satisfactory explanation for all. It needs to be taken into account, however, when dealing with those texts where it may be applicable.

---

1. Erhard Blum has an excursus that is not particularly helpful (*Die Komposition der Vätergeschichte*, WMANT 57 [Neukirchen-Vluyn: Neukirchener Verlag, 1984], 471–75). His hermeneutical-philosophical discussion is limited; the exploration of biblical text is for the most part negligible. Whybray assesses the issue critically (*Making of the Pentateuch*, 63–72).

Once these three elements are properly weighed and evaluated, we believe that no need can be demonstrated for continuous sources based on the evidence of the differing divine names. Two claims we make are involved in this conclusion. First, biblical text often provided alternatives and options for its users. There is no need to hypothesize the combination of sources to explain this, for it was a normal part of the creation of biblical narrative. Second, differences of divine name within a tradition may say something about the origin of that tradition but need not say anything about the question of belonging to a continuous source.

2. Concern for Genealogies

Genealogies are the very stuff of ancestral narrative; their presence is hardly surprising in the stories of Israel's ancestors. Genealogies are either linear or segmented (i.e., branched, as in a family tree), although the two forms may be mixed.[2] All genealogies are characterized by fluidity. Outside the OT, they occur only rarely; within the OT, they are found predominantly in Genesis and Exodus and in Chronicles and Ezra–Nehemiah. This sits comfortably with the traditional assumption of a late date for the final composition of Genesis–Exodus. Naturally, it says nothing of the age of the genealogies; the preservation of ancient records is possible, but it is also not necessary. The functions of genealogies vary, as Robert Wilson remarks: "In contrast to the multiple functions of segmented genealogies, linear genealogies have only one: to ground a claim to power, status, rank, office, or inheritance in an earlier ancestor" (*ABD* 2:931). The derivation of genealogies from outside sources is taken for granted. To quote Wilson again: "The various ways in which the biblical writers incorporated genealogical material into their work suggests that they understood the idiom of genealogy and were able to use it creatively throughout the biblical period" (*ABD* 2:932). Genealogies can also be used metaphorically; a "whole political system can be conceived as one large family and described by using the idiom of genealogy" (*ABD* 2:931). The upshot is simple. The presence of genealogies cannot be used as evidence for a single author, for they point to an interest or attitude that may stretch across several circles or generations.

3. Concern for Ages and Dates

A concern for ages and dates is evident across texts in Genesis; ages, and occasionally dates, are obviously relevant in ancestral contexts. In biblical text, dates of accession and length of reign are also regularly noted for kings; ages at accession are given only for the kings of Judah.[3] Dates are not infrequently noted in relation to prophetic utterances.[4] Such ages and dates can be expressed in a vari-

---

2. For what follows on genealogies, see Robert Wilson, "Genealogy, Genealogies," *ABD* 2:929–32; cf. Wilson, *Genealogy and History in the Biblical World* (New Haven, CT: Yale University Press, 1977).

3. For kings in general, see 1 Kgs 15:1–2, 9–10, 25, 33, and so on. For the kings of Judah, see 1 Kgs 14:21; 22:42; 2 Kgs 8:17, 26; 11:21; 14:2, 21; 15:2, 33; 16:2; 18:2; 21:1, 19; 22:1; 23:31, 36; 24:8, 18.

4. For example, Jer 1:2–3; 25:1, 3; 28:1; 32:1; 36:1, 9; 39:1–2; Ezek passim; Hag 1:1, 15; 2:10; Zech 1:1, 7; 7:1.

ety of formulas. Without going into detail at present, it can be said that noting ages is particularly appropriate within ancestral material such as Genesis and Exodus. As with genealogies, ages and dates cannot be used as evidence for a single origin or a specific period of time.

Examined closely, both the connections between passages are doubtful, and the overall characteristic features claimed for P are doubtful. Absent both connections and characteristic features, the concept of P, whether as individual theologian or as cohesive group, is in trouble. The concept of P becomes doubtful. What is common to passages traditionally assigned to P can be accounted for by an origin in the priestly circles associated with the Jerusalem temple or other circles with similar interests. Such writings may well replace the Priestly Writer (whether author or editor, individual or group)—with major implications for the understanding of the Pentateuch.[5] By way of example, without pretending to be comprehensive, we may note areas where such circles can be seen operating, circles with intimate connections of interest and evident distinction of identity. Such similarity and difference is present around the texts of creation and flood, in the difference of *El Shaddai* traditions from otherwise similar concerns, in the texts around the instructions for the sanctuary, its construction, and its place in the camp and on the march—and so on. The interweaving of diversity and identity proves remarkable.

The presence of marked diversity within priestly circles coupled with the reality of clear identity need not be thought surprising. For example, there are Americans, British, French, Germans, Italians, Spaniards, and many others. No one of these peoples would be confused with another; yet the diversity within each of them is huge. The analogy could be honed more finely, but the basics are clear. Within a well-defined family, marked differences can coexist. So it is in many cases; so it was within the priestly circles of ancient Israel. There is no P in the Pentateuch; there is priestly writing, of course—by a variety of priestly thinkers.

The "Text-as-Base-for-User" Approach

Old Evidence, New Paradigm

The evidence for this approach is in (1) the brevity of many of the story texts and (2) the presence of options and variants in them. In the early 1900s, Hermann Gunkel in his Genesis commentary noted the brevity of these texts. At first, he estimated that the average story text would have lasted scarcely a half-hour; a little later, he reduced this to scarcely a quarter-hour. Had he taken a quarter-hour to time them, under five minutes would have been closer to the mark. For two or three centuries, the presence of options and variants in the texts has been essential

---

5. The text traditionally attributed to P shapes up as a document and not editing; see A. F. Campbell, "The Priestly Text: Redaction or Source?" in *Biblische Theologie und gesellschaftlicher Wandel: Für Norbert Lohfink SJ*, ed. G. Braulik, W. Groß, and S. McEvenue (Freiburg im Breisgau: Herder, 1993), 32–47.

for the literary-critical distribution of the traditions across two or three sources (J, P, and E). In the mid-eighteenth century, Jean Astruc saw differences and distributed the Genesis text across sources; scholars have been doing the same sort of thing ever since. A new paradigm is overdue. Most of the story texts are far too short to have been a record of performance; Gunkel was right, but his explanation was inadequate and insultingly anti-Semitic.[6] Many of the story texts contain options and variants. Astruc was right, but his solution was inadequate, because distributing these "repetitions" across continuous sources was not the only possibility.

Reflection on the difference between the production and use of literature in ancient Israel and today suggests that a paradigm shift involving two major transformations of mind-set may be needed, regarding, first, the nature of the text and, second, the role of the user (such as storytellers and others).[7] We do not propose this change with regard to all biblical text and not even with regard to all biblical narrative text. What is proposed may be applicable to some, perhaps many, cases of biblical narrative text. It is proposed not as a matter of dogmatic certainty but as a possibility, to be envisaged and evaluated, accepted or declined as appropriate.

The Nature of the Text

People today are used to regarding the biblical text as canonical Scripture. However, many of the texts involved here were, at the stage under discussion, precanonical, not regarded yet as Scripture. We are also used to treating the canonical text as final text—to which nothing is to be added or taken away—to be expounded for the purposes of policy, preaching, teaching, and so on. Given the brevity of the texts, however, it is possible that many of the precanonical texts under discussion were not written to be *expounded* but to be *expanded*—that is, enlarged or developed for the purposes of entertainment, instruction, and so on. Some texts may preserve optional variants and the like. For our entertainment, we today rely on novels, cinema, television, and more; a much earlier age may have placed greater reliance on the storyteller.

The Role of the User (Such as Storytellers and Others)

Because many of the narrative texts contain what may be understood as variants, options, or even contradictory traditions, it is possible that storytellers (and other users) took it for granted that they would choose between these options and that the presence of such options in the text would be signaled. What source critics tend to call "repetitions" are an excellent example of one class of variants or options. Here, the variants from the tradition were recorded in the text so as to be available for the storyteller's choice. As a rule, only one option would have been actualized in a given performance of a story. Many of the narrative texts pre-

---

6. Campbell, "Storyteller's Role."
7. Campbell's "Storyteller's Role" (*CBQ* 64) will be used in this regard; its detailed arguments will not be repeated here.

served to us, at an average of ten verses or so, are far too short to record the performance of a story; they need to be expanded.[8] Storytellers could be relied on to fill those gaps in a story that needed to be filled rather than left open.[9] Part of the role of the storyteller may have been to choose among options, to expand the story from its base text, and in the course of that expansion to smooth out gaps that needed filling.

Users today normally read the canonical text as end-text, to be *expounded*. Users in ancient days, in contrast, may have used the precanonical text as a base-text, to be *expanded*. The condensed text reported on past performances of a story; it could have served as a base for reflection and for further storytelling. In other words, in a precanon world, users came to some texts as beginning points, expecting to find choices to make; with the canonical text, in contrast, users come to some texts as fixed points, expecting to find information to receive.

From this, we identify the paradigm shift that can account for the brevity and layered quality of much narrative biblical text: ancient narrative texts were often written initially to be *used by ancient storytellers and others*; they were not written with a view to being *read by moderns* as Bible.[10] Is it unthinkable?

The core insight of this "text-as-base-for-user" understanding involves a threefold shift of focus:

from	*to*
(a) the ability of a modern reader	(a) the ability of an ancient user
(b) analyzing and dissecting	(b) selecting from and expanding
(c) a dense final text	(c) a condensed base text

This paradigm shift in the understanding of the nature and function of some biblical narrative text is the foundation of much that we do in this book. In practice,

---

8. The length of passages can be measured, but intuition has primacy for reflection on their use. Susan Niditch thinks it "entirely possible that the telling of pan-Israelite stories was aided by notes or some sort of written texts" (*Oral World and Written Word: Ancient Israelite Literature*, Library of Ancient Israel [Louisville, KY: Westminster John Knox, 1996], 122). Stephanie Dalley points to something similar in some Sumerian and Akkadian literature, "bare skeletons which were fleshed out in practice by skilled narrators" (*Myths from Mesopotamia: Creation, the Flood, Gilgamesh and Others* [Oxford: Oxford University Press, 1989], xvi). One senior OT scholar (James A. Sanders) described much of the biblical text as "*signals*" for telling stories." Documents from medieval England are not the same as biblical stories, but the early preference for hearing something rather than reading the text itself is worth noting; see M. T. Clanchy (*From Memory to Written Record: England 1066–1307* [London: Edward Arnold, 1979], esp. 202–30).

9. To take two examples from the books of Samuel: (1) David emerged from the cave behind Saul, who had just eased nature; the three thousand troops who had been searching for David did not seize him (1 Sam 24). A royal gesture of restraint or a royal word of command would fit naturally into the telling of the story; it was not necessary to use up valuable parchment for the purpose. (2) A boy saw Jonathan and Ahimaaz and told Absalom; Absalom's servants knew where to go to look for them (2 Sam 17). A storyteller might easily have explained how the two were recognized and why the house in Bahurim was singled out.

10. If a nametag is needed for this approach, it would have to be something like "user theory" or a "text-as-base-for-user" approach ("user-base" for short), applying within the literary context of ancient Israel.

that "use" included expanding and selecting. The implication for ancient users is twofold:

1. Narrative text often required expansion to be turned into the telling of a story.
2. Narrative text often preserved variant versions or optional details, therefore requiring choice on the part of the storyteller.

Concurrently with this, from our study of biblical text, our experience of biblical editors as skillful and intelligent forced the question whether, in many cases, the signals in the text pointed to editors seeking to conceal their interventions, or to disclose them. In our judgment, ancient editors may often have sought to disclose their interventions, and ancient compilers did not seek to conceal variants or options.

We do not propose abolishing the old and replacing it with the obligatory new. Instead, we advocate an alternative paradigm as a possible option on occasion. Over the last few centuries, the biblical text has been looked at in many ways. We urge "a change in the perception and evaluation of familiar data" to allow for a new and alternative possibility.[11]

What we propose as a possibility, then, does not supplant all aspects of past understandings of biblical text; instead, it may complement them. It certainly does not apply to all biblical text, not even to all nonpoetic text; it may apply to some prose texts—certainly not to legal texts, possibly not to prophets, and not to Job or Wisdom and, of course, not to all narrative text. In principle, it applies only to storytelling texts and not necessarily to all of these (so for the Pentateuch, roughly rather less than 45 percent of the whole). Where the insights of past research often flowed from the Pentateuch to the narrative traditions from Joshua onward, here the insight flows rather from the storytelling in the books of Joshua to Kings to the Pentateuch.

The literary industry of ancient Israel is as yet little understood, both as to its products and the uses to which they were put.[12] The copying of manuscripts before the invention of printing meant a limited distribution; whatever the outcome of the debate about literacy in ancient Israel, a literacy that allowed for access to sophisticated texts such as the Pentateuch was no greater then than now,

11. Thomas S. Kuhn, *The Structure of Scientific Revolutions* (1st ed, 1962; 3rd ed., Chicago: Univ. of Chicago Press, 1996), x–xi. Kuhn continues: "Paradigms gain their status because they are more successful than their competitors in solving a few problems that a group of practitioners has come to recognize as acute" (ibid., 23). The Documentary Hypothesis was such a paradigm—and successful. It has ceased to function effectively. What another physicist remarks remains right even when the ellipses (occupied by string theory, space and time, etc.) are filled in differently: "Because these features . . . require that we drastically change our understanding . . . , they will take some time to get used to, to sink in at a comfortable level" (Brian Greene, *The Elegant Universe: Superstrings, Hidden Dimensions, and the Quest for the Ultimate Theory* [New York: Norton, 2003], 5).

12. Valuable groundwork has been laid by scholars such as André Lemaire and Susan Niditch (A. Lemaire, "Schools and Literacy in Ancient Israel and Early Judaism," in *The Blackwell Companion to the Hebrew Bible*, ed. L. G. Perdue [Oxford: Blackwell, 2001], 207–17; Niditch, *Oral World*). Beyond production and use, there are issues of ownership and responsibility, storage and access, and so on.

with the consequent restriction of use to specific circles. The limited length of many shorter narrative units needs explanation. The economics of the industry is largely unknown to us. A valuable comparison comes from Lindisfarne, among the monasteries of ancient Britain; according to Simon Schama, a single Bible there required five hundred calfskins.[13] We know of the materials in use at Qumran; the implications of cost for the distribution of manuscripts in ancient Israel, to the best of our knowledge, remains unexplored.

Our proposal allows for the final canonical and scriptural status of the biblical text. It calls for an understanding of the beginnings of that text as written text, incorporating precanonical reports of the past performance of stories, reports that preserved the salient highlights of a tradition and made them available for selection and expansion. The proof of the pudding is in the eating; if this proposal proves helpful in understanding the text, it will be a valued possibility. What this proposal does for Genesis, and indeed much of the Pentateuch, is not dissimilar from what Gospel research has done for the infancy narratives of Luke and Matthew. Rather than viewing the biblical text as a composite put together from reminiscences of historical tradition, it is possible to see it responsibly as theological reflection expressed in narrative form.

Further Implications of This Paradigm Shift

With both the need for sources and the existence of P in doubt, the existence of a Yahwist (J) is also in question. J or JE (Yahwist and Elohist taken together; of late, more cautiously termed "nonpriestly") have often been the exegetical counterweight to P. There are repetitions and different divine names; there is the difference of styles: lively for J, pedantic for P. Given explanations that dispense with the need for such sources, the existence of a Yahwist becomes less likely. Fondness for the Yahwist narrative has been trending downward for some time, to put it mildly. As Solomonic theologian, the Yahwist was extolled by von Rad.[14] Frowns came from many, probably first from Schmid.[15] Viewed as later than the Deuteronomistic History, the narrative was maintained by Van Seters as semifictive history rather than as possibly authentic theology.[16]

13. Simon Schama, *A History of Britain: At the Edge of the World? 3000BC–AD1603* (London: BBC, 2000), 51. Small wonder that the monastery at Qumran had a tannery associated with it.

14. Gerhard von Rad, *Old Testament Theology*, vol. 1, *The Theology of Israel's Historical Traditions* (Edinburgh: Oliver & Boyd, 1962). For example, pp. 48–49. Similarly, Peter F. Ellis, *The Yahwist: The Bible's First Theologian* (Notre Dame, IN: Fides, 1968).

15. Hans Heinrich Schmid, *Der sogenannte Jahwist: Beobachtungen und Fragen zur Pentateuchforschung* (Zurich: Theologischer Verlag, 1976). Recently, there is the volume of collected papers, J. C. Gertz, K. Schmid, and M. Witte, eds., *Abschied vom Jahwisten: Die Komposition des Hexateuch in der jüngsten Discussion*, BZAW 315 (Berlin: de Gruyter, 2002). Its farewell to the Yahwist is often accompanied by clinging rather too closely to P and relying rather too trustingly on nineteenth- and twentieth-century work practices. More radical approaches are needed. They are not found in Christoph Levin's *Der Jahwist*.

16. John Van Seters, *The Life of Moses: The Yahwist as Historian in Exodus–Numbers* (Louisville, KY: Westminster/John Knox, 1994), 457–58. See also his *Prologue to History: The Yahwist as Historian in Genesis* (Louisville, KY: Westminster/John Knox, 1992), 328–33.

Westermann had opted for a nonexclusive approach, "a transmitter, a storyteller, and a theologian,"[17] a position with venerable antecedents: "It is no surprise therefore that, for Gunkel, the Yahwist became the 'brother Grimm' of the OT: he was not an author, but a *collector*. The antipathy of Gunkel toward the concept of author had to do with the idea that most of the biblical texts actually derived from oral tradition."[18]

The Yahwist, whether understood as an individual figure or a cohesive group, has been generally seen less as a recorder of tradition and creator of narrative than as a compiler and organizer of much that was already in existence. As Lawrence Boadt observed: "We can be certain that J did not write from whole cloth. He brought together old poems, stories, and songs of the exodus that were alive in the cult."[19] Given a base of traditions and cycles of tradition, compilers are essential to reach a compiled text, the present biblical text. It will always be possible to name one of these compilers the Yahwist, responsible for the organization of much of the nonpriestly material in the Pentateuch. However, when the level of discontinuity and difference within the compiled traditions is realized, it is unlikely that any description of a Yahwist will emerge that resembles the images common in the past, such as Boadt's "the Yahwist forms the heart of the Pentateuchal structure" and Alberto Soggin's "with J there comes into being the first nucleus of the Pentateuch as we have it today."[20] Compilers may have given the text its stages along the way and its final shape at the end. It is unlikely—but of course possible—that a single theologian of genius is to be credited with the preservation and organization of the traditions of ancient Israel.[21] The possible, however, is not the same as the necessary; and we refrain from suggesting it.

Along with these considerations, the fragmentation involved in providing continuous sources in biblical text renders the process of source analysis increasingly dubious. When the use of differing divine names, such as *elohim* and *yhwh*, can be seen as markers allowing for variants and options within narrative text, the justification for fragmenting these texts to produce two or more sources is highly questionable. The evaluation of a hypothesis of sources or a hypothesis of hermeneutical markers will have to be based on the plausibility of the narrative texts that emerge. In most cases, our judgment favors the hermeneutical markers; readers will form their own.

---

17. Claus Westermann, *Genesis 12–36* (Minneapolis: Augsburg, 1985), 571.

18. Thomas Römer, "The Form-Critical Problem of the So-Called Deuteronomistic History," in *The Changing Face of Form Criticism for the Twenty-first Century*, ed. M. A. Sweeney and E. Ben Zvi (Grand Rapids: Eerdmans, 2003), 240–52, see p. 241. For a wide-ranging introduction to the Yahwist, see Jean Louis Ska, "The Yahwist, a Hero with a Thousand Faces: A Chapter in the History of Modern Exegesis," in *Abschied vom Jahwisten*, ed. J. C. Gertz et al., 1–23.

19. Lawrence Boadt, *Reading the Old Testament: An Introduction* (New York: Paulist, 1984), 98.

20. For Boadt, *Reading the Old Testament,* 98; for Soggin, *Introduction to the Old Testament: From Its Origins to the Closing of the Alexandrian Canon* (Philadelphia: Westminster, 1976), 101.

21. As was claimed by von Rad, for example: "We have to realize that in fact we owe all the information that we have about the early ages in Israel solely to the work of the Jahwist who preserved and rearranged it" (*Old Testament Theology,* 1.50).

Other Matters

The Elohist

The separation of the E material in the Pentateuch into two documents, the early Elohist and the later Priestly Document, began at the end of the eighteenth century (Ilgen, 1798).[22] In 1948, in one of the more methodically solid studies of recent times, Martin Noth argued for the existence of an Elohist narrative; in our judgment, E barely survived his scrutiny.[23] In 1981, at the end of his work on Gen 12–36, Westermann denied that the so-called E texts there can be understood to present a tradition parallel to J.[24] The need for an Elohist source has faded from the scene.[25]

The Impact of Pentateuchal Traditions on Other Biblical Text

We need to ask whether the traditions now in Genesis–Deuteronomy are significant in the rest of the Bible. From Joshua to 2 Kings, there may be two or three occurrences for Moses that reflect early traditions (prescinding from Josh 13–14), and nothing early for Joshua, Abraham, Isaac, or Jacob. In Table 1, under "ancestors," we have included the triads with Abraham, Isaac, and Jacob/Israel; the names occurring in these triads have not been given a second listing subsequently under the individual names. Table 1 displays the occurrences.

From this, we see that it is unlikely that the pentateuchal traditions had significant impact on other biblical text before the century 722–622 BCE. This may indicate that there was neither need nor appropriate place for these traditions of the ancestors within the books from Joshua to 2 Kings (with the exception of Moses and Joshua in the early part of Joshua). It may say more. After 722, the people of Israel had been reduced to a unity (Judah); around 622, occurrences of the triad of three ancestors may be found in Deuteronomy.[26] Overall, the prophetic literature does not gainsay these observations. The Jacob traditions are present in Hos 12, marginally pre-722. Both Isaac and Jacob are found as synonyms for Israel in Hosea; in Amos, Isaac only; reference to the exodus is present in Amos 2:10; 3:1; 9:7.[27] Like any issue of dating, uncertainty remains.

---

22. From Kraus, *Geschichte der historisch-kritischen Erforschung*, 154.

23. Martin Noth, *A History of Pentateuchal Traditions* (German original, 1948; Chico, CA: Scholars Press, 1981), 21–37; finally, "What has been preserved of the E material is in parts so fragmentary that it is impossible to attempt sketching a complete picture of it in any degree" (37).

24. Westermann, *Genesis 12–36*, 571–72. He is negative on the presence of an Elohist in chs. 12–25, even after 21:1–7. Regarding fragments in chs. 25–36, he concludes: "A better explanation is that each of these [layers] is an elaboration that has its own reason and meaning" (572).

25. See Antony F. Campbell and Mark A. O'Brien, *Sources of the Pentateuch: Texts, Introductions, Annotations* (Minneapolis: Fortress, 1993), 161–66.

26. For the ancestral generation in Deuteronomy, see Thomas Römer, *Israels Väter: Untersuchungen zur Väterthematik im Deuteronomium und in der deuteronomistischen Tradition*, OBO 99 (Freiburg, Schweiz: Universitätsverlag, 1990, and Norbert Lohfink's response, *Die Väter Israel's in Deuteronomium. Mit einer Stellungnahme von Thomas Römer*, OBO 111 (Freiburg, Schweiz: Universitätsverlag, 1991). For the named triad, see Suzanne Boorer, *The Promise of the Land as Oath: A Key to the Formation of the Pentateuch*, BZAW 205 (Berlin: de Gruyter, 1992).

27. For Moses, the occurrences are Isa 63:11–12; Jer 15:1; Mic 6:4; Mal 4:4, and they are late; there is nothing for Joshua or Sinai; for ancestors, Abraham 7x, Isaac 3x (Amos 7:9, 16; Jer 33:26), Jacob 90x and Israel 508x (in the latter two, mainly for the people, occasionally for the individual ancestor, but late).

Table 1: Occurrences of Pentateuchal Traditions
in Other Biblical Text

	Josh	Judg	1 Sam	2 Sam	1 Kgs	2 Kgs
MOSES	passim *(editorial)*	4x *(4:11, early?)*	2x *(12:6, 8, late)*	nil	4x *(late)*	12x *(late)*
JOSHUA	passim	6x *(late)*	nil	nil	1x *(16:34, late)*	nil
ANCESTORS (3)	nil	nil	nil	nil	1x *(18:36, late)*	1x *(13:23, late)*
ABRAHAM	2x *(ch. 24, late)*	nil	nil	nil	nil	nil
ISAAC	2x *(ch. 24, late)*	nil	nil	nil	nil	nil
JACOB	2x *(ch. 24, late)*	nil	1x *(12:8, late)*	nil	1x *(18:31, late)*	1x *(17:34, late)*

early = before the 7th century   *late = not before the 7th century*

Meaning

With the unfortunate assumption of inept editors, who were capable of mindless mutilation and assembled texts by a process of mechanical piecework, the possibility of meaning in a text is greatly reduced.[28] With a thorough revision of the understanding of how the pentateuchal text came into existence, better conditions exist for meaning to be recovered. An interpreter's job is not done when "roughnesses" in the biblical text have been explained by appeal to the process of development; rather, it is then that the interpreter's job is begun. When a modern argues that something should be cut out of the text, the prior and necessary step is to justify why it got there in the first place.

What Is Possible Need Not Be Necessary

Once said, this statement—"what is possible need not be necessary"—is obvious; for a long time it was not said. To our knowledge, it was first said by Martin Noth;[29] but whether it was often practiced by Noth is a matter of opinion. For

---

28. Not thoughts from a distant past, alas, but reflecting an influential U.S. scholar (F. M. Cross), published in the late twentieth century.

29. Noth, *Könige I. 1–16*, BKAT 9/1 (Neukirchen-Vluyn: Neukirchener Verlag, 1968), 246.

a very long time the practice of critical biblical circles was to take for granted that, if a textual operation could be shown to have been possible, no further evidence was needed to assume that the origin of the text had been explained. In our view, to the contrary, the degree of need must be demonstrated; it should not be confused with possibility. That perception is at the heart of this book.

Biblical Editors Skillful and Intelligent

The discovery of the Qumran scrolls has opened a previously unknown world. In the Judean desert, an exclusive community existed, and associated with it was an industry producing parchment and copying scrolls. More important, the scrolls showed that a variety of versions of the biblical text existed, of which the Masoretic Text was only one. With this discovery, a greater understanding of the literary process has become possible, including the realization that "an author often served, when the need or the occasion arose, also as the editor, transmitter, scribe or copyist of his own works or the work of others."[30] Editors and transmitters need have been no less wise than authors and creators. Our own observation, particularly in regard to the Deuteronomistic History, has confirmed the skill and intelligence of those editing biblical text in ancient times. Modern editors have several techniques available for indicating editorial intervention, including brackets ([ ]), annotations [ed.], change of font, and so on. It should not surprise us that the ancients, especially with their respect for tradition, should want to draw attention to their activity. Given the intelligence of audiences and users of the texts, one may assume the capacity to exploit the possibilities that editors offered.

The Limits of the Modern Scholar

The modern emphasis on subjectivity—extending from literary theory to quantum physics—obliges scholars to take into account their own subjectivity and that of others. The myth of the objective scholar is indefensible, in principle and in practice. The interpreter's subjectivity can never, and should never, be isolated from the act of interpretation. It is true of judgments about today; it is true of judgments made about the past. The empathy needed to bridge a gap millennia wide should eliminate the temptation to think as though what we have in the Bible is all that ancient Israel had too. We know so much more than was known in generations past; there is still so very much that we do not know and will not know.

Summary and Preview

When the criteria for attributing text are reassessed and the storyteller's role is taken into account—within a new paradigm—we can maintain the continuity and integrity of narrative text (thereby avoiding fragmentation) and envisage an

---

30. Shemaryahu Talmon, "The Textual Study of the Bible—A New Outlook," in *Qumran and the History of the Biblical Text*, ed. F. M. Cross and S. Talmon (Cambridge: Harvard University Press, 1975), 321–400, see p. 336.

openness to the diversity and variation of storytelling (offering options). Without pentateuchal sources, three factors need to be emphasized regarding much narrative biblical text: (1) variant origins of traditions, (2) variant options for storytellers, and (3) variant versions of stories.

When these three factors are taken into account, an outcome emerges for the Pentateuch that is at least possible. According to this understanding, we entertain the possibility that Genesis begins with stories exploring the human condition, which are placed at the beginning but were quite probably written late (Gen 2:4b–11:9). Human existence and the boundaries of human living are explored in three passages (Gen 2–3; 4; 11:1–9); human existence and the relationship with God are explored in one other major text (Gen 6:5–9:17). In Genesis, duality (in the form of continuous sources or continuous editing) succumbs to variant origins, options, and versions; as a result, pentateuchal sources are not needed. Duality is present in the narrative of Israel's exodus from Egypt; there are two narratives from Moses' call to the Reed Sea. One of these continues on to the sanctuary at Sinai (ending with Exod 40:38); the other most probably stops with the Song of Moses at the Sea of Reeds (Exod 15:1–18). The books of Leviticus and Numbers have an integrity of their own. Within the Pentateuch as a whole, the book of Deuteronomy correlates with Genesis One (Gen 1:1–2:4a). Genesis One can be understood as a faith statement about an ideal world, as it might have come from the hand of its creator; Deuteronomy can be understood as an exhortation to Israel to realize that ideal.

It is important that the stories exploring the human condition, placed at the beginning of Genesis, be recognized for their potential. *It is important* to envisage the possibility that Genesis One, as a faith statement about an ideal world, may be correlated with Deuteronomy as an exhortation to Israel to realize that ideal. *It is important* to explore the traditions of Israel's ancestors and of Israel in Egypt and at Sinai. *At the same time*, in all of this, *it is also important* not to lose sight of a fundamental paradigm shift: the narrative text may often be a base for the operations of storytellers and other users, needing to be expanded, containing for the storyteller's selection variant versions of a story and variant options for a story. With these perceptions in place, the biblical text of much pentateuchal narrative can be freed from the burden of undue complexity unfairly placed upon it.

Chapter 3

Outcome

What changes does the "text-as-base-for-user" approach bring to interpreting the Pentateuch? It is important in two areas. First, with storytelling texts, (a) the brevity of the texts implies their expansion if the story is told or discussed, and (b) the practice of preserving options in the texts involves their identification and may require selection by the user (unless the contrast itself is the subject of reflection). Beyond these, see discussions in appendix 4 for frequent reliance on user skills. Second, with nonstorytelling texts (e.g., Exod 19—Num 10), the "user-base" approach allows for attention to the concerns of specific sections, without the need to achieve artificial continuity.

The task of this chapter is to present an outline of one possible outcome for our understanding of the Pentateuch. It is an outline, because it is brief; it is only *one possible outcome*, because in due course there may be others. This outcome exploits the "user-base" approach to the text; it is not, however, limited to it. Interpretation of the text is liberated from the need to tease out material for continuous sources or editing. Stylistic qualities, including repetition, may heighten the meaning of the text. Other insights from modern biblical scholarship are brought to bear where they are helpful or required. For a one-paragraph summary of what follows, see the introduction (above, p. 7).

Outcome in Genesis A: Nature of Humanity

Beyond the benefits, just noted, of the "text-as-base-for-user" approach for story-telling, a further consideration has a major impact on the early chapters of Genesis. Principally because of the likely absence of P, interpreters are liberated from the need to see sources beginning with Gen 1:1 and Gen 2:4b. The texts, therefore, need not be looked at as reflecting the beginnings of humanity but rather as studies in humanity, placed at the beginning. Viewed as the beginning of the pentateuchal sources, the early chapters of Genesis were inevitably associated with the *beginnings* of humankind. Freed from the sources, these chapters can more easily be seen as reflections on the *nature* of humankind—and for that reason placed at the beginning.[1]

Genesis 1:1–2:4a

The opening chapter of Genesis is magnificent. It has dominated discussion of the biblical thinking about creation in ways that are unfair to it and also to so many other creation texts, because its dominance led to their being ignored.[2] Despite its biblically unique structure over seven days, its implications for Israel's worldview and its correlation with Israel's Sabbath have been largely disregarded. The question of what happens in hermeneutic understanding when two different accounts of creation are juxtaposed in one text has not been adequately taken into account. The possibility that Genesis One (Gen 1:1–2:4a) serves more as an image of an ideal world than as an account of God's creative activity has to be taken most seriously.

It opens with the all-time great headline in literature:

> *bĕrē'šît bārā' 'ĕlōhîm*
> IN THE BEGINNING GOD CREATED THE HEAVENS AND THE EARTH.

The precise syntax has bothered Jewish and Christian scholars since at least the Middle Ages. It is controversial in its grammar, which has implications for its content; it is best understood as a principal sentence, "a heading that takes in everything in the narrative in one single sentence."[3]

At the beginning, the world was what one might have expected: a chaos, a desert waste, incapable of supporting life (v. 2). By the time of God's Sabbath rest at the end of the process, the world is in right and proper order, awash with life. God's action in the process has been majestic and sovereign.

---

1. A different approach to these chapters is taken by Erhard Blum, *Studien zur Komposition des Pentateuch* (Berlin: de Gruyter, 1990), 278–85. More recently, see Markus Witte, *Die biblische Urgeschichte: Redaktions- und theologiegeschichtliche Beobachtungen zu Genesis 1,1–11,26*, BZAW 265 (Berlin: de Gruyter, 1998). Joseph Blenkinsopp argues for seeing the traditional J text as a postexilic supplement to P ("A Post-exilic lay source in Genesis 1–11," in *Abschied vom Jahwisten*, ed. J. C. Gertz et al., 49–61.

2. For example: Job 26:6–13 and 38:4–38; Ps 104:5–30; Prov 8:22–31; Gen 2:4b–25; also references such as Isa 51:9–10; Job 7:12; 9:13; Ps 74:12–17.

3. Westermann, *Genesis 1–11* (Minneapolis: Augsburg, 1984), 94.

The words that describe the initial situation are unsurprisingly ambiguous. They can reach back toward the chaos: a fierce wind swept over the waters. They can reach forward toward God's action to come: the spirit of God hovered over the waters. The ambiguity pales into insignificance as the voice of God is proclaimed: "Let there be light" (v. 3).

God does things and orders things done, but overall it is God's word—"and God said"—that is in sovereign control. However, rather than following the text through the stages of the process, it can be appropriate for us here to view the whole and admire the product.

The symbolism of light replaces the former darkness and chaos. The waters above are safely separated from us. The dangerous forces of the sea are kept at bay. The life-giving fertility of the earth abounds with food from plants and trees. The skies supply lights and stars, for days and nights, for months and years, for seasons. Vitality is everywhere. Fish fill the waters; the birds fill the air; the animals are all over the earth. To crown it all, there is humankind, made in the image and likeness of God, male and female, and blessed by God ("and indeed, it was very good," 1:31).

There has been a smooth procession of days, from evening to morning, from evening to morning. Six of them. On the seventh day, God stopped and rested—in the sounds of the Hebrew language, God sabbathed. What could be more ideal! The feared unknown of chaos has been replaced by the welcome familiarity of order: darkness by light, uncertainty by security, barrenness by plenty, emptiness by life, the unpopulated by people. This is a faith claim: all is according to the sovereign will of God. And God willed a world where six days of work were followed by a seventh day of rest and Sabbath. No matter how much chaos and darkness may encroach on this image of the ideal, God, who is committed to this ideal, will ultimately work God's will upon this our world. It is an amazing tribute to the faith of some in ancient Israel to have made this claim—above all, if this text, as is generally thought, was given its final form around the time of exile, at the absolute nadir of Israel's fortunes.

There is an ideal quality to this text where the opening to world and life comes to closure in the repose of God.

The differences between Genesis One (short for Gen 1:1–2:4a) and Genesis Two (short for Gen 2:4b–25) are so clear and have been so frequently rehearsed that further discussion here is unnecessary. One understanding of the two would allow for the preservation of variant traditions. Another would allow that the focus of Genesis One is not so much information on the process of creation as the presentation of an ideal for the created world. Similarly, Genesis Two is focused less on the process of creation and more on providing a situation within which the realities of human life can be explored. As the image of an ideal world, Genesis One is complete in itself.

The chapters in Genesis that follow fall into three groups: (1) the human capacity to have come from the hands of God and have moved to the horrors of violence (Gen 2:4b–4:24); (2) the possibility of a far-from-holy human existence alongside an all-holy God (Gen 5–10); (3) another story of human failure, in its own way a parallel to Gen 2–3 (Gen 11:1–9). (Enhancements and the like are relatively few and are treated in appendix 4, below.)

Genesis 2:4b–4:24

The first group comprises Gen 2:4b–4:24. In the first story, a pair (the man and the woman) stands for us all, being in a situation where the boundaries of their living are made clear (there is just one: "You may freely eat of every tree of the garden; but of the tree of the knowledge of good and evil you shall not eat" [2:16–17]). The boundary is not observed. They go beyond the boundary in the garden, so beyond the boundary of the garden they are obliged to go. Intimacy, trust, and harmony with the environment are eroded. Israel knew, as we know, that if appropriate boundaries are observed, life is better.

Cain is confronted, as was Israel and as are we, with the inequality of human life. He did not come to terms with it, failed to handle the situation, and killed his favored brother. God's intervention involves the issue of justice and mercy. Cain's banishment and fear imply a broader context than the garden ("anyone who meets me" [4:14]). The Cain story moves on to Lamech, from family to generations, seven from the beginning in fact. In association with the advance of culture, the story underscores the place of violence in human society: "I have killed a man for wounding me. . . . If Cain is avenged sevenfold, truly Lamech seventy-sevenfold" (4:23–24).

Israel learned from experience, as we learn, that all the way along the range from the occasional pettiness and at times viciousness of interpersonal power to the massiveness of despotic power, power tends to corrupt, and appropriate boundaries seldom prevail.

Genesis 5–10

The "list of the descendants of Adam" in Gen 5 is, in fact, a beginning in its own right (vv. 1–2). The descendants after Adam—made in the likeness of God, created male and female, and blessed and named "humankind" (ʾādām)—are listed as Seth, Enosh, and so on. Cain and Abel do not feature, with differences for the generations after Cain. Genesis 4:25–26 doubles back massively in order to cast a bridge over this gap. The gap is still there (see appendix 1, pp. 111–12). Ten generations take the text from Adam to Noah (5:3–32).

The flood text is not the Bible's best-told story and is uneven. It has been badly misunderstood as reporting only the destructive action of a wrathful God (not the grieving God of Gen 6:6). It is among the Bible's best pieces of theology, for it grapples with one of the deepest of theological issues: how a far-from-holy humankind can remain in relationship with an all-holy God. It remains mystery: it is in the realm of myth. A single story is told that begins with destruction and ends with its opposite. Nothing is resolved; the story is told and belief is affirmed.

The flood text itself is obviously a composite. It opens with God's observation "that the wickedness of humankind was great in the earth, and that every inclination (*yēṣer*) of the thoughts of their hearts was only evil continually" (Gen 6:5). To this is added the comment that "the earth was corrupt in God's sight, and the earth was filled with violence" (6:11). As a result, God was regretful and grieved (6:6) and determined to make an end of all flesh (6:13). After the flood, God is presented as saying: I will never again curse the ground because of humankind, "for the inclination (*yēṣer*) of the human heart is evil from youth"; nor will I ever again destroy every living creature (8:21). Life will go on (8:22). The text goes on, in ch. 9, to describe features of the new earth: there will be "fear and dread" in the animal world (9:2) and killing and murder in the human world (9:5); the death penalty will be imposed on those who shed human blood (9:6). Life will go on (9:7). With this less-than-perfect world, God is presented establishing an unconditional and everlasting covenant never again to destroy (9:8–17).[4]

As Noth has pointed out, composite texts of this kind, where one version is interwoven with another, are the exception rather than the rule.[5] Other examples are the crossing of the Sea (Exod 14) and the story of David and Goliath (1 Sam 17–18). Here, the major components of the composite text end with the same message (cf. 8:21–22 and 9:1–7, 8–17): God's long-term coexistence with our less-than-perfect world.

A ten-generation genealogy, from Adam to Noah, leads up to this story; another genealogy leads on from the story to a repeopled earth (Gen 5–10).

The two little vignettes in 6:1–4 and 9:18–28 are deftly located, in the first case, after the genealogy and before the story and, in the second case, after the story and before the genealogy. Their interpretation is far from simple and will not be developed here.

Genesis 11:1–9

The story of the tower of Babel (Gen 11:1–9) is an odd passage that may blend versions of the story. Coming after ch. 10, with its multiplicity of families, languages, lands, and nations repeopling the earth, ch. 11 has a nameless group migrate from the east, the whole earth having one language. Akin to the situation of the couple in the garden who have become like God (Gen 3:22), they set out to make a name for themselves and build a tower "with its top in the heavens." They are prevented from doing this by being scattered abroad, their language confused. While thematically evoking Eden (Genesis Two), the Babel tradition is out of kilter with what precedes it in ch. 10. As for what follows in the present text, 11:1–9 provides some sort of buffer between the family of Shem, with a multibranched genealogy extending widely over their territory (10:21–31),

---

4. Horst Seebass speaks of 9:1–17 as a "monumental elucidation" of 8:20–22 and later speaks of 8:20–22 as "belonging indisputably to the most important [verses] of the whole Bible" (*Genesis I: Urgeschichte [1,1–11,26]*, [Neukirchen-Vluyn: Neukirchener Verlag, 1996], 206, 220). For 9:8–17, see appendix 3.

5. Noth, *Pentateuchal Traditions*, 249–50. Among possibilities, the flood text can be understood as a combination of pentateuchal sources or as a base narrative with adequate indications of an alternative version—with options or expansions included.

and the ten-generation linear genealogy that makes the link between Shem and Abram (whose name will be made great, 12:2).

Summary

It is helpful to recognize the thematic structure in the composite text that is Gen 1–11. Genesis One, as we have seen, is likely an image of the ideal, a picture of how a perfect world might have looked as it came from the hands of its creator. Genesis 2–4 brings the user's gaze back to reality and the human capacity to transgress whatever boundaries are part of that reality. Genesis 5–10 moves to theological contemplation: the paradox of the coexistence of a sinful world and its sinless creator. Finally, the Babel story brings us back to our everyday sinful world, scattered and divided. Israel's theologians may have visualized Israel's destiny as bringing this sinful world closer to the picture of the ideal. It is an appropriate preamble to what follows.

Reflection

Given the significance of Gen 1–11, a pause for reflection is in order. The task of interpreting text, and in its own right the present text, cannot be a solely scholarly one. Of hermeneutic necessity, it involves the mutual interaction of text and person, what the text brings to the person and what the person brings to the text. The infinite variety of human experience must generate infinite potential for the mutual encounter with a text, limited only by adequate awareness of one's human experience and fidelity to one's informed perception of the phenomena of the text. This is a book not of interpretation but of rethinking. It may open the way to interpretation; it cannot undertake full interpretation. On occasion, we offer limited pointers to interpretation, based on our experience of the present text; in a book such as this, there is not space to venture more.

Outcome in Genesis B: Ancestors of Israel

The Biblical Text of Genesis 12–36 as It Presents Itself

For the purposes of this book, the discussion of Gen 12–36 is separated into two phases. First, we examine the text as it presents itself to the reader or user. As presented by the text, there is one family line: Abraham is the father of Isaac and Isaac the father of Jacob. Second, also present in the text, however, are discordances in this regard (i.e., the information that, at various points, appears to subvert this presentation), discussed below (pp. 52–54). This separation between what the text claims "as it presents itself" (pp. 30–52) and the discordances enshrined within this presentation in the text (pp. 52–60) is important for our task of exploring Israel's working out of its theology and self-understanding. The family sequence of Abraham, Isaac, and Jacob is a central affirmation in the text; nevertheless the same text enshrines the difficulties regarding this sequence.

As the identification of text shows clearly (see appendix 4), the impact of our recommended approach is considerable. It is not to be confused with former literary-critical and form-critical procedures. Most of the unevenness in the sequence of the biblical narrative can be seen to result from the need to combine in one sequence narrative traditions from different origins. In a "user-base" approach, the much-discussed evident duplication boils down—for the ancestral narratives in their entirety (i.e., Gen 12–36)—to the equivalent of some eighty verses of enhancement, preserving variants and options (i.e., a tad more than three verses per chapter). A simpler text results, in place of the complexity of the continuous sources.

Abraham Cycle

For understandable reasons, the Abraham cycle (Gen 11:10–25:18) is far and away the most complex of the Genesis narrative cycles.[6] As has long been recognized, at the core there are Abraham family traditions. Along with it, there are also the traditions of Abraham and Lot that somehow belong together. Other traditions exist that are associated with Abraham (e.g., 12:10–20 and 20:1–18; 15:1–21; etc.). The place of *El Shaddai* has long been recognized; the alignment of these concerns as a separate interest is new.

We are tempted to begin directly with Abraham in Gen 12:1–3, but the ancestor has to be grounded in his family and its distant roots. The cycle of traditions begins with the genealogy from Shem to Terah (Gen 11:10–32; note that this genealogy is not identical in style with that of Gen 5). Once identified, Abraham is given his marching orders (*lek lĕkā*; "Go") with the massive promise attached. He goes through the land, from Shechem to Bethel, ending up at Hebron (13:18). But midway he goes from Bethel to Egypt; on return to Bethel, after Abraham separates from Lot, God says: "Rise up, walk through the length and the breadth of the land, for I will give it to you" (13:17). This "walk through" is the last we hear of any such physical intimacy with the land until a burying place is purchased there (Gen 23). The land is to be shown Abraham in 12:1, is promised to Abraham's seed in 12:7, and the gift to Abraham himself in this context is mentioned only within the enrichment (13:14–17). With 13:18, he is at Hebron.

The somewhat uneven sequence of the narrative results from the combination of material from three origins (the Abraham family traditions, Abraham traditions, and the Abraham-Lot traditions; see appendix 4). The issue of Abraham's age is appropriate for an ancestral story (v. 4b). The little enrichment in 12:5a specifies the necessary possessions, easing the inclusion of the Abraham-Lot traditions; Sarah is available for vv. 10–20. The enrichment in 13:14–17 offers the option of further reflecting on the divine promise of the land (cf. Gen 28:14); the invitation to "walk through the length and breadth of the land" allows a smooth modulation into Abraham's move to Hebron (13:18).

---

6. For a valuable survey of recent research on Gen 12–25, see Thomas Christian Römer, "Recherches actuelles sur le cycle d'Abraham," in *Studies in the Book of Genesis: Literature, Redaction and History*, ed. A. Wénin, BETL 155 (Leuven: Leuven University Press, 2001), 179–211.

If there is to be a nation, there have to be descendants. Genesis 15 affirms the promise of descendants but hardly helps to provide them. Sarah sends Abraham to Hagar, whose child is Ishmael (Gen 16). Isaac is promised and named (Gen 17:19), the promise reiterated without any name (Gen 18:10), and finally Isaac arrives (Gen 21:1–7). He grows and is weaned; apart from Gen 24, we do not hear of him until after Abraham's death. Ishmael receives more attention (Gen 16 and 21).

At the start of the cycle, Abraham is hardly in Canaan before he leaves it for Egypt (12:10–20). For reasons that we may not fully understand, it appears to have been necessary that this episode be located here at the beginning. Later, the separation of Abraham and Lot happens at Bethel; but, as the text stands, Abraham had journeyed on into Egypt and then had to come back to Bethel. Much the same story is told a second time for Abraham at Gerar (Gen 20); it is the beginning of Abraham's life in Canaan without Lot. At Gerar again, it is told for Isaac (Gen 26:1–11); this too comes at the beginning of Isaac's dealings with the Philistine king, Abimelech. In some way, the stories carry an assurance of God's protection in the isolation of a foreign land.

Back from Egypt, Abraham and Lot separate. Abraham makes Lot an unlimited offer—almost unwisely generous—and Lot takes the best of the land, the well-watered plain of the Jordan. In what we here see as an enrichment, God makes Abraham an even more generous promise: everything in sight, without restriction (13:14–17). In terms of what lies ahead, God's action is fine; in terms of its immediate context, the promise is troubling—the Jordan plain is in sight and in Lot's possession. Abraham's generosity to Lot redounds to Abraham's credit, despite Lot's future being limited; given that future, God's generosity to Abraham will not renew the conflict that the separation sought to avoid.

The text continues to enhance the figure of Abraham. In the tradition of Gen 14, Abraham rescues Lot. In the tradition of Gen 18—intimately interwoven with the promise of a child to Sarah—God informs Abraham (after reference to Gen 12:2–3) of the forthcoming fate of Sodom and Gomorrah, allowing Abraham to intercede at length for the doomed cities (for Gen 18–19, see appendix 2). According to Gen 19:29, looking in on the story from the outside, it was due to Abraham that Lot was spared.

A reflective pause is in order, allowing for thought regarding the Abraham family traditions and the Abraham-Lot traditions. Land and descendants would appear to be central to Abraham's needs and God's promise in Gen 12:1–3. Beyond divine promises, however, both land and descendants receive minimal treatment in the traditions preserved for us. Fuller treatment is given to accounting for relationships and establishing separation. Lot is there at the beginning; after the overthrow of Sodom and Gomorrah, he is relegated to a cave in the hills, becomes the ancestor of Moabites and Ammonites, and vanishes from the narrative. He is family and he is distanced. Similarly, Ishmael is son to Abraham, ancestor of the Ishmaelites, and distanced from Israel. An initial separation from Ishmael occurs with ch. 16 and a final separation in ch. 21; an initial separation from Lot is in ch. 13 and the ultimate separation in ch. 19 (Moabites and Ammonites). Ishmael's descendants are noted in Gen 25:12–18; no more is heard of him beyond Gen 28:9, where Esau goes to him and marries his daughter. In its own way, that emphasizes the strange tension of being both in the family and out of the picture. Tradition has a distance between the brothers. Esau will be at Mt. Seir, Jacob at Succoth. Esau, the outsider whose wives are considered troublesome (Gen 26:34–35), seeks to overcome his troubles by marrying within the family, but to an outsider (daughter of Ishmael). The emphasis in these traditions is on Israel's relationship with its neighbors and its distinctness and difference from them.

Before the first conception of a son, Gen 15:1–21 affirms the promises of descendants and land, encapsulates the whole history of Israel down to the exodus and beyond, and seals it with a covenant.[7] Brueggemann may be right to say that "this chapter is pivotal for the Abraham tradition,"[8] but that does not determine its origin. There is agreement that it is not an original Abraham tradition, but rather artificial theologizing. As Westermann observes, "it is scarcely possible any longer to ascribe either vv. 1–6 or vv. 7–21 to the oldest layer of the patriarchal story";[9] Scullion says Gen 15 comprises "artificial narratives constructed around and for the purpose of communicating the promises."[10] In Gen 17, beginning the *El Shaddai* traditions, the all-important word is "to be God to you and to your offspring after you" (v. 7). The promise is assured by covenant, associated with descendants and land as a perpetual holding, and expressed in circumcision. There will be an heir from Sarah: Isaac, not Ishmael; but Ishmael will be taken care of (made fruitful and exceedingly numerous, the father of twelve princes and a great nation [v. 20]). The birth of Isaac is noted in 21:1–7, bringing together in the present text aspects of 18:9–15 and 17:15–21. In 21:1–7 itself, attribution to sources or strands is most uncertain; decisions about how to use what is there can be left to a storyteller's skills. In 21:1, the duality of visitation and conception is possible (echoing 18:14). In 21:2, a similar duality (conception and birth) is present, with *elohim* signaling an alternative to v. 1 (cf. 17:21). Verse 3 may come from the Abraham family traditions; it may come from *El Shaddai* concerns (cf. 17:19). Verse 4 may belong to the *El Shaddai* traditions, reflecting the concern for circumcision (17:10–14). Verse 5 suggests closure, in which case vv. 6–7 are enrichment, with two reminiscences given to Sarah

---

7. See John Ha, for whom Gen 15 is a compositional unity and probably exilic (*Genesis 15: A Theological Compendium of Pentateuchal History*, BZAW 181 [Berlin: de Gruyter, 1989]). More recently, see Thomas Römer, for whom Gen 15 was probably the last text integrated into the Abraham cycle ("Recherches actuelles," 198–210, see pp. 203, 206. For J. C. Gertz also, the final form (including vv. 11, 13–16) is postpriestly ("Abraham, Mose und der Exodus: Beobachtungen zur Redaktionsgeschichte von Gen 15," in *Abschied vom Jahwisten*, ed. J. C. Gertz et al., 63–81, esp. 73–74).

8. Walter Brueggemann, *Genesis*, Int (Atlanta: John Knox, 1982), 140.

9. Westermann, *Genesis 12–36*, 215.

10. John J. Scullion, *Genesis: A Commentary for Students, Teachers, and Preachers* (Collegeville, MN: Liturgical Press, 1992), 129.

(cf. 18:12–15 for v. 6 and 17:17 for v. 7); note the introductory clauses, "And Sarah/she said" (vv. 6–7). Verse 7, with its "nursing," modulates from the birth (v. 2a) to the weaning (v. 8). The Hagar and Ishmael story begins with v. 8.

In the present text, Gen 21:22–34 provides a suitable bridge, preparing for Isaac and Abimelech in 26:12–33 (there is much in common between the two); it is possible that the passage points to an absorption of Isaac traditions into the Abraham cycle or, the reverse, development of Isaac's out of Abraham's.[11] Genesis 22:1–19, the sacrifice of Isaac (the *Aqedah* in Jewish tradition), requires the reminder that its readers encounter a text; they do not contemplate an event. Presented as a divine command to sacrifice Isaac, it is the most radical threat to the promise made Abraham; Israel's destiny is at stake. Israel needed to believe that God ruled the world and that God was committed to taking care of Israel; Gen 22:1–19 is an extraordinarily dramatic presentation of that belief. Even Westermann agrees that "it originated relatively late."[12]

Genesis 23 is frequently treated as a significant acquisition of land in Canaan by Abraham. As burial place, Machpelah has evident importance within the *El Shaddai* traditions (see below) and is a pointer to family unity. Genesis 23:17–18 is largely duplicated in 23:19–20. Verse 17 has the field, Machpelah, and Mamre; so does v. 19. Verse 18 has the purchase made in the presence of the locals; v. 20 notes the purchase from the locals. The use of the verb *q-w-m* in both vv. 17 and 20 (NRSV, "passed") is rare (cf. Lev 25:30; 27:19—conveyancing). Given the importance of this cave in the *El Shaddai* material, it is likely that its purchase and first use attracted *El Shaddai* attention. Pointers to this are v. 1 (the formulation of Sarah's age, see below) and v. 2aβ ("at Kiriath-arba [that is, Hebron] in the land of Canaan"; 23:19; 25:9; 35:27; 49:30). It is possible, therefore, that a short notice reported Sarah's death, Abraham's grief, and Sarah's burial (23:1–2, 19–20). In this scenario, vv. 3–18 are an enrichment of unknown origin. To attribute their presence to the *El Shaddai* circle, with its interest in this grave, is attractive; but there is not compelling evidence to do so.[13]

Last in the sequence, before the involvement with Keturah, is Gen 24:1–67. Alexander Rofé has cogently described the chapter as "a very late composition, written in the fifth century BCE."[14] (We will discuss this in greater detail below.)

---

11. The issue of the twelfth-century Philistines in these traditions needs mention. It can be accommodated (Kenneth A. Kitchen, *On the Reliability of the Old Testament* [Grand Rapids: Eerdmans, 2003], 339–41); it can be problematic (Blenkinsopp, *Pentateuch*, 128). See also Westermann, *Genesis 12–36*, 347.

12. Westermann, *Genesis 12–36*, 355. J. C. Gertz, following Veijola, affirms it as postexilic (*Tradition und Redaktion in der Exoduserzählung: Untersuchungen zur Endredaktion des Pentateuch*, FRLANT 186 [Göttingen: Vandenhoeck & Ruprecht, 2000], 273).

13. See, with differences, Westermann, *Genesis 12–36*, 371–72.

14. Alexander Rofé, "An Enquiry into the Betrothal of Rebekah," in *Die Hebräische Bibel und ihre zweifache Nachgeschichte: Festschrift für Rolf Rendtorff zum 65. Geburtstag*, ed. E. Blum, C. Macholz, and E. Stegemann (Neukirchen: Neukirchener Verlag, 1990), 27–39, see p. 27. For Westermann, Gen 24 is "unquestionably later" than the stories of Gen 29 and Exod 2 (*Genesis 12–36*, 384); according to Scullion, "the story is generally regarded as late . . . for the following reasons [four are noted]. . . . These arguments together would set the composition of the story in the post-exilic period" (*Genesis*, 188).

Generally speaking, the Abraham cycle in the present text is constituted by what we have called above the Abraham family traditions, the Abraham-Lot traditions, and the *El Shaddai* material. Beyond these, others are termed Abraham traditions, coming from Israel's pool of traditions, shaping Israel's perceptions of itself. Already mentioned are the episodes in Egypt and Gerar (12:10–20; 20:1–18); also Gen 15:1–21; 21:22–34; 22:1–19; and 24:1–67. A number of passages enrich the traditions in which they are now found, including Gen 16:10–14; 18:20–21; 22:15–18; and 24:7, 25, 30, 40b, 61, 62b. For less important details, see the text listing and discussions below in appendix 4.

Overview: Abraham Cycle

The move toward the making of the final text is a logical step.[15] The possible scenarios are many, and detailed proposals are necessarily speculative. In this book, we refrain from speculating.

The Abraham traditions are operating on at least two levels: (1) Abraham's concern for land and descendants; (2) a sequence of promise, response, and renewed promise. As to the first, the land is limited and the primary descendant (Isaac) restricted to a few verses (21:2–4, 8). As to the sequence, the promise is first in 12:1–3, and Abraham's first failure to trust is in Egypt; rescued in Egypt, he is generous to Lot and finds God more generous still. In passing, we may note that the thread of the Lot story can function as a countertheme: Lot chooses the best (ch. 13), is captured and then rescued by Abraham (ch. 14), and only escapes Sodom and Gomorrah with his life through God's loyalty to Abraham (19:29). Genesis 15 resumes the sequence (of promise, response, and renewed promise), with Abraham's doubts providing the impetus for God's renewed promise with an expanded trajectory. Abraham's trust succumbs to Sarah; he acts and Ishmael is on the scene. God's promise of an heir is renewed with its fullest expression (ch. 17); then God acts and Isaac is born. Ishmael has been moved aside but elevated (17:18–20). The ultimate test of trust is in ch. 22; Abraham trusts his God, but loses his son (22:19—Isaac is unmentioned). Sarah is buried (ch. 23), Isaac is married (ch. 24), and with Abraham's end (in ch. 25) the cycle can conclude. Through it all, God's commitment is given to a less-than-perfect human being.

The present text offers the storyteller or the user options built in at a number of points (e.g., the options around the doom of Sodom and Gomorrah). Passages such as Gen 15 and Gen 17 are not so much optional variants for storytelling as pieces for large-scale theological reflection.

Isaac

Genesis 25:19–34 is focused on Esau and Jacob and belongs within the Jacob cycle. All that is left as possible independent Isaac tradition is now in Gen

---

15. For moves in this direction, see Blum's work in his two monographs (*Vätergeschichte* and *Studien*) and subsequent studies that explore the stages of development that ended in the compiled text. For a discussion in English, see Damian J. Wynn-Williams, *The State of the Pentateuch: A Comparison of the Approaches of M. Noth and E. Blum*, BZAW 249 (Berlin: de Gruyter, 1997).

26.[16] Within Gen 26, the theme of blessing comes early (vv. 3–5), with the Deuteronomistic overtones of God's oath to Abraham and the obedience of Abraham to God; the promise is within the story of the couple and the king (vv. 1*–11), with its echoes of Gen 12:10–20 and Gen 20.[17] The precise correlation of "the land that I shall show you," in which Isaac is to settle (root: *š-k-n*), the land in which he is to reside "as an alien," and "all these lands" that will be given to him and his descendants is uncertain and may be left to the skills of the storyteller; the drift is clear. If, as we believe, v. 2 is original, with an enhancement in vv. 3–5, the "settle" (root: *š-k-n*) of v. 2 implies a longer period of occupation than v. 6's "dwelt" (JPS; root: *y-š-b*), that is, in the meantime, he dwelt in Gerar.

The narrative goes on to Abimelech's dealings with Isaac, the pastoralist (vv. 12–33). First in the valley of Gerar, wells are specifically referred to as having been dug by Abraham (vv. 17–22); then Isaac and Abimelech, in Beer-sheba, solemnize a peace treaty, the account ending with an etymology for Beer-sheba. Ahuzzath, Abimelech's adviser, is not mentioned in 21:22–34, but Phicol, commander of Abimelech's army is. Some elements, at least, recur. It is difficult to draw conclusions from this, but absorption of Isaac traditions into the Abraham cycle is possible. The final note, on Esau's initial marriages (26:34–35), may well be attributed to the *El Shaddai* concerns.

Jacob Cycle

The Jacob cycle opens with the beginning of what we may call the Jacob family traditions (found within 25:19–34).[18] The passage offers glimpses of tension, which is resolved, to some degree only, in the last two chapters of these traditions (Gen 32–33). At the beginning, the barren wife conceives, and a pithy divine oracle sums up the gist of what is to come; beyond merely sons, nations and peoples are in view.[19]

> Two nations are in your womb,
>   and two peoples born of you shall be divided;
> the one shall be stronger than the other,
>   the elder shall serve the younger.
>
> (25:23)

The narrative moves from birth to birthright, from infancy to adulthood. Esau is firstborn and the elder; in his hunger, coming in from the field, he sells his

---

16. As late, intrusive, artificial, and borrowing from the Abraham cycle, see Alfred Marx, "Genèse 26,1–14A," in *Jacob: Commentaire á plusieurs voix de Gen 25–36*, ed. J.-D. Macchi and T. Römer, *MdB* 44 (Geneva: Labor et Fides, 2001), 22–33. In this context, see Noth's imaginative traditio-historical view of the Isaac traditions as more ancient than those of either Jacob or Abraham (e.g., *Pentateuchal Traditions*, 106, 109).

17. See John Van Seters, *Abraham in History and Tradition* (New Haven, CT: Yale University Press, 1975), esp. 167–91. The potential difference between the stories as independent versions and as part of the extended narrative needs to be taken into account.

18. For a close study of the whole cycle, see Blum, *Vätergeschichte*, 66–270.

19. The issue of nations and peoples recurs with the identification of Esau as Edom in Gen 36. The interplay of 25:22 (sons), 23 (oracle), 24 (twins) is intricate.

birthright (25:29–34). At the end, on the news of Jacob's return, Esau with four hundred men is coming to meet his brother. "Jacob was greatly afraid and distressed" (32:7 [Heb. 32:8]). The meeting, and Jacob's return to his country, end with reconciliation between the two, but also their separation (33:16–17). In between, this tension between the brothers is, as it were, in remission, subtly replaced by other tensions. At the end, the statements of the birth oracle foretelling Jacob's strength and Esau's service are ignored; in fact, they appear to be reversed—Jacob's weakness contrasts with Esau's superiority. The promise at the beginning is not fulfilled at the end.

The family traditions also contain other tensions. Because of tension, Jacob leaves his own and goes "to the land of the people of the east" (29:1). At Bethel, on the way, he receives God's promise: "I am with you . . . and will bring you back to this land" (28:15). There is tension over both the acquisition of his wives (ch. 29) and the acquisition of their children (29:31–30:24). There is also tension over the acquisition of Jacob's wealth (30:25–31:54). On Jacob's return to his own, the tension with Esau is resolved—but not completely. The issue of Bethel recurs in the present text (ch. 35), but in traditions that may not belong to the Jacob family traditions.

Once under way, the Jacob narrative is compact and continuous. The winning of his wives merits only a few verses in the text, although the process took more than a few years. When it comes to the arrival of the children, a variety of factors betrays a composite origin for the text; no amount of scholarly ingenuity has provided a satisfactory account of these origins. Similar differences of origin lie behind the narrative of Jacob's acquisition of wealth. As with Abraham, his wealth is affirmed; the detailed specifications are not given (with the possible exception of Gen 32:15–16 [Heb.; NRSV vv. 14–15]). The present text is composite; nevertheless, it is the text we have. To ignore its being composite would be as foolish as to imagine that its difficulties can be totally resolved. Some pointers along the way will help.

At the core of the cycle, the continuity of the narrative thread extends from Jacob's departure to his return. Fear of Esau precipitates the departure and surfaces at the return. Before the departure, there are issues of birth and rivalry (25:19–34); after the return, there is a further cluster of tradition (chs. 34–36).[20] Within the continuity of the narrative thread, variant versions are preserved at four points: (i) the birthing and naming of Jacob's sons; (ii) the gaining of Jacob's wealth; (iii) Jacob's parting from Laban; (iv) Jacob's meeting with Esau.

The present text of the Jacob cycle begins with the traditions of rivalry between Esau and Jacob from birth (25:19–34), follows with the Isaac traditions (26:1–33, see above) without mention of the two sons until Esau's first marriages (26:34–35), and modulates into the lengthy story of Jacob's deceitfully obtaining his dying father's final blessing, at the instigation of Rebekah (27:1–40; cf.

---

20. It is possible that 25:22–23 is an enhancement emphasizing the national focus (Israel/Edom). Verses 21 and 24 appropriately account for the birth. However, see Blum, *Vätergeschichte*, 69–79.

v. 4, "before I die"). The motivation for Jacob's departure is to hand. The issues of the origins of parts of this text are discussed below. Chapters 24 and 27 contain similarities, and if Gen 24 is deemed late, it is unlikely that Gen 27 would differ much in date. In this case, the material involving both Isaac and Rebekah is likely, as a whole, to be of similar date (possibly, quite late). If Gen 24 is deemed late, there are also implications for Gen 29:1–14; these are discussed below. The limits to the Isaac-Rebekah material under consideration are Gen 24:1–29:14; naturally, not all the material within these limits would need to be of the same origin or date.

Jacob's move to Haran, via Bethel, is reported in 28:10–22.[21] The association of Jacob with Bethel is a challenge to interpreters, as is the text itself. In the present text, Jacob is there on his way out to the east. Later, well after his return, he is told by God to settle there (35:1); he does not but (in the present text, after a stay of substantial but unspecified length at Succoth and Shechem) passes through Bethel on his way south. In the present text, God appears to him there twice (28:13–17; 35:9–13). God deals with Abraham twice; both times, God promises the land: to Abraham's offspring (at Shechem, 12:7) and later to both Abraham and his offspring (near Bethel, 13:14–17). The gift of the land to Abraham is not mentioned in ch. 28 (cf. 28:13, "I will give to you [Jacob] and to your offspring"); the gift to Abraham (and Isaac!) is noted at 35:12, although no mention is made of Bethel as the place of that appearance (perhaps to accommodate the inclusion of Isaac).

The marked differences in the two versions that report the divine speech to Jacob at Bethel are worth noting. There are five elements in the speech attributed to YHWH in 28:13–15.

    i. self-designation of God (YHWH, God of Abraham and Isaac)
    ii. gift of the land ("to you and to your offspring")
    iii. abundance of descendants ("like the dust of the earth," compass points)
    iv. universal blessing ("for all the families of the earth")
    v. divine promise ("I am with you . . . and will bring you back")

There are three elements in the speech attributed to *Elohim* in 35:11–12.

    i. self-designation of God (*El Shaddai*)
    ii. abundance of descendants (a nation, a company of nations, kings)
    iii. gift of the land (to Abraham and Isaac; to you and your offspring)

In 28:13 Abraham and Isaac are named in relation to God, but in 35:12 they are named in relation to the gift of the land. In both places the land is given "to you

---

21. On Jacob at Bethel, see Blum, *Vätergeschichte*, 7–65; also Wynn-Williams, *Pentateuch*, 108–47.

and to your offspring," but in 35:12 it is given in association with the prior gift to Abraham and Isaac. The abundance of descendants is quite differently described. The use of "dust of the earth" for this comparative purpose occurs only at Gen 13:16 and 28:14 (both with the four points of the compass in the context); beyond this, in 2 Chr 1:9, it is used in reference to the people ruled by Solomon. The triad of "nation," "company of nations," and "kings" is unique to Gen 35:11. Even the "company of nations" alone is found in only one other text, Jer 50:9 (but cf. 28:3; 48:4). The last two elements in ch. 28 (vv. 14b–15) are not repeated in 35:11–12. The formula of the universal blessing is identical with that in the promise to Abraham (12:3b), adding only and appropriately "and in your offspring."

The Bethel traditions in ch. 35 can be treated separately from the Bethel traditions of ch. 28.[22] To a large extent, the present text of ch. 28 is part of the Jacob family traditions, involving Jacob's journey to the east. This narrative sequence can be understood as ending with Jacob's arrival at Succoth and Shechem (ch. 33). Genesis 34–36 are then understood as enhancements or expansions of the family traditions, perhaps from the *El Shaddai* circles (see below). In this understanding, ch. 35 must be treated in its own right, and not simply as a variant version of ch. 28.

In Gen 28:10–22 the change of divine name (from *elohim* to *yhwh*) in vv. 13–15 may point to an enhancement of the text, transforming a reported dream experience into a theophany, with accompanying divine speech.[23] Noth and source critics traced the transformation to a blending of sources; Blum and others trace it to a variety of reworkings of the text.[24] Any approach, however, must account for the "why?" that is, what meaning can we discover in these changes? Elements of the language are late; aspects in the presentation are unexpected. The

---

22. Despite Horst Seebass, *Genesis II: Vätergeschichte II (23,1–36,43)* (Neukirchen: Neukirchener Verlag, 1999), 313.

23. Without going into detailed argument, once one recognizes that elements preserved in a text are not necessarily part of the primary narrative of the text, and once the role of the storyteller or user is given due place, this much-controverted passage is not particularly difficult. The underlying core is the report of a dream experience (28:10–12, 16 [introd.], 17). Several versions of a sanctuary story can be based on this: (i) as above; (ii) with the addition of vv. 18–19, celebrating a stone pillar in the sanctuary; (iii) with the addition of vv. 20–21a, 22, relating a tithe to the sanctuary; (iv) with the addition of vv. 20–21, focusing the story on Jacob's commitment to Yahwism (attached to YHWH in some way, probably but not necessarily through the YHWH-speech in vv. 13–15). Finally, there is the version, enhanced with a YHWH-speech (vv. 13–15), that forms part of the Jacob journey story. Elements like vow (despite 31:13) and tithe are associated with a sanctuary; the promise, in this case, is to be associated with the journey.

The alternation of divine names in vv. 20–21 may be understood as a move from the generic to the personal: if god (i.e., the god of this place) will be with me . . . then YHWH (i.e., the god of this place) will be my god. The last clause (v. 21b) cannot be considered superfluous ("entbehrlich"; against Noth [*Pentateuchal Traditions*, 35 n.133]). Verse 22, with its involvement of second-person address ("you give me . . . I give to you"), belongs to a version of the sanctuary story associated with the dream experience (against Blum, *Vätergeschichte*, 88–98, esp. 91 n.19). Verse 21b (Jacob's vow) to the best of our knowledge is observed; within the narrative, v. 22 (Jacob's tithe) is not.

24. Wynn-Williams, *Pentateuch*, 83.

dilemma can be put simply: if this is an early text, why the late elements; and, if a late text, why the unexpected aspects?[25]

Three questions stand out in relation to the divine speech. Why is there no mention here of the gift of the land to Abraham and Isaac, as in 35:12? In what scenario is the gift of the land to Jacob and his descendants significant? In what scenario is the promise to bring Jacob back to the land significant? Yet another question is central to the report of the dream experience: in what scenario is Jacob's Bethel experience significant? As with origins, so with meaning: to speculate on possibilities lies outside the scope of this book. The complexity and diversity of the past are evident, and origins in the past are out of reach.

The narrative has Jacob continue his journey. The expression used in 29:1 is unique, literally: lifted up his feet. A land in the east is mentioned in Gen 25:6, in relation to the sons of Abraham's concubines; a "people of the east" is not mentioned elsewhere in Genesis (but 4x in Judg, and 2x in each of Isa, Jer, and Ezek, with two other occurrences).

The issues of Gen. 29:1–14 have been mentioned and are further discussed below. By the end of 29:30, Jacob has two wives and their two maids. In the context of 29:1–14, his wives come from within a single household, whose head claimed descent from Terah. Technically it might be said that Isaac's charge to his son was to go to "the house of Bethuel, your mother's father; and take as wife from there one of the daughters of Laban, your mother's brother" (28:2; cf. v. 6) and that Jacob's marriage to Leah and Rachel fulfilled that charge. Two factors cause unease, however. First, the founding of Jacob's family from four women— the two wives and their two maids—is not particularly consonant with Isaac's charge. Second, Bethuel is not mentioned in what follows, and Laban is identified in relation to Nahor (cf. 29:5).[26]

The untroubled text begins with 29:15. It is most instructive to realize that the text at the core of the Jacob cycle is substantially different in composition from much of the text in Genesis that precedes it. Clearly the process of growth of the text, and probably its transmission, has been different from that of other texts in Genesis—different, for example, from what has been encountered so far in Gen 1:1–11:9 or 11:10–25:18. Nevertheless, insights central to this book remain fruitful here, such as the recognition of narrative texts that preserve alternatives, with enhancements, expansions, bridging passages, and so on. The Doc-

---

25. Late elements: (i) God's self-designation ("I am YHWH") is a late usage (Lev 52x; late Isa 22x; Ezek 84x); in Genesis, it occurs twice only (15:7; 28:3; cf. with *El Shaddai*, Gen 17:1; 35:11; otherwise, Job 13:3); (ii) the association of God with Abraham and Isaac; (iii) "to you and to your offspring" (Gen 13:15; 17:7, 8; 26:3; 28:4, 13; 35:12). Unexpected aspects: (i) Abraham and Isaac are mentioned, but the gift of the land to them is not; (ii) the universal blessing is given to Jacob without mention of Abraham. Three other aspects are worth noting: the issue of return, promised in the divine speech; the significance of the location at Bethel; and the issues associated with the two versions of Jacob's vow—to become a YHWH worshiper (initial or renewal?) and to pay a tithe "of all that you give me" (unmentioned later).

26. The reference to Bethuel is surprisingly restricted (22:23; 24:15, 24, 47, 50; 25:20; 28:2, 5) and stops with ch. 28. This rather strongly suggests a separate tradition.

umentary Hypothesis looked for continuous sources. Here, at the core of the Jacob cycle, as recent critics have recognized, there is no place for continuous sources. In these texts, we have a composition—whether at one time or over the course of time—that brings together a variety of offerings. We may think of such offerings as sources, but they are not source documents, not pentateuchal sources.

The story of Jacob's marriages (29:15–30) is straightforward narrative. The section on Jacob's children (29:31–30:24) is focused on the wordplay associated with their names. The names of the sons are given exclusively by Rachel and Leah; the concerns reflected in the names are the concerns of Rachel and Leah and do not extend beyond the world of these two women. The structuring of the passage is evident, but the meaning of the structure is not. The first four sons are born to Leah, the next two to Bilhah, Rachel's maid, the next two to Zilpah, Leah's maid, the next two to Leah, and finally Joseph to Rachel. The sequence is unlikely to be natural; the structure appears artificial. Although the preceding text summarizes Jacob's feelings toward the two women as "he loved Rachel more than Leah" (29:30), the first three sons are named against a background of explicit hatred for Leah ($\check{s}\check{e}n\hat{u}^{\flat}\hat{a}$ = hated, scorned; the NRSV's "unloved" is unduly mild); the fourth is Judah. Bilhah's two are named by Rachel in terms of conflict— "struggle" and "wrestle"; Zilpah's, on the other hand, are named by Leah in terms of good fortune and happiness. At this point, the mandrakes are brought into play, although without clarity; Leah's Reuben brings them to his mother, but Rachel exercises control. More is involved than we are told. The mandrakes play a role in the naming of Issachar. With the naming of her sixth son, Zebulun, Leah returns to the theme of gaining her husband's favor. No explanation is offered of Dinah's name. Joseph's naming by Rachel is richly ambiguous (v. 24b); as participle, "the LORD is adding," it may refer to Joseph being born to Rachel after sons born to Bilhah, while as jussive, "may the LORD add," it may refer to a future son, Benjamin.

Both divine names (*elohim* [6x] and *yhwh* [5x]) are present, in both the narrative and the wordplays on the names. The text using *yhwh* (29:31, 32, 33, 35; 30:24) surrounds that using *elohim* (30:6, 17, 18, 20, 22, 23 [prescinding from 30:2]). Despite this distribution, it is not helpful to allocate the texts to Yahwist and Elohist sources.[27] For three of the names—Issachar, Zebulun, and Joseph— the potential for two explanations is present. Although certainty about the origins and meaning of the text is impossible, it seems likely that the central focus is on the wordplays, selected from traditions that employ either or both divine names. It is clear that there is more background involved than is divulged to the user; Leah is "hated," the episode of the mandrakes, needed for one tradition of Issachar's naming, conceals more than it reveals (as noted, Rachel is given a controlling role there, 30:15). The comparison with Gen 49 is instructive: there the

---

27. Westermann's distribution of the text over an older "rivalry" layer and a later "genealogical" layer is a good example of the possible that is both unnecessary and unlikely (*Genesis 12–36*, 471–72); Seebass: too fragmentary to reconstruct completely (*Genesis II/2*, 345).

issues are tribal, here, they are familial.[28] The reasons for the fascination with the wordplay and the relationships is unclear. Might it, in the realm of symbol deep in the unconscious, have some echo of Israel's awareness of being little in terms of world power and Israel's belief of being loved in terms of God? A structured text that has been assembled under the power of some such fascination is best left undisturbed, especially when no compelling reason is alleged to disturb it. The passage is stark evidence that at some point in the history of ancient Israel some people had no qualms about mingling the divine names, if desired.

The following text (Gen 30:25–43), however, is a different kettle of fish.[29] It is puzzling to interpreters now and was probably puzzling to interpreters then. It may have been made more so by improvements and enhancements. The complexity of negotiating style (i.e., vv. 28 and 31) could be a storyteller's delight (cf. Gen 23:11, "I give it to you"—but it cost a pretty penny). Westermann's observation that "the accumulation of complicated steps . . . would not be possible in an oral narrative"[30] does not adequately value the role of the storyteller and the text as a base for storytelling. The written text preserves the options, and the oral storyteller chooses among them. Among the options were the inclusion of either the goats or the black lambs. The text is *enhanced*; it is not *compiled* from traditions. Interpreters will remain aware that a story requires narrative plausibility. The many issues involved here require plausibility, not reality—for example, the effectiveness of such breeding techniques, the restriction of mating to watering times, the number of years needed for Jacob to build up wealth by these means (cf. 31:41), and so on. The point of the story is made in the final narrative comment: "the man grew exceedingly rich" (30:43).[31]

Jacob has by now gained family and wealth; the narrative task now is getting the man, his wives, family, and wealth back home. The text maintains what may be a studied ambiguity regarding "return." References such as "the land of your ancestors" (31:3) and "the land of your birth" (31:13) name neither the land nor the ancestors (although 31:13 associates God with Bethel). It is not until 31:18 that Isaac and Canaan are mentioned. This is totally in line with the present text, but it scarcely places an obstacle in the way of hypotheses of an originally different tradition.

The undoubted complexity in the text recounting Jacob's departure from Laban reflects something of the options available.[32] What begins as fearful flight

---

28. Noted by Westermann, *Genesis 12–36*, 472–73.

29. Noth comments that "Gen. 30:25–43, which is very difficult to understand in its details, cannot be divided successfully into two sources" (*Pentateuchal Traditions*, 29 n.94).

30. Westermann, *Genesis 12–36*, 480, in agreement with Gunkel.

31. For "exceedingly [$mĕ'ōd mĕ'ōd$]" outside Genesis and Ezekiel, see esp. Num 14:7; 1 Kgs 7:47; 2 Kgs 10:4.

32. According to Noth, the passage is distributed between J and E, with secondary additions (*Pentateuchal Traditions*, 25, 29, 34–35); similarly Gunkel, *Genesis*, 331–42. According to Westermann, the narrator is the Yahwist; there is no Elohist source in Gen 31 (*Genesis 12–36*, 490). There are "two different expansions completely independent of each other" (ibid.). For the record, *yhwh* occurs once in v. 3 and once in v. 49; *elohim* as name occurs six times within the chapter. The divine names are not helpful for the attribution of text. The treatment of vv. 4–16 as a first expansion is superficially attractive; unfortunately, it does not account for the complexity in the subsequent text.

ends in amicable concord. The text as we have it gives storytellers plenty of scope for skilled embroidering. A primary version of the story is enhanced by two thematic concerns: the theft of Laban's household gods and details of the accord between Laban and Jacob. Verse 2 has been read as repetition but need not be, for the views of Laban's sons were shared by their father.[33] Verse 19b abruptly injects the note needed for the theme of theft of the household gods (*těrāpîm*) and the dream warning that goes with it (cf. vv. 24, 29, 42b)—itself a potential option. The complaint, "Why did you steal my gods?" (v. 30b), is followed up in vv. 32–35 and v. 37 (quite different in concern from vv. 38–42a, but associated with vv. 32–35 by Laban's search [root: *m-š-š*]). Verse 42b offers a final reference to the dream warning.

The details of the accord between Laban and Jacob are hardly satisfactory under any assessment of the text. Verse 44b ("let it be a witness between me and you") is unsatisfactory—probably corrupted, certainly grammatically impossible.[34] The LXX expands with an appeal to God as well: "And he said to him, 'Look, there is no one with us; look, God is witness between me and you.'" The expansion in vv. 45–53 may well reflect attempts to fill this lacuna, while providing a variety of options. That Jacob's household participated in a meal is twice attested (vv. 46, 54). In these two options, the protagonist is Jacob. Two further interpretations are provided with Laban as protagonist, concerning his daughters (vv. 48–50) and concerning territory limits (vv. 51–53). The little expansion in 32:2b–3 (Heb.; NRSV 1b–2) provides for a geographical identification.

In the story, the description of Laban's behavior goes well beyond what preceded in ch. 30 (e.g., 31:6–7, 38–40).[35] Furthermore, in Jacob's dream there is reference to Bethel and the vow made there (31:11–13; note the use of different word for "goats" from ch. 30).[36] The conclusion: at the time this version was formulated, the Bethel tradition was part of the larger narrative; at the same time, these texts are at the service of storytellers, and space must be left for their role. Verse 15 raises the possibility of a dowry tradition, otherwise unknown. Within 31:18, there is specific reference to Paddan-aram, Isaac, and the land of Canaan. It is one of two possible remnants of so-called P dealing with the story of Jacob (the other is within 33:18a).[37] With the existence of P understood as certain, a case could be made for this; but with the existence of P understood as uncertain,

33. Brueggemann may be right to see 31:3 as an echo of 12:1 (*Genesis*, 257). It is the only use of YHWH in the passage; its "land, fathers, kindred" echoes 12:1. If so, v. 3 is affirming the unity of the family. What Abraham leaves when departing for Canaan, Jacob returns to when departing for Canaan.

34. A covenant (intangible accord) is not a sign or witness; pillars and heaps fulfill that function—one such may perhaps be foreshadowed here. The grammatical impossibility is a feminine subject, "covenant," and a masculine verb, "let be" (Westermann, *Genesis 12–36*, 498).

35. So Seebass, *Genesis II/2*, 360–61. In storytelling, such variations naturally are to be expected; characters in the narrative shape their story according to their audience in it.

36. Westermann reorders vv. 11–13, which he regards as secondary (*Genesis 12–36*, 491–92).

37. See Noth, *Pentateuchal Traditions*, 14; Westermann, *Genesis 12–36*, 493, 527–28; also Campbell and O'Brien, *Sources of the Pentateuch*, 32–33; Rolf Rendtorff, *The Problem of the Process of Transmission in the Pentateuch*, JSOTSup 89 (German original, 1977; Sheffield: JSOT, 1990), 140–44.

even unlikely, the case for a gloss or editorial overview is much stronger. An editorial locking of this story into what preceded it in the final text is the more likely. Something similar at 33:18aβ is likely. Other details need not be dealt with here.

The departure from Laban has been negotiated and sealed by covenant. Jacob has his family and his flocks in the hill country of Gilead; he is a made man. The only danger lies ahead: Esau, named here as his brother.[38] Life with Laban and leaving it were essential to setting up Jacob as an independent figure. Jacob's encounter with Esau is essential for Jacob's survival as an independent figure. The encounter itself and, above all, the preparation for it have received considerable attention in Israelite narrative tradition. For Westermann, Jacob's prayer (32:10–13 [Heb.; NRSV 9–12]) is at the center of ch. 32, framed by the two embassies to Esau.[39] For us, in the broader sweep of the narrative, it is Jacob's encounter with God at the Jabbok (the night's wrestling) that is flanked by two accounts of the preparations and two accounts of the encounter.

Much is left unsaid. Why should Jacob fear that Esau might kill them all, "the mothers with the children" (32:12 [Heb.; NRSV 32:11])? The matter of the birthright and blessing of twenty years ago is possible as cause, but it is left unsaid. Esau has become "my lord" and has four hundred men at his disposal. What has happened in twenty years that we are not told? Jacob's "my lord" may reverse God's birth oracle, but it is unlikely, nor is it said. Does it reverse Jacob's deceit (in ch. 27)? Again, this is unlikely and not said. The gift/present is clear in the text, described as such in 33:10 (*minḥātî*) while the use of "my blessing" for Jacob's gift in 33:11 (*birkātî*) may leave an opening to ch. 27. The division into two companies is not followed up in the text. Offspring, uncountable "as the sand of the sea" (for Jacob, 32:13 [Heb.; NRSV 32:12]), were promised in the text to Abraham in these terms (Gen 22:17), not Jacob. There is a wealth of tradition to be drawn on here; the text does not unfold it all.[40]

We have options to be exercised in the telling of the story, rather than two versions of the same story. The division into two companies, the gift sent ahead, and protective ordering of the family party can be combined. As noted, the division into two companies is not followed up in the present text. Where the actual encounter with Esau is concerned, two contrasting versions appear to be present, one emphasizing heartfelt reconciliation and the other leaving space for suspicion. In the first case, Gen 33:4 strongly suggests heartfelt reconciliation: "Esau ran to meet him, and embraced him and fell on his neck and kissed him, and they wept." In the other (33:12–17), deceitfully Jacob lies (he does not "come to

38. The apparent ease of journeys, from Haran to Gilead or from Seir to the Jabbok, is a pointer to the quality of the unreal that attaches to these "ancestral" stories.

39. *Genesis 12–36*, 504. That the "two embassies" are rather two versions of Jacob's preparations can be seen from the duplication of vv. 14a and 22b (Heb.; NRSV vv. 13a and 21b).

40. For further discussion of the Jacob-Esau traditions, see Konrad Schmid, "Die Versöhnung zwischen Jakob und Esau (Genesis 33,1–11)," in *Jacob*, ed. J.-D. Macchi et al., 211–26. We regret that Schmid's *Erzväter und Exodus* was not available to us at the time of writing; the wide range of its contribution precluded later incorporation.

my lord in Seir" [v. 14]); Esau can be construed as untrusting (let us journey together. . . . let me leave some of my people with you) until he is sure of his superiority.[41] Of course, a storyteller might choose to combine both approaches; heartfelt reconciliation could be used as a cover for lingering caution.

The text of chs. 32–33 is comfortably understood as a narrative with enhancements or options. Whether it is fully integrated with what precedes remains open for discussion. In the earlier narrative, Jacob was received by Laban as a kinsman (29:14–15) rather than as the alien he claims here (cf. 32:5 [Heb.; NRSV 32:4]). The description of Jacob's wealth as "oxen, donkeys, flocks, male and female slaves" goes beyond the description in ch. 31; the enumeration of the gift argues against a possibly formulaic understanding (32:15–16 [Heb.; NRSV 32:14–15]). Seir has not been mentioned before this (except for Gen 14:6) and Esau's presence there is not accounted for. For all that, the narrative ends with Jacob settled at Succoth and shortly to move to Shechem. Jacob's further travels can be left to ch. 35; Esau's status can be left to ch. 36. It may not be out of place to note in this context, however, that 36:6–8 paints a thoroughly different picture from ch. 33 and has the brothers separate on the same grounds that Abraham and Lot did in Gen 13:6. An attempt to read 36:6 in relation to 35:29b would be valiant; but in the light of the varying traditions, to say nothing of the encounter in ch. 33, it would be untenable.

The story of Dinah (Gen 34) is almost totally self-contained. Dinah's birth was reported in 30:21 (perhaps with this story in view, given the absence of any reflection on her name); the story of rape and conflict suitably motivates the move south in ch. 35 (esp. v. 5). Westermann speaks of a family narrative and a tribal narrative that have been brought together by a compiler, presupposing Deut 7 and close to the language of P (therefore a late date).[42] Noth did not accept the two-narrative account. "Alongside the basic material we do not have elements of a second independent narrative but a series of additions . . . not fragments of a variant narrative."[43] Alternative views are advanced by Blum and Seebass.[44] For details, see appendix 4.

Treating Gen 35 as a single block consisting of various traditions assembled appropriately here around the themes of Bethel and burial is an attractive proposition. For all the differences within the chapter, there is enough in common to render the single block a genuine possibility.

There is a unity to vv. 9–15, from God's appearance to Jacob through to Jacob's naming of Bethel. A number of features are significant:

41. A different interpretation is of course possible. Westermann: "Esau knows quite well that it [Jacob's final remark] is not meant to be taken seriously. . . . Generously and with the best of intentions ["in guter Absicht und Großzügigkeit"] Esau makes yet another offer (v. 15)" (*Genesis 12–36*, 527); unfortunately, Westermann gives no evidence to support this view. The issue is taken up by Blum, who, however, feels the need of reconciliation to balance the conflict begun with Gen 25:21ff. ("Genesis 33,12–20: Die Wege trennen sich," in *Jacob*, ed. J.-D. Macchi et al., 227–38, see pp. 229–31).

42. *Genesis 12–36*, 535–37.

43. *Pentateuchal Traditions*, 30 n.99.

44. Blum, *Vätergeschichte*, 210–16; Seebass, *Genesis II/2*, 418–35.

1. Jacob is presented as coming from Paddan-aram; unless broadly interpreted, this repeats what was achieved in 33:18 (identical wording in
   Hebrew) and bypasses the stay at Shechem.
2. Jacob's name is changed; this repeats 32:29 (Heb.; NRSV 32:28).
3. The first part of *El Shaddai*'s address (v. 11) echoes 28:3 and ignores
   28:14.
4. The second part of *El Shaddai*'s address, the promise of the land (v. 12),
   refers to Abraham and Isaac, as might be expected, but does not mention any relationship.
5. God "goes up" from Jacob; this echoes 17:22.
6. Jacob sets up a stone pillar (v. 14); this repeats 28:18.
7. At the end of the passage, Jacob names the place Bethel (v. 15); this
   repeats 28:19.

Two conclusions emerge from these observations: (1) the passage belongs securely
among the *El Shaddai* traditions, and (2) the passage bypasses 28:10–33:20.

The synchronic implications will be taken up shortly (pp. 49–50). Two aspects
are of interest diachronically. First, if given "early" status, the passage would need
to be seen as the beginning of the moves to integrate Jacob, the Aramean outsider, with Abraham and Isaac, developed in the *El Shaddai* traditions. Second,
if given "late" status, the passage is decidedly odd, clashing with the established
tradition.

The surrounding verses (vv. 1–8, 16–29) can be interpreted as "domesticat-
ing" this oddity or as advancing a little the process of integration. An ambiguity
in vv. 1–8 makes them particularly suitable for this purpose. In v. 1, God speaks
to Jacob at a time and place that is not specified; in v. 5, a terror falls upon the
cities, preempting pursuit. It is not said whether the journey involved was from
Paddan-aram (v. 9) or from near Shechem (v. 4; cf. 34:30). The cities along the
route are not specified, either outside Canaan or within it. Jacob is given the foreign gods (*ʾĕlōhê hannēkār*, not *hattĕrāpîm* as in 31:19, etc.) as well as assorted
ornaments to dispose of (v. 4; Heb. root: *ṭ-m-n*). Do the foreign gods here echo
the "household gods" stolen by Rachel, or rather refer to a situation akin to that
depicted in Josh 24:14, 23?

Although the reference to Bethel, and God's appearance to Jacob there, helps
with the process of integrating vv. 9–15 into the broader narrative, all is not
straightforward. The command of God to "settle there" is not obeyed; the command to build an altar is. Jacob calls the place "El-bethel" (v. 7), but the earlier
text has him sent to Bethel (v. 1) and arrive at Luz, in the land of Canaan, "that
is Bethel" (v. 6). The report of Deborah's death links back to Gen 24:59.

Verses 16–21 resume the journey and move to Rachel's death in childbirth,
completing the number of the twelve sons. The scene evokes 30:24 and what precedes it. The sons are enumerated in vv. 22b–26. The location of "the tower of
Eder" is unknown; given the multiplicity of traditions associated with Jacob, precision might not be helpful (cf. "tower of the flock," Mic 4:8).

The burial of Isaac by both Esau and Jacob (vv. 27–29) echoes Abraham's burial by Isaac and Ishmael (25:9). The linguistic associations with the *El Shaddai* traditions have been noted in relation to the Abraham cycle (pp. 33–35; see below, 50–52).

All in all, it is probably allowable and economical to view ch. 35 as a unitary collection of texts, under the umbrella of the *El Shaddai* traditions, appropriately located here after the conclusion of the Jacob family traditions. In this context, it is worth recalling the traditions affirmed in Hos 12 (which, if original, belongs around 750 BCE).[45] Five elements are involved:

1. Rivalry with his brother, in the womb
2. Wrestling with God
3. Encounter with God at Bethel
4. Flight to Aram
5. Service there for a wife

The first two (conflict with his brother in the womb and in his prime with God) and the fourth are unequivocal. The encounter at Bethel could be reflected in either ch. 28 or ch. 35. The only uncertainty with regard to the fifth is whether it speaks of one wife only or, through the parallelism, speaks of two. While a variety of difficulties beset the interpretation of the Hosea text, it is clear that Esau is not mentioned beyond the rivalry in the womb.[46] Hosea offers no motivation for the flight to Aram; nor does Hosea mention any encounter with Esau on return. Jacob's fear of Esau (over the blessing; near the Jabbok) is not mentioned. Flight and return are present, however, in Hosea; anything different must contend with this text. The Jacob-Esau tradition appears to have been in a relatively fluid state.

This fluidity in the tradition is visible at the start of the following chapter (Gen 36:1–8), which begins with Esau's wives (Adah daughter of Elon, Oholibamah daughter of Anah, and Basemath daughter of Ishmael) and the sons born to him in Canaan (Eliphaz, Reuel, Jeush, Jalam, and Korah). The identities of the wives, of course, do not tally with the earlier traditions (i.e., Judith daughter of Beeri, Basemath daughter of Elon, and Mahalath daughter of Ishmael).

Verse 5 ends with a description of the list as "sons of Esau who were born to him in the land of Canaan." Verse 9 begins with the list of the descendants of Esau, "in the hill country of Seir." Whatever their origin, vv. 6–8 function in the present text as a bridge between these two lists.

The picture painted in vv. 6–8 of the brothers' situation needs close attention. According to 36:7, the possessions of Esau and Jacob were "too great for them to

---

45. For Hos 12 as evidence of the Jacob oral tradition, see Albert de Pury, "La tradition patriarcale in Gen 12–35," in *Le Pentateuch en question: Les origines et la composition des cinq premiers livres de la Bible à la lumière des recherches récentes*, ed. A. de Pury (Geneva: Labor et Fides, 1989), 259–70, esp. 265–67.

46. See de Pury, "La tradition patriarcale in Gen 12–35."

live together." So Esau moved away, establishing "some distance from his brother Jacob" (36:6), settling in the hill country of Seir; "Esau is Edom" (36:8). This picture of the "distancing" differs from Jacob's "flight" in ch. 28. As noted above, a transition is required for Esau to acquire wealth and status (400 men) in Seir. Jacob's "twenty years" in Aram amply allows for this in the narrative. However, the picture of vv. 6–8 makes no mention of Jacob's flight. Jacob's service to Laban in exchange for his wives (in lieu of a dowry) does not easily agree with the picture of Jacob and Esau whose "possessions were too great for them to live together." Two conflicting traditions appear to be present as to how the brothers acquired their wealth. In one case (chs. 30–33), it was acquired outside Canaan, for Jacob in Aram, for Esau in Seir. In the other case (36:6–8), both acquired their wealth in Canaan. An attempt to reconcile the conflict by harmonization, basically situating 36:6–8 after Jacob's return from Aram and having a homesick Esau return for some time from Seir (cf. 35:29), is rather too complicated to carry conviction. The hypothesis of conflicting traditions is more plausible, especially given the likelihood of Isaac's death some twenty or so years earlier (cf. 27:4). The echo of Abraham and Lot is clear (cf. Gen 13:6), but its meaning is not so clear.

Recovery of Israel's past is likely to be less important than understanding Israel's present. Genesis 36:6–8 echoes the memory of Abraham and Lot, with Ammon and Moab in the background. The memory is benevolent. The initial ill feeling around Isaac and Ishmael is reflected in the initial rivalry of Jacob and Esau. While the unfolding for Jacob and Esau (in Gen 30–33) is different from that of Isaac and Ishmael, its benevolence is distinctly ambiguous. In Ps 137:7–9, benevolence is dead. The challenge to interpreters is to elucidate these understandings. Esau bulks larger in Israel's traditions than does Isaac; this is unlikely to be by chance. The operative concerns are likely to be associated with the issues of affinity and distinctness.[47]

After 36:1–8, the rest of the chapter falls into four sections, with much repetition of names in the first three: (i) the sons or descendants of Esau, ancestor of the Edomites; (ii) the tribal chiefs of the Edomites; (iii) the sons or descendants of Seir, the Horite, with their tribal chiefs in vv. 29–30; (iv) the kings of Edom.[48] It is clear that the chapter is not to be distributed across documentary sources. Noth attributes it, brokenly, to P—perhaps along the lines of the principle that our scholarly forebears did *not* formulate but may have used: if it is pedantic and boring, it is P.

Observations of the *El Shaddai* traditions (see pp. 50–52) suggest the possibility that, as a group, chs. 34–36 belong there.

47. For general information on Edom, see J. R. Bartlett, "Edom," *ABD* 2:287–95; more specifically, Bert Dicou, *Edom, Israel's Brother and Antagonist: The Role of Edom in Biblical Prophecy and Story*, JSOTSup 169 (Sheffield: Sheffield Academic Press, 1994).

48. The kings of Edom here are listed in the simple linear system, found also within the Prophetic Record (see Antony F. Campbell, *Of Prophets and Kings: A Late Ninth-Century Document* [*1 Samuel 1–2 Kings 10*], CBQMS 17 [Washington, DC: CBA, 1986], 139). Westermann (for unavowed reasons) is quite clear on the origin of this list: "the Edomite king list (from the chancery of the last king of Edom) came into the chancery of the king of Jerusalem" after David had subdued Edom (*Genesis 12–36*, 561).

Overview: Jacob Cycle

At the core of the Jacob cycle, two tasks had to be accomplished by Jacob: the bringing into being of a family and the bringing into being of an asset base to support that family. The establishment of a family is narrated in twenty-nine verses (Gen 29:31–30:24), the establishment of an asset base to support that family in nineteen verses (Gen 30:25–43). The narrative of the acquiring of the necessary assets unfolds pretty much as expected: negotiation between Jacob and Laban, manipulation by both. The narrative of the establishment of a family, in contrast, has thoroughly unexpected characteristics. Jacob is given almost no role whatsoever. In 30:1–2, he argues angrily with Rachel over responsibility for her barrenness; in 30:4, he goes into Rachel's maid, Bilhah; in 30:16, he comes in from the field; in seven other places, he gets indirect mention (e.g., she bore to Jacob a son). As noted above, the whole passage revolves within the world of two women, Rachel and Leah. While explanations are given for the names of the eleven sons, these explanations are totally concerned with the world of the two women. This is not the world of men; it is not the world of tribes. What is the significance at any time of this passage in this place?

In Israel's ancestral stories, the Jacob cycle is preceded by the Abraham cycle and followed by the Joseph story. Within the Jacob cycle, the two core passages (Gen 29:31–30:24 and Gen 30:25–43) are flanked by the action narratives of Jacob's coming to Laban and Jacob's flight from Laban. On both sides of these are further narratives of action. At the center of these ancestral stories of Israel are two unusual passages, one utterly inner-oriented and the other utterly outer-oriented, one marked by the activity of women and the other by the activity of men. This book is not the place to explore the ramifications of this observation. These core texts are unlikely to be concerned with the history of Israel, but rather with aspects of inner meaning. Greek mythology, for example, is less a reflection of history than an exploration of aspects of human living. In this case, the inner meaning is obscure, but it is where interpretation must begin.

The present text presents an unchallenged picture of Isaac's son coming to his mother's folk in the old country, obtaining a family there and wealth, and returning to Canaan. An arguably earlier text, reflecting a putative earlier picture, cannot be recovered. These issues will be discussed below. The potential lateness of the texts associated, above all, with Rebekah suggests that the concern to create an ancestral sequence from Abraham and Sarah through Isaac and Rebekah to Jacob with Rachel and Leah was itself a late concern. Although historians are tempted to see the origins of the northern tribes reflected in the Jacob cycle, the texts are not there that would provide full support.

To summarize: the symmetrical organization of the present text of the Jacob cycle is striking. Relations with Esau begin the cycle and end it; within it are the two encounters with God, at Bethel and at the Jabbok; next are the dealings of Jacob and Laban, concerning arrival (wives) and departure (wealth); at the center is the childbearing of Rachel and Leah (daughters of Laban), Bilhah and

Zilpah (lineage unknown), and Jacob's acquisition of wealth.[49] The two passages—childbearing and wealth-getting—reflect the inner world of two women and the outer world of two men. In this may lie something of the power of the Jacob cycle.

Within the present text of the Jacob cycle, Esau's role bulks large. Hosea 12 has the rivalry in the womb and Jacob's flight without any mention of the fear of Esau as its cause; Jacob's return is implicit ("he strove with God"), but without any mention of Esau at all. The role of Esau in the present text is similar to that of Lot in the Abraham-Lot traditions and of Ishmael in the Abraham family traditions. All three are family; all three are distanced. Two needs appear in the text: identity in unity and identity in distinctness. There is evident unity: Abraham and Lot are uncle and nephew; Ishmael and Isaac are brothers; Esau and Jacob are brothers. There is evident distinctness: Lot disappears into a cave in the hills, and the Ammonites and Moabites disappear from the story; Ishmael is sent away from Abraham's family; Esau has moved to far-off Seir. The relationship of Israel with its neighbors is important, the relationship of Israel with itself equally so. Israel is to be blessed; so are all the families of the earth.

This is a complex brew: divine and human; unity and distinctness; women's world and men's world—and so much more. It does not yield up its secrets easily. Perhaps there are no secrets, only aspects of the mystery of being human.

The *El Shaddai* Traditions

The *El Shaddai* material needs special investigation. The texts involved are Gen 17:1–26; quite possibly 21:4; 23:1–2, 19–20; 25:7–18 (see discussion); possibly 26:34–35 and 27:46–28:9; probably all of 35:1–29 (certainly vv. 9–15 and vv. 27–29; probably vv. 1–8, 16–26); 48:1–7; probably 49:1a, 29–33.[50] Given the emphasis on circumcision and interest in Esau, it is not unlikely that chs. 34 and 36, together with ch. 35, belonged within the *El Shaddai* material.

The tone is set by Gen 17. God (*elohim*, but also named *yhwh* in 17:1) appears at the beginning (17:1; also 35:9) and "goes up" at the end (17:22; also 35:13).[51] The concerns of the text are summed up in 17:7–8: (i) God's commitment to Israel, expressed in covenant; (ii) offspring (Hebrew: seed); (iii) land. The covenant is signified in circumcision; the line of offspring will begin with Isaac; Ishmael is to be special (v. 20: "I have heard you"). Genesis 21:4 is a logical consequence of Gen 17. Where 21:1–7 as a whole is concerned, the text is complex and requires that suggestions be tentative (see above, in the Abraham cycle).

---

49. Clearly and appropriately, chs. 34, 35, and 36 stand outside this symmetrical organization as additions to the whole. For the symmetry especially, see the graphic layout in Brueggemann, *Genesis*, 213. But the emphasis is on the two women, not the births and not the offspring. "Undoubtedly, this presentation of sons [born in rivalry, envy, and dispute] is a mapping of the tribes of Israel" (ibid., 253); it is really surprising to realize that it is not. The giveaway is that word "undoubtedly."

50. Gen 43:14 stands on its own as an isolated occurrence of the name *El Shaddai*; the occurrences in Genesis are: 17:1; 28:3; 35:11; 43:14; 48:3.

51. *yhwh* in 17:1, *elohim* in the other three.

Sarah's death and burial are treated in Gen 23. In Gen 25:7–18, the place of *El Shaddai* tradition in the report of Abraham's death and burial is clear enough (see the following discussion). Isaac and Ishmael are brought together to bury their father Abraham in the cave of Machpelah; similarly, in 35:29, Esau and Jacob bury their father Isaac there. For Ishmael, the inclusion of 25:12–18 in the *El Shaddai* traditions reflects the blessing and "twelve princes" of 17:20 and 25:16.

A number of relatively minor details tie the account of Abraham's burial into the *El Shaddai* traditions. First, the ages of Abraham (25:7), Sarah (23:1), Ishmael (25:17), and Isaac (35:28) are expressed in a way that occurs nowhere else in the Bible: the noun for "year" (*šānâ*) is expressed with each element (i.e., hundreds, tens, and units) and the direction of the count is from the greater (hundreds) to the lesser (units). It may seem trivial, but all other cases are different. Second, the three verbs that express death—"to breathe one's last," "die," and "be gathered to one's people"—are found together in three cases only: Abraham (25:8), Ishmael (25:17), and Isaac (35:29); note also 49:33 for Jacob ("breathed" and "gathered").[52] For verbs that are far more widely used, this restricted combination is significant. Third, the gracious combination of "a good old age" with "full of years" (in prose) and "gathered to his people" pulls together elements that are relatively rare; they do, however, draw together Abraham, Ishmael, Isaac, and Jacob.[53] All three elements together occur only in Gen 25:8. Although these observations hardly constitute an overwhelming demonstration of a separate origin for the *El Shaddai* traditions, they do suggest a certain coherence of expression within the group and a separateness from other formulations of a similar kind. The Hebrew phrase describing the length of Abraham's life (the days of the years of his life) is not used elsewhere in Gen 12–36.[54] Six of the ten occurrences of Paddan-aram occur within this group (see also 48:7, Paddan); the term does not occur outside Genesis.[55]

The program is laid out in Gen 17: the relationship expressed in an everlasting covenant solemnized in circumcision, the promise of descendants, and the land of Canaan as a perpetual holding. Next, the heir, Isaac, is affirmed; the mother, Sarah, is buried; the ancestor, Abraham, is buried with her by his sons, Isaac and Ishmael; a note is given of Ishmael's descendants and the length of his life; Jacob's link into the family in the old country is ordered by Isaac, and Esau's association with Ishmael noted; Jacob's name is changed to Israel and the promise of land to Abraham and Isaac repeated for Jacob and his offspring; Isaac is buried by his sons Esau and Jacob; Jacob lays claim to Joseph's sons, Ephraim and Manasseh, in the matter of

---

52. Hebrew: *wayyigwaʿ* and *wayyāmot* and *wayyēʾāsep ʾel ʿammāyw*.

53. The occurrences: "a good old age"—Abraham (15:15; 25:8), Gideon (Judg 8:32), and David (1 Chr 29:28); "full of years"—Abraham (25:8), Isaac (35:29), Job (42:17), and David again (1 Chr 29:28); and finally, "gathered to his people [plural]"—Abraham (25:8), Ishmael (25:17), Isaac (35:29), Jacob (49:33), Aaron (Num 20:24; Deut 32:50), and Moses (Num 27:13; 31:2; Deut 32:50).

54. It is used five times in the rest of the Hebrew Scriptures: Gen 47:8, 9; 2 Sam 19:35 [Heb.; NRSV 19:34]; Ps 90:10; Eccl 6:3.

55. The other four occurrences are Gen 25:20; 31:18; 33:18; 46:15.

inheritance. Finally, Jacob's death and his desire to be buried in the cave at Machpelah, with Abraham, Sarah, Isaac, Rebekah, and Leah, are reported. Although scarcely continuous, there are memories here, synthesizing the story of the ancestors and affirming the existence of the ancestral traditions in a unified and legitimating whole.

Whether the *El Shaddai* material is editorial work on an existing text or derives from traditions belonging in particular circles and drawn on for the composition of an extended text is a question that remains open. Following on Gen 17, the circumcision of Isaac (21:4), the length of Sarah's life, and the death of Abraham are matters of tradition; they scarcely constitute continuous narrative. Much the same can be said of Esau's wives and Jacob's being sent to the house of Bethuel. As noted, the additional chapters on Dinah, Jacob, and Esau (chs. 34–36) may belong to the *El Shaddai* tradition. Jacob's blessing of Manasseh and Ephraim (48:1–7) and the death of Jacob (49:1a, 29–33) bring the traditions to a close.

The concern for the sequence of Abraham, Isaac, and Jacob is clear. Abraham is buried by Ishmael and Isaac (25:9); Isaac is buried by Esau and Jacob (35:29); Jacob charges his sons to bury him with his ancestors (49:1a, 29). There is a surprising concern for Ishmael ("father of twelve princes . . . a great nation," 17:20) and the note that Esau married finally within the family, but with Ishmael's daughter (28:9). A further concern is the issue of circumcision. It is scarcely surprising; what is surprising is that circumcision occurs in Genesis only in chs. 17 and 34, and in 21:4. It is not noted for Esau and Jacob. Nothing is reported of the circumcising of Jacob's sons, merely the demand at 34:15 "that you will become as we are." Given the interest in Ishmael and Esau, the focus on circumcision, and the ways already noted that Gen 35 differs from the earlier Bethel traditions (cf. also Gen 36:6–8), it is likely that the *El Shaddai* traditions included Gen 34–36 (and Gen 25:12–18 to include the twelve sons of Ishmael). The association with the Abraham-Lot traditions (cf. Gen 13:6 and 36:7) and the Rebekah material (cf. Gen 25:20) is there; in our judgment, without further evidence, it is too slight to build on. Nevertheless, the possible association of these traditions with some sort of relationship to the surrounding peoples of the south (Ishmael, Esau/Edom, Moab, Ammon) is worth noting.

The central concerns of the *El Shaddai* traditions would then be: the unified family of Abraham, Isaac, and Jacob, closely associated with Ishmael and Esau; the importance of circumcision for the identity of this family; the place played by Bethel in the family story. The importance of this family concern may not be clear, but it may be the driving force in the text.

Discordances Enshrined within the Biblical Text in Relation to This Presentation Above

As we noted above, the ancestral traditions in the present text clearly present Abraham, Isaac, and Jacob as descended in one family line. Some four areas in the text might be said quietly to question this: (1) a full cycle of tradition is lacking for Isaac; (2) the links between Isaac and Jacob are possibly of late date;

(3) the Jacob cycle is not without its problems for this descent from a single family; (4) appearances do not favor the Joseph story's being early. Fidelity to the biblical text means that these issues need attention.[56] Our questioning does not arise directly from the "user-base" approach. The issues are raised by the text in any critical approach. On the other hand, the presence of options in narrative texts may have facilitated the preservation of these variant traditions.

1. The present text contains a cycle of traditions associated with Abraham (concerned with heir and land) and a cycle associated with Jacob (concerned with wives, family, and wealth), but there is no equivalent cycle for Isaac.[57] There are further problems. Beyond Gen 25:21, hardly a text in Genesis that indicates the father-son relationship for Isaac and Jacob is immune to challenge as witness to an old tradition.[58] The birth oracle in Gen 25:23 has the elder serve the younger, that is, Esau serve Jacob. In the stories that follow, this is not the case. At the end (chs. 32–33), separation is achieved, but Esau is presented as the more powerful. If Esau and Edom are identified, Edom breaks loose from Israelite (Judean) control in the late ninth century (cf. 2 Kgs 8:20–22). Within this context, the "breaking loose" of Esau from his brother (Gen 27:40) has considerable significance.

In the present text, Gen 26 is appropriately situated in the years that must be allowed to elapse between Esau's surrender of his birthright and his marriages to Hittite women. Isaac is portrayed as "the blessed of the LORD" (26:29); Esau is put at a distance—he despised his birthright (25:34) and made his parents' life bitter (26:35). Esau's surrender of his birthright evokes the Jacob cycle. "Blessed of the LORD" Isaac may have been, but in the text he is a shadowy figure. Genesis 26 can be seen as significantly reflecting aspects of the Abraham cycle. Adjusted for context, there are the famine, the promise, the episode with his wife, the wealth obtained, land, and the dealings with these same Philistines (for Abraham, 21:22–34). Given the birth of sons to Isaac already (and leaving aside the Abraham-Lot material), this summarizes much of the Abraham narrative.

2. If Gen 24 is considered late, as may well be the case,[59] issues of relationship in the ancestral texts become fluid; Rebekah, as Isaac's wife, is a major link between Abraham and Jacob within the family of Terah. Although it is possible that an earlier version of ch. 24 has been replaced leaving no trace, it is unlikely

---

56. For many, the origins of the text and its present structure are to be understood in relation to the *toledoth* formula (*ʾēlleh tôlēdôt*; 10x in Gen and 3x elsewhere: Gen 2:4; 6:9; 10:1; 11:10, 27; 25:12, 19; 36:1, 9; 37:2; and Num 3:1; Ruth 4:18; 1 Chr 1:29). Given respectful and careful consideration of the occurrences in Genesis and the literature about them, we do not see how they can be used as a key to the structure of the book of Genesis (cf. esp. Gen 25:19; 36:1, 9; 37:2). Variant translations are offered and various qualifications are indicated, in our opinion, to little avail. While many of these occurrences are certainly of interest, we do not find that they add insight to the structure of Genesis as a whole.

57. In the present text, outside Gen 26 almost nothing is said of Isaac, this long-awaited son. In Gen 21, the child Isaac is the reason for banishing Ishmael; in Gen 22, the only son Isaac is nearly sacrificed. In the present text, mentions come at Gen 24:62–67 (his bride); 25:7–11 (his father's burial); 25:19–26 (his sons' birth).

58. See, for example, Gen 25:26b; 27 passim; 31:18, 53; 32:10 (Heb.; NRSV 32:9); 35:27; 46:1.

59. See Rofé, "Betrothal of Rebekah" (see the discussion later).

and unnecessary.[60] Similarly, it is possible that earlier versions of the Jacob-Esau traditions existed (cf. Hos 12) but not necessary. Other adjustments might have been made; it is possible, but again the evidence is not there to make it necessary (see below). What Gen 24:1–67 does is bring Rebekah into the ancestral narrative. She becomes Isaac's bride; she will become Jacob's mother and will be instrumental in Jacob's going to Haran. As far as extensive text goes, Rebekah is the primary link between Abraham and Jacob.

3. Other areas in association with Jacob raise potential problems. Traditions of Bethel can be appropriate to far-off antiquity, to the northern kingdom, or to the period after the exile (Zech 7:2). The putting away of foreign gods (Gen 35:2–4) can be set in antiquity and also has overtones of returning exiles. In this context, we note the divine command, "Go to Bethel and settle there" (35:1); Jacob went to Bethel, but it is never reported that he settled there. Where settlement is concerned, it may be problematic that the first generation occupied land in the Hebron area; there is no mention of this for the second generation, settled near Beersheba; and the third generation is most closely associated with Succoth-Shechem in the north. The locations of Beer-lahai-roi (25:11b) and "the tower of Eder" (35:21) can be surmised but have not been preserved with any precision. The Jacob references in Hos 12 have been noted.

4. Finally, there is the story of Joseph and his brothers. It or its equivalent is needed for a pentateuchal composition (combining Genesis with Exodus), but it is not needed earlier. It is noteworthy that the local lad (Joseph) becomes almost the equal of Pharaoh (see Gen 41:40–44), controller of the food supply for one of the great powers of the ancient world (41:48, 55, 57), and head of Treasury par excellence for Pharaoh—all the money (47:14–15), flocks (47:16–17), land of Egypt (47:19–20), and even the people (47:19, 21) are brought by Joseph under Pharaoh's control. Such elements are unlikely to be early.[61]

Further Questions Raised by the Jacob Cycle

The Abraham family traditions concern descendants and land; the Jacob family traditions concern family and wealth. A major difference such as this demands examination. Three factors heighten the difference. First, in Gen 24 the story is emphatic that Abraham's son is not to go back to the old country (24:5–8 [twice]); on the contrary, the bride is to come to Isaac (cf. 24:5–8, 39–41). In the

---

60. Illustrated by the attempt of Seebass (*Genesis II/2*, 251–52).

61. Walter Brueggemann, however, would consider the "royal, urban ethos of Solomon" a plausible locus for the narrative, in which God's purposes are achieved "by the ways of the world which seem to be natural and continuous" (*Genesis*, Int [Atlanta: John Knox, 1982], 288–89). The extent of the power claimed for Joseph hardly seems to be in the category of "natural and continuous." Donald Redford remarks that, in the Hyksos period, "Joseph's sudden rise to power would be plausible, since the Hyksos were semitic-speaking Asiatics like himself" (*A Study of the Biblical Story of Joseph (Genesis 37–50)*, VTSup 20 [Leiden: Brill, 1970], 187). Redford might have been more skeptical if he were not about to demolish the early chronological parallels. One must ask whether the "sudden rise to power" is at all plausible in whatever circumstances. Those who have come to power seldom share it with foreigners jailed allegedly for attempted rape, even those successful in interpreting dreams.

Jacob family traditions, however, Jacob goes to the old country, marries there, and eleven of his twelve sons are born there. Second, Ishmael, the child of Hagar the maid, is sent away from the family; on the other hand, the children of Bilhah and Zilpah, the maids, are constituent members of the family. Third, Abraham is portrayed leaving Haran at YHWH's command, suggesting YHWH worship; when Jacob leaves Laban, however, the gods taken by Rachel are "*teraphim*" (NRSV "her father's household gods," Gen 31:19; cf. 35:2, "Put away the foreign gods (*ĕlōhê hannēkār*) that are among you"). For each of these three, we can ask why it should be so. One answer is, because it happened that way. As in all such cases, the question then moves to, why did Israel tell this story prominently in its traditions? Another answer given is, because the originators of the traditions wanted it that way. The question then becomes, why did they want it that way?

Within the present text of this Jacob cycle, features occur that invite speculation. While they allow possibilities to be entertained, they do not warrant the recovery or reconstruction of earlier texts. With this caution, it will help to spell out something of these possibilities here.

If we turn first to evidence from outside Genesis, Deut 26:5 and Hos 12 need attention. According to Deut 26:5, "A wandering Aramean was my ancestor." If nothing else, the going down to Egypt and living there as an alien, few in number, identifies the ancestor as Jacob. A Jacob whose family was founded in Haran, in Aram (Syria), and only subsequently journeyed to Canaan, would fit this description. The present text of Genesis does not, however, allow for this, but a hypothetical past text might have. In contrast, however, as noted, Hos 12 (if original, in the eighth century) points to a Jacob tradition with flight and return.[62] In Amos 1:11, Edom is condemned "because he pursued his brother with the sword . . . he maintained his anger perpetually." Formal considerations suggest the text is a later addition in the book of Amos.[63] Historically, however, some cause is needed to account for the violence of Israel's early hostility toward Edom (cf. 1 Sam 14:47; 2 Sam 8:12–14 [text uncertain]; 1 Kgs 11:14–17 [David and Joab: killed every male in Edom]; and late, Ps 137:7–9). Suffering in later times could have surfaced ancient memories. As a potential cause of Jacob's flight, such hostility might have been available.

Three scenarios emerge as examples of possible hypotheses to explain these and other features in the Genesis text.

First Scenario: Jacob as One of Two Possible Original Ancestors   Although reported in the Genesis text, it is odd that Jacob, a third-generation migrant, should be presented as not only returning to the old country in search of a wife, but also spending some twenty years there (31:38, 41), working to acquire two wives and founding a family of twelve (eleven of them sons), before returning home. In the present text, motivation for flight is provided by Esau's desire to kill (27:41–45)

---

62. As noted, see de Pury, "La tradition patriarcale."
63. See H. W. Wolff, *Joel and Amos*, Hermeneia (Philadelphia: Fortress, 1977), 139–41, 160; J. L. Mays, *Amos*, OTL (London: SCM, 1969), 35–36.

and by Rebekah's desire for peace (27:46). From the point of view of a hypothetical past, it is possible that behind these Jacob traditions there was once an
origin of Israel in Aram, akin to the Abraham tradition of origin in Haran. Such
a hypothesis is coherent with Deut 26:5, but traditions for it cannot be recovered
from the present text of Genesis. (Note that even the gift of the land can be associated with Jacob—"that I gave to my servant Jacob" [Ezek 28:25; 37:25].)

Second Scenario: Reflecting an Early Flight by Jacob   Jacob's "flight" to Aram is
present in Hosea (12:13 [Heb.; NRSV 12:12]); a specific reason is not given.
Jacob's journey to Aram is begun with Gen 28:10; it is not expressly described as
flight. In a different scenario, with a hypothetical reconstruction assuming Jacob's
presence in Canaan, an early cause for flight could have been provided by the
hostility of Edom. Esau goes his way (25:34), while later Jacob leaves Beer-sheba
and goes toward Haran (28:10). Flight is not mentioned. Israel's storytellers can
be trusted to handle such contexts appropriately. A hypothesis of Jacob's flight
motivated by the actions of Edom rather than Esau is possible, but traditions for
it cannot be recovered from the present text.

Third Scenario: Creating a Single Family from Abraham, Isaac, and Jacob   Unquestionably, the present text of Genesis has Abraham and Sarah as parents of Isaac,
and Isaac and Rebekah as parents of Jacob. Equally unquestionably, as noted earlier, the present text has no cycle of tradition for Isaac. Speaking generally, the text
locates Abraham at Hebron and Isaac at Beer-sheba, and it has Jacob build at Succoth (33:17), buy at Shechem (33:19), and journey vaguely south to pitch his tent
"beyond the tower of Eder" (35:21; location unknown). The multiple locations
for the three generations, with minimal contact between them, leaves the impression of something odd. Also problematic is God's order to settle at Bethel, which
is included in the text (35:1)—but is not obeyed. Similarly problematic is the presence of foreign gods during the stay at Succoth and Shechem that are to be buried
before going to Bethel (35:2–4). Enough uncertainty is present to allow the
thought that a single family may have been created from a diversity of traditions.

Contributory Factors within the Genesis Text

A number of factors in Gen 24–29 contribute to make the scenarios just noted
at least thinkable. The relevant factors are noted under the following texts.

Genesis 24   Alexander Rofé's judgment—that Gen 24 is "a very late composition, written in the fifth century BCE"[64]—is widely shared.[65] Rofé argues his case

---

64. Rofé, "Betrothal of Rebekah"; see above.
65. As Blum's thorough work notes (*Vätergeschichte*, 383–87), the affirmation of Gen 24 as late
goes back at least to Noth (see *Pentateuchal Traditions*, 104, 199), von Rad (see *Genesis*, 259), Sandmel (*JBL* 80), and Winnett (*JBL* 84). Among others in agreement since, we may list: Seebass, *Genesis II/2*, 251–52 (for the final form); Soggin: a late, postexilic composition, from the writing table
("Schreibtisch"), not from oral tradition ("Volksmund"), in its origins (*Das Buch Genesis* [Darmstadt:
Wissenschaftliche Buchgesellschaft, 1997], 329–30; Römer, "Recherches actuelles," 188, 195; Ska,
"Cycle d'Abraham," 170; Van Seters, *Pentateuch*, 129–30, 138).

on multiple grounds: language and syntax, legal institutions, theology (prayer, promise as oath, angels, divine intervention), dependence on earlier tradition, and literary style.[66] Although the case may not be watertight in every detail, it is nevertheless highly likely.[67] The text is different from surrounding traditions and likely to be a late composition.[68] When this conclusion is brought into association with the observations here regarding the Rebekah traditions, wide-ranging implications for the ancestral narratives are unavoidable.

Without the Rebekah tradition, the link is through Isaac: Isaac prayed for his wife, who was barren, his prayer was heard, and she (25:21, in apposition, Rebekah) conceived and bore Esau and Jacob, with the final notice of Isaac's age at the time of the birth (Gen 25:21, 26b). Later, Laban describes Jacob as "my bone and my flesh" and "my kinsman" (Gen 29:14–15). These can be general terms, understood simply as "my countryman" (e.g., BDB lists among the meanings of אָח "member of same tribe . . . of same people"; for "bone and flesh" see 2 Sam 5:1; 19:13–14 [Heb.; NRSV 12–13]). Rebekah is not named outside Genesis. Obviously, in the texts noted below, Rebekah features frequently and much more is said.

Genesis 25:19–34   Isaac and Rebekah feature largely, but in only two verses (25:19–20). There is the opening *tôlĕdōt* formula for Isaac son of Abraham; then the statement that Abraham fathered Isaac (v. 19). Next, Isaac's age at his marriage to Rebekah daughter of Bethuel the Aramean from Paddan-aram, sister of Laban the Aramean (v. 20). Isaac is mentioned twice as Abraham's son (v. 19); Rebekah is situated in relation to both her father (Bethuel) and her brother (Laban), and being an Aramean is specified for each. The text is unusually full and detailed, making its point heavy-handedly. The repetition in v. 19 emphasizes Isaac as Abraham's heir; the repetition in v. 20, however, emphasizes Rebekah's ties to the family back east (cf. 28:5). Given this heavy-handedness, it is possible that the kinship specifications in v. 20 ("daughter of Bethuel the Aramean of Paddan-aram, sister of Laban the Aramean") were inserted.[69]

In vv. 21–34, Rebekah is mentioned twice: at the end of v. 21, in apposition, "Rebekah, his wife"; and in v. 28, preparing for ch. 27. The references are perfectly acceptable in the text as they stand. They are also perfectly susceptible to being understood as additions (in v. 21, the proper name; for v. 28, the entire verse).

66. Rofé notes similar results from "distinct argumentation," achieved by B. Diebner and H. Schult, "Alter und geschichtlicher Hintergrund von Gen 24," *DBAT* 10 (1975): 10–17.

67. Gary Rendsburg has accepted the presence of Aramaisms in Gen 24, but queried whether they are better explained as a "literary device" providing "local color" for a story set in Aram rather than by postexilic origin ("Some False Leads in the Identification of Late Biblical Hebrew Texts: The Cases of Genesis 24 and 1 Samuel 2:27–36," *JBL* 121 [2002]: 23–46). Much else from the chapter favors the late-origin explanation.

68. "The Rebekah story is unique. . . . It is also uniquely woman-centered" (Thomas L. Brodie, *Genesis as Dialogue: A Literary, Historical, and Theological Commentary* [New York: Oxford University Press, 2001], 281).

69. For Jean Louis Ska, the text is composite and postexilic, coloring the reading of Gen 25–35 ("Genèse 25,19–34—Ouverture du cycle de Jacob," in *Jacob*, ed. J.-D. Macchi et al., 11–21).

Genesis 26:34–35 and 27:46 and 28:1–9   At the end of ch. 26, Esau's marriages to two Hittite women (= locals) are noted, and they are said to have made life bitter for Isaac and Rebekah. At the end of ch. 27, Rebekah speaking to Isaac refers negatively to Hittite women in the context of marriage. This provides the bridge to the passage in which Isaac sends Jacob to find a wife among the daughters of Laban (28:1–5). The figures are named in relation to Rebekah, as Jacob's mother: Bethuel, "your mother's father"; Laban, "your mother's brother" (v. 2). At the end of the passage (28:1–5), what is to come is anticipated; Isaac sends Jacob off, and Jacob (obedient to his father and mother, v. 7) goes to Paddan-aram, to Laban, more than usually fully identified as "son of Bethuel the Aramean" and "brother of Rebekah, the mother of Jacob and Esau" (v. 5). A final comment after this has Esau take note (apparently bypassing ch. 27 [cf. 28:6]) and marry Mahalath, "daughter of Ishmael son of Abraham" (v. 9).

These passages sandwich the splendidly told story of ch. 27. They offer a blend of issues of country and issues of family. In Abraham's instructions (Gen 24), while the bride is to be family, Isaac is emphatically not to leave the country. In Jacob's case, he is to leave the country.[70] Esau had married "Hittite" wives; Jacob was to marry "family." Even when Esau married "family," his wife, his third, was the daughter of Ishmael. The choice of a daughter of Ishmael cannot be without significance in the text. The concern for marriage within the clan is evident; similar concerns are most evident in the postexilic period.

Genesis 27   This is not the place to put on record a full study of Gen 27. Careful study of its language, however, leads to the conclusion that it is unlikely that Gen 27 is an early text; it is probable that it is not earlier than the seventh century.

Full discussion of the evidence that points to a late date for this chapter would occupy about half this book. Here, therefore, we restrict ourselves to a list of the relevant verses that contain late language, indicating in parentheses (and in English) the words involved. Nonspecialists will have an overview; specialists will assess the Hebrew.

> Verses 3, 5, 7, 19, 25, 30, 31, 33 (a. to hunt; b. game); *otherwise*: mainly late.
>
> Verses 4, 7, 9, 14, 17, 31 (savory food); *otherwise*: Prov 23:3, 6.
>
> Verses 4, 19, 25, 31 (the use of *nepeš* [being–soul–person–self]) pronominally with the verb "to bless"); *otherwise*: some early occurrences (e.g., Judg 16:16; 1 Sam 20:4; Hos 4:8; perhaps Judg 5:18; 1 Sam 2:16), notably more common later (Jeremiah, Ezekiel, Third Isaiah, Psalms, etc.).
>
> Verse 10 (so that; Heb. *baʿăbur ʾašeř*); *otherwise*: nil.

---

70. In Rebekah's instructions, to save his life (27:42–45); in Isaac's instructions, to take a wife (28:2).

Verse 12 (to mock); *otherwise*: 2 Chr 36:16.

Verses 12, 13 (a curse); *otherwise*: Deut 11x, Jer 9x, and sundry others.

Verses 12, 21, 22 (to feel); *otherwise*: Gen 31:34, 37; Exod 10:21; Deut 28:29; Job 5:14; 12:25.

Verse 15 (best, desirable); *otherwise*: Dan 6x; Ezra 8:27; 2 Chr 20:25.

Verse 33 (violent trembling); *otherwise*: Dan 10:7.

Verse 34 (very bitter); *otherwise*: nil.

Verse 35 (deceit); *otherwise*: note Gen 34:13, possibly *El Shaddai* circle; many others, mainly late.

Verse 36 (to reserve); *otherwise*: Num 11:17, 25; Ezek 42:6; Eccl 2:10.

Verse 37 (to sustain); *otherwise*: a few early examples but many late, including Lev 14x, Num 4x, Pss 11x.

Verse 40 (break loose, roam); *otherwise*: Jer 2:31; Hos 12:1 (Heb.); Ps 55:3 (Heb.).

Verse 40 (to break); *otherwise*: late.

Verse 41 (a. to hate, bear a grudge); *otherwise*: Gen 49:23; 50:15; Ps 55:4 (Heb.); Job 16:9; 30:21. (b. days of mourning); *otherwise*: Gen 50:10; Deut 34:8; Isa 60:20; Esth 9:22.

Three conclusions follow from these observations. First, both chs. 24 and 27, involving Rebekah, are likely to be late (not earlier than the seventh century). Second, without the Rebekah material, the link from Abraham to Jacob is fragile. Third, the present text is emphatic—discordances notwithstanding—that there is a single familial sequence: Abraham–Isaac–Jacob. If the late dating (for Gen 24 and 27) is confirmed, the consequences for the sequence Abraham, Isaac, and Jacob must be accounted for *in any understanding* of the Pentateuch.

From the point of view of the history of text, it may be that a Jacob tradition has been integrated with an Abraham tradition, the process facilitated by the Isaac and Rebekah traditions. Such a Jacob tradition, flourishing in the north, may have been "decapitated" with a view to this integration. We will refrain from speculating. There are implications for a history of Israel and any correlation with the fall of Samaria, Jerusalem, the exile, and return. The ultimate question is theological: what does this quest for unity say of Israel's experience of itself and of its God? Who am I? Who are we? Who is God?

With this text, Israel's tradition has the course of Israel's election by God determined by the choices of two mothers: Sarah, who preferred Isaac over Ishmael, and Rebekah, who preferred Jacob over Esau.

Genesis 29:1–14   The unusually full and detailed references to Rebekah and her family noted above draw attention to five places in these verses where the phrasing concerning Rebekah is equally unusual. Three are in v. 10, two in vv. 12–13. In v. 10, the scene at the well has Jacob see Rachel, the daughter of Laban, "his mother's brother," and twice more refers to the flock of Laban, "his mother's brother." The verse is overly full. In v. 12, Jacob tells Rachel that he is kin to her father, and "the son of Rebekah"; in v. 13, Laban hears about Jacob, "son of his sister." The references here are easily explained; they are equally easily dispensed with. The association of Laban with Nahor is restricted to a question on the lips of Jacob (v. 5); again, it is easily explained and equally easily dispensed with.

What is particularly interesting about the phenomena signaled here for Gen 29:1–14 is that they allow for a preexisting text that may have been expanded. In this case, there is the possibility of Jacob having come to Haran from somewhere else. The "somewhere else" is not necessarily specified. The opening verse (29:1) with its "the land of the people of the east" may have more to do with the geographical location of the narrator than with the journey of Jacob. The narrator is situated west of the land; Jacob's itinerary is left open.

Review

The result of these observations on text from Gen 24 to Gen 29 needs to be cautiously formulated and properly understood. While showing differences of age and origin, the present text is comprehensible; at the same time, allowance could be made for a different scenario if the need for it could be shown. It must be emphasized that such scenarios are hypotheses, exercises of imagination that may be invited by aspects of the text; the text necessary for them cannot be recovered from what we have.

The final text says what it says: Abraham, Isaac, and Jacob were three generations of one family. The discordances it contains point to possibilities and invite reflection. No amount of reflection will (or should) reverse the final text. If research increases the likelihood of earlier disunity, it is appropriate for thought or theology to explore the implications of Israel's conceptual drive for this unity. The revealing of God to Israel in the past of its traditions may have mattered less than the finding of God by Israel in the present of its experience, located within the flow of those traditions. Beyond this, however, the lateness of the Rebekah texts effectively rules out any thought of an early Yahwist.

Outcome in Genesis C: The Joseph Story and Associated Text (Genesis 37–50)

Joseph Story

The brilliance of the Joseph story—and it is brilliant—is not in the telling of how an arrogant and obnoxious smart-aleck kid brother made it to the top of the Egyptian political machine; that was a feature of some of Israel's Diaspora literature. The brilliance is rather that the story makes it plausible that this whiz kid should crack emotionally under the weight of his compassion for a doting and overloving father. As literature, it is a study of human beastliness and the realities of reconciliation.

As literature, it has been transformed by two developments: (1) With regrettably exaggerated claims (see below), second-raters have fiddled the plot beyond all credibility. (2) If accepted as possibly once an independent story, in the present text the Joseph story has become the link between the ancestors of Israel and the exodus from Egypt.

Stories of a local's meteoric rise to power or favor in a foreign state are found elsewhere in Israel's literature. In the late but canonical book of Daniel, King Nebuchadnezzar of Babylon, like Pharaoh, has a dream. Where the wise men of Babylon fail, Daniel tells Nebuchadnezzar both his dream and its meaning. For this, he receives the king's adulation and is made "ruler over the whole province of Babylon and chief prefect over all the wise men of Babylon" (Dan 2:48). Later Daniel's interpretation at Belshazzar's feast of the inscription written on the wall by the moving hand earns him a royal proclamation that "he should rank third in the kingdom" (Dan 5:29).

In the canonical book of Esther (Hebrew), Esther, a local in exile, is portrayed becoming queen to King Ahasuerus, ruler of the Medes and Persians. "The king loved Esther more than all the other women; of all the virgins she won his favor and devotion, so that he set the royal crown on her head" (Esth 2:17). Her uncle Mordecai, who had adopted her, at the end of the book is placed "next in rank to King Ahasuerus" (Esth 10:3). In the deuterocanonical book of Judith, Holofernes, chief general of the army of King Nebuchadnezzar, second only to the king (Jdt 2:4), is encamped in the plain of Esdraelon with a massive army, on the verge of destroying Israel. Judith, a lovely widow, arrives at the encampment, and Holofernes and his attendants say of her: "No other woman . . . looks so beautiful or speaks so wisely!" (Jdt 11:21). Persuaded to come to Holofernes' private banquet, she is so stunning that "Holofernes' heart was ravished with her and his passion was aroused" (Jdt 12:16). He drinks himself into a stupor, and she cuts his head off and so saves Israel. She is the local and she goes to the top.

The stories cover a remarkable extent of territory and time. Daniel is set in Babylon and Esther in Susa, at the eastern extremities of Israel's world; both stories are set in the time of exile. Joseph is in Egypt, to Israel's west, set in ancestral times. Judith's story, by contrast, is set in Israel itself, in the plain of Esdraelon, supposedly in the period before Israel had fallen to the Assyrians. The two men win their way to the top by the interpretation of dreams; the two women achieve their aims by beauty and strength of character.[71]

---

71. For the characterization and dating of the Joseph story as Diaspora short story ("Diaspora-novelle") and its comparison with the book of Esther, see A. Meinhold, "Die Gattung der Josephs-geschichte und des Estherbuches: Diasporanovelle I," *ZAW* 87 (1975): 306–24, and "Die Gattung der Josephsgeschichte und des Estherbuches: Diasporanovelle II," *ZAW* 88 (1976): 72–93 (date: between 650 and 425 BCE, "Diasporanovelle I," 311); D. B. Redford, "between the mid-seventh

Compared with the story of Joseph, a markedly different tone permeates the stories of Daniel, Esther, and Judith. In these latter, the rhetorical embroidery is greater, the aura of weakness and persecution evident, with a correspondingly great emphasis on prayer and appropriate observance. The language of Genesis may be more restrained, but thematically the distance is not great; God's role is palpable. Says Joseph: "God has revealed to Pharaoh what he is about to do" (Gen 41:25, 28); says Pharaoh: "Can we find anyone else like this—one in whom is the spirit of God?" (41:38). Once again, the victim and underdog (an oppressed alien, God's outsider) gets the top job. The fantasy of quasi-supreme power in Egypt is probably conceivable only within a Diaspora situation.

This is before second-raters fiddled the plot beyond all credibility. As we said earlier, "it is noteworthy that the local lad (Joseph) becomes almost the equal of Pharaoh (see Gen 41:40–44), controller of the food supply for one of the great powers of the ancient world (41:48, 55, 57), and head of Treasury par excellence for Pharaoh—all the money (47:14), flocks (47:16–17), land (47:19–20), and even the people of Egypt themselves (47:21–25) are brought by Joseph under Pharaoh's control." Food supply (ch. 41) is one thing; money, flocks, land, and people (ch. 47) are another. Famine, and the move to Egypt, has been a theme earlier in the text. Joseph's position in control of Egypt's food supply may pose a challenge to the suspension of disbelief; the moves to include money, flocks, land, and people push well beyond the bounds of credibility.

Because of famine, Jacob's family must come down to Egypt to find food (cf. Gen 12:10), and in due course Jacob himself must come. The presence of the ancestral family in Egypt allows the welding together of the ancestral traditions and the exodus traditions.[72] The nature of the Joseph story does not require the two to be combined; a return to Canaan could have happened by other ways than the exodus (cf. Gen 50:7–14). The story of Joseph must be looked at in its own right.

Of themselves, these reflections have nothing to say about the history of ancient Israel; they are involved with the study of literature. *Hamlet* and *Macbeth*, although deservedly ranking among the great dramas produced by the human spirit at its creative best, are not sources for the history of events in Denmark or at Dunsinane. The story of Joseph is a skillfully told story; it need not be a source for Israel's history.

---

and mid-fifth centuries B.C." (*Story of Joseph*, 252); J. A. Soggin: late but not post-Maccabean (*Das Buch Genesis*, 427–36, see p. 430). For Konrad Schmid, the Diaspora aspect is unquestionable ("fraglos"); he thinks of an earliest date in relation to a possible northern Israel Diaspora in Egypt (from 720) but not as late as postpriestly ("Die Josephsgeschichte im Pentateuch," in *Abschied vom Jahwisten*, ed. J. C. Gertz, 83–118, see pp. 108–14). Note Gunkel, "The very late form of the Joseph accounts also explains why only very little historical information echoes in them" (Hermann Gunkel, *Genesis*, trans. M. E. Biddle [German original: 3rd ed., 1910; Macon, GA; Mercer University Press, 1997], 383).

72. George W. Coats, "The Joseph story functions as a bridge, theologically and structurally, between the patriarchs and the exodus" (*Genesis: With an Introduction to Narrative Literature*, FOTL 1 [Grand Rapids: Eerdmans, 1983], 266, cf. p. 261). That this was not the original purpose of the Joseph story, see Konrad Schmid, "Josephsgeschichte im Pentateuch," in *Abschied vom Jahwisten*, ed. J. C. Gertz, 83–118.

Before discussing the Joseph story itself, a detour has to be devoted to the story of his brother Judah. In its place in the present Genesis text (ch. 38), it is located after the episodes with Joseph in Canaan (ch. 37) and before those in Egypt— precisely where it has to be. In ch. 37, Joseph is said to be seventeen; his brothers, shepherding their father's flock, are not much older. In ch. 38, Judah, fourth of the brothers, has had a wife and three sons, with the youngest, Shelah, grown to marriageable age (cf. 38:14). The story, therefore, must be placed after ch. 37; it cannot be placed any later if it is to be kept in Canaan.[73] The events relate to the life of a wealthy farmer; apart from the identities, they could come from almost any time in Israel's history. The text is most likely story rather than report for three reasons. First, options appear to be present regarding whether lineage or marriage is the story's focus. On the one hand, Onan resents raising offspring [seed] for his brother (38:8, levirate marriage [cf. Ruth; Deut 25:5–10]); the focus suggested is lineage, not marriage.[74] On the other hand, when Tamar sees that she has not been given as wife to Shelah, the third son (38:14), the focus seems to have shifted from lineage to marriage. Only when marriage is apparently out of the question does the story have Tamar focus exclusively on concern for lineage. Second, Tamar's stratagem succeeds, almost adventitiously; Hirah could so easily have advised his friend against patronizing a wayside prostitute when a professional at Timnah at the end of the day might have been more advisable. Third, at her request Judah gives the "prostitute" his signet, cord, and staff. These three proofs of identity prepare for a great ending to the story, but, in the reality of event, the request for all three might have risked rousing suspicion on Judah's part. Finally, while he may be assumed to have been sexually needy, nothing is said of her situation, and yet she conveniently conceives. Whatever facts are presupposed, the text is probably best understood as story.[75] The naming of her sons, of course, does not determine the dating of the story.

The picture painted of Judah, a son of Jacob and farmer in the land of Canaan, does not coexist comfortably with the picture of Joseph, son of Jacob, reaching the heights of political power in Egypt, bringing his brothers down there twice, and finally his father and family. The two pictures are not wholly incompatible, but the text does nothing to ease their coexistence. Judah has had a wife and three sons, and the third has grown to marriageable age; Joseph acceded to power over Egypt, aged thirty (41:46), with seven plenteous years and seven years of famine to follow. Compatibility of timing is not impossible, but compatibility of image is strained. In the Joseph story, the brothers are treated as a unity (cf. 42:1–3); in

---

73. Robert Alter begins his valuable introduction to biblical narrative with an analysis of this story in its place, and the evidence for the "careful splicing of sources by a brilliant literary artist" (*The Art of Biblical Narrative* [New York: Basic Books, 1981], 3–12, esp. 10).

74. For the context of levirate marriage, cf. A. D. H. Mayes, *Deuteronomy*, NCB (London: Oliphants, 1979), 328–29. Issues of property, family name, and a woman's security in society are involved.

75. Westermann, endorsing Emerton, appears not to consider the possibility that story need not be the mirror image of event (cf. *Genesis 37–50* [Minneapolis: Augsburg, 1986], 50).

the Judah story, that is not so (cf. 38:1). The user of the text may well relish both stories and be left to wonder which seems more nearly to approximate the unfolding of God's world: that a son of Jacob should patronize his own daughter-in-law as a prostitute near Enaim, on the road to Timnah (38:14–16), or that the Pharaoh of Egypt should say to a son of Jacob: "You shall be over my house, and all my people shall order themselves as you command; only with regard to the throne will I be greater than you" (41:40).

Good stories can usually be told in more than one way, and this is true of the Joseph story. Variants exist; they do not need to be parceled out to reconstruct earlier documentary sources.[76] From the beginning, features are there to suggest an overall story rather than a fragmented one.[77] Joseph is a dreamer (37:5–11); the interpretation of dreams will bring him to power in Egypt (chs. 40–41). Joseph has two dreams: the first angered his brothers, as he dreamed their sheaves bowed down to his (vv. 5–8); the second involved the whole family, with sun, moon, and eleven stars bowing down to him (vv. 9–11; note that Rachel is long dead). Dominance over his brothers fires the narrative until ch. 44; with reconciliation and the breakdown of Joseph's composure, dominance over the brothers is not dissipated but rather is complete and includes their father.[78] It stays that way until the end.

If these basic building blocks are needed for the total narrative, can the various repetitions and doublets be accounted for as enhancements, enriching the story with options and the like? Exposure to the text affirms this. Starting with ch. 37, a good example is found in the verses concerning Reuben. The text allows great scope for storytelling, with ambiguities surrounding Reuben's proposals and intentions. Later in the narrative, Reuben's voice recurs with the righteousness of the one who was ignored (42:22), reinforced by the offer he makes (42:37). In these early stages, the Reuben motif is a valued enhancement.[79] Reuben's proposal can be understood as a protest against actual killing, without adopting the enhancement offered by v. 22b; he then silently concurs with Judah over sale to

---

76. Recent studies have moved in the direction of treating the Joseph story as a unified whole. For example: Redford, "The present writer sees no alternative to rejecting the view that 'J' and 'E' . . . are present in the Joseph Story" (*Story of Joseph*, 253); Coats, "[the Joseph story] appears to be from one source . . . efforts to reconstruct the earlier stages seem hopelessly hypothetical" (*Genesis*, 265; see also Coats, *From Canaan to Egypt: Structural and Theological Context for the Joseph Story*, CBQMS 4 [Washington, DC: CBA, 1976]); Westermann, "Recent scholarship shows a marked tendency to the unity thesis" (*Genesis 37–50*, 20). Westermann quotes a damningly revealing comment from Wellhausen regarding the source division in chs. 37–50: "One suspects that this section, like the rest, is a synthesis of J and E; our earlier results impose this solution and would be profoundly affected were it not demonstrable" (ibid., 19). With respect, it is not demonstrable.

77. At a cost of fragmentation of verses and dislocation of text, a putative early version of the Joseph story can be isolated and a process of development sketched; the cost renders the process suspect (cf. Hans-Christoph Schmitt, *Die nichtpriesterliche Josephsgeschichte: Ein Beitrag zur neuesten Pentateuchkritik*, BZAW 154 [Berlin: de Gruyter, 1980]). For discussion of the context possible for such an early version, see David M. Carr, *Reading the Fractures of Genesis: Historical and Literary Approaches* (Louisville, KY: Westminster John Knox, 1996), 277–83.

78. For the role of these initial dreams, see Campbell and O'Brien, *Sources*, 227–37.

79. See Campbell and O'Brien, *Sources*, 225–28.

the Ishmaelites (followed up in 39:1). There will be no killing. The enhancements (vv. 22b, 28aα, and 29–30) allow for different versions. With v. 22b, Reuben is revealed to have other plans; he is silent, naturally, while Judah proposes the sale. With v. 28aα (to: "out of the pit"), the Midianites intervene, and as Reuben finds Joseph gone (vv. 29–30), his plans evaporate.[80] The sale to Potiphar by the Midianites (37:36) allows for a further version in which the Ishmaelites are bypassed and the sale made by the Midianites themselves in Egypt.

To an ancient storyteller, the text offers multiple options, only one of which would be actualized in any given telling of the story. Which telling makes for the best story? One option: Joseph stripped, dropped down the well, and left to die; no Reuben rescue, no Ishmaelites, no Midianites. Another option: Joseph sold to passing Ishmaelites. Another option: Joseph "lifted" by the Midianites (assuming the brothers were lunching over the hill, out of earshot of Joseph's cries and out of eyesight of the pit), thwarting any sale by the brothers (and any rescue by Reuben, if that had been introduced), and leaving open the option of the Midianites selling to Potiphar (cf. 37:36) or to the Ishmaelites (cf. 39:1). A further option: no sale of Joseph, but the rescue planned by Reuben (cf. v. 22b) and thwarted by the Midianites.

After Joseph's transfer to Egypt, the story's essential move is to bring him into contact with two of Pharaoh's household, one of whom will bring him into contact with Pharaoh. The text offers the user two options to introduce this move, identifiable by contrasting terminology. First, there are an Egyptian, described as Joseph's master (Egyptian: 39:1, 2, 5), and Potiphar, described as captain of the guard (37:36; 39:1; 40:3, 4; 41:10, 12). Potiphar is described as a *sārîs* of Pharaoh, a term used also of the baker and cupbearer (40:2, 7); the term can mean "official" or "eunuch." Second, there are two terms for the prison, *bêt hassōhar* and *mišmar*. The essential contact with Pharaoh's baker and cupbearer begins with 40:5. One lead-in to this can begin with Potiphar (37:36), who places the offending baker and cupbearer in Joseph's charge (40:4). An alternative lead-in can begin with "the Egyptian, Joseph's master," whose wife accuses Joseph of attempted rape; her husband throws him into prison (*bêt hassōhar*), where the chief jailer puts him in charge of all the prisoners. Following either lead-in, the narrative can continue from 40:5.

An alternative lead-in, more extensive than the other, designates God as YHWH (occurring eight times in ch. 39 and nowhere else in the Joseph narrative). Simple division into J and E sources does not, of course, explain this; no version of the Joseph story would stop with ch. 39. In this option, Joseph is jailed in order to bring him to the attention of the prisoner, who will in due course bring him to the attention of Pharaoh, because of his skill as an interpreter of dreams. It is significant that ch. 39, with its emphasis on YHWH, comes at the start of Joseph's time in Egypt. "The LORD was with Joseph" (39:2, 21) is

---

80. In v. 28a, the subject of "they sold him" can be the brothers (from v. 27) or, with the enhancement, the Midianites.

emphatic throughout (cf. vv. 3, 5, 23); the theologically identical claim is made for David. The emphasis on the god of Israel is important here and, once established in the narrative, need not be reasserted.

It is noteworthy that in the final stages of these introductions certain terms are mingled: for example, (i) *bêt hassōhar* and *mišmar* (40:3, cf. v. 5); (ii) place of confinement (39:20; 40:3, 5); (iii) king as equivalent to Pharaoh (39:20; 40:1, 5); (iv) the *mišmar* in conjunction with his master's house (40:7). Storytellers would follow their chosen line through these without difficulty. Details of narrative skill—such as the "pit" (NRSV, dungeon) in 40:15 (also 41:14) echoing the pit of ch. 37, following the reference to "the land of the Hebrews"—cannot be explored here.[81] Allowance also has to be made, in a text of this sort, for the possibility of editorial tidying and linking.

Much of the potential duplication alleged within 41:34–57 falls into the category of what is possible but, without further evidence, not necessary. Details need not be discussed here; the single story line is adequately maintained. Jacob's knowledge that there was "grain" (*šeber*) in Egypt indicates that the fact of bread in Egypt (41:54) was due to Joseph's prudent storage over the preceding seven years. Verses 54–57 need not be tampered with. The general statement in v. 54b is followed by the unfolding of the intensifying famine throughout Egypt with the corresponding enhancement of Joseph's power; the piling up of references to the famine may be good narrative technique. Rearrangement of the text to isolate Egypt from the surrounding lands, while possible, is not necessary.

Regarding source division in ch. 42, a glance at what has been done allows three statements to be made: it is possible, but with substantial gaps for J; it is probably quite unnecessary; it is certainly forced. Westermann endorses Redford and Rudolph: "the planned architecture of the middle part [vv. 6–25] would be destroyed by separation into different sources."[82] Reuben's "Let us not take his life. . . . Shed no blood" (back in 37:21–22a, without Noth's emendation to Judah) was ambiguous—let him not die at all or let him not die at our hands—until 37:22b brings good intentions to the rescue. A storyteller who worked Reuben's good intentions into the storyline for whatever reason might well have prolonged this shaft of light among the brothers with 42:22, 37—especially with Joseph overhearing (v. 23). The tension between vv. 27–28 and v. 35 can be exaggerated; in vv. 27–28 only one brother opens his sack and then tells the others. It is only at journey's end (v. 35) that the others open their sacks and see for themselves their own silver in each sack. A storyteller wanting to focus on the anxiety for the rest of the journey might include v. 27; another might focus instead on the surprise at the end.

If a late date is assumed, 43:14's *El Shaddai* is hardly surprising. In the old man's mouth, it is not out of place; other possibilities, however, exist. The repetition of

---

81. Westermann comments: "It is a hole . . . as seen from the point of view of the prisoner" (*Genesis 37–50*, 77).

82. *Genesis 37–50*, 104.

the motif of the money in the sack (44:1–2) can be allowed as available to the storyteller; it is not used in the follow-up at 44:6–12. Source division has been argued for 45:3–4.[83] But v. 3b can be understood to allow for v. 4; the brothers were too frightened to speak, requiring a second try by Joseph. Other minor differences in vv. 1–15 are easily surmountable. The theme of God's preservation of life in vv. 5b–8 is a global accounting for the whole episode. The earlier reconciliation, effected by Judah, that brought about Joseph's tears is a portrayal of inner-family dynamics; as such, it is not in tension with the overview. With 45:15, the issue of Joseph's reconciliation with his brothers is substantially complete.

In all that has happened so far, the transactions have been strictly between Joseph and his brothers; Pharaoh has not been involved. Suddenly, Pharaoh is informed "Joseph's brothers have come" (45:16; cf. 45:2). Naturally, this can be accounted for, and an ancient storyteller would have been able to take it in stride. Nevertheless, what follows—with its "best of the land . . . fat of the land" (v. 18) and gift of wagons—smacks of the exaggeration to come. An enhancement is perhaps possible. The gift of garments (45:22) is significant for symbolizing reconciliation here, reversing 37:23 (an observation courtesy of Michael Kolarcik).

The subsequent theophany, marked off by Beer-sheba in 46:1 and 46:5, is strongly redolent of the language of 26:23–25. There is repetition between the concern for the old man, the little ones, and the wives in the wagons (v. 5) and the listing in vv. 6b–7: Jacob, all his offspring, sons and grandsons, daughters and granddaughters, all his offspring. There is no neat point where a Joseph story ends and secondary expansions accumulate. It is possible—no more than that—to conclude the Joseph story with 45:15, 25–26; 46:1a*, 6–7.[84] The story ends with Jacob and his extended family in Egypt. It is tempting to include 46:28–30. The Hebrew syntax of 46:28, as it stands, requires a name; the sentence has none. In the narrative text, prescinding from the list in vv. 8–27, the nearest subject is "Jacob," to be found in v. 6b. With the omission of vv. 8–27, it is not impossible. There is no neat and tidy point for the story to end—not really here and not between here and Gen 50:26 inclusive.[85]

Overview: Joseph Story

Within the context of moving Israel into a position of privilege, the Joseph story is compact and dense, exploring a dysfunctional set of relationships within a family and the achievement of reconciliation in the midst of it all. In Canaan, Joseph has two dreams; in the Egyptian jail he interprets two dreams; for Pharaoh he interprets another two dreams. No wonder the story has his brothers come down to Egypt twice. In Canaan, he is portrayed as arrogant to his brothers and they

83. See Campbell and O'Brien, *Sources*, 180 n.41.

84. Readers of translations will realize that in Hebrew these sentences begin with the equivalent of "and"; 46:1, in particular, begins "And Israel set out . . ." The NRSV's "So" (45:25) and "When" (46:1) are appropriate in their context, but may not be when the context changes.

85. See Konrad Schmid's discussion and difficulties, "Josephsgeschichte im Pentateuch," in *Abschied vom Jahwisten*, ed. J. C. Gertz, 83–118, see pp. 95–106.

as beastly to him; having achieved power in Egypt, Joseph is portrayed being as beastly to his brothers as they were to him. The story finds a goodness in Judah, who offers himself as substitute for Benjamin. Confronted with this offer, Joseph must also be aware that the suffering inflicted by the brothers on his father is being matched by the suffering he himself is inflicting upon the old man (cf. esp. 44:27–31). Joseph breaks down in tears: "I am Joseph. Is my father still alive?"

It is a story of admirable complexity. There is the issue of Joseph's meteoric rise to such power in Egypt that one might only dream about. Coupled with this are both Joseph's tears (42:24, 43:30) and his tyranny. The outcome of it all is reconciliation with his brothers and reunion with Benjamin and his father. The drama and plot of this story are not about the coming of Jacob's family to Egypt. The story had to bring Benjamin and Jacob down to Egypt, for that is where reconciliation leads. The coming down to Egypt is not the essence of the story, but its outcome. The story is useful for bringing Israel into Egypt, but bringing Israel into Egypt is not the essence of the story.[86]

After the Joseph Story

What follows the Joseph story can be dispatched briefly enough. With few exceptions, the remaining text can be assigned to later additions that elevate Joseph's status and power. The list of seventy persons (46:8–27) comes from Israel's pool of traditions. Joseph's family is presented to Pharaoh and settled in Goshen. After that, the overkill begins: finances (47:14–15); livestock (47:16–17); land (47:19–20); even people (47:19, 21). Joseph's sons, Ephraim and Manasseh, are blessed by their grandfather. This blessing is followed in ch. 49 by Jacob's blessing of his sons, the tribes of Israel; this is widely recognized as an independent passage. The difference from 29:31–30:24 is particularly evident. The burial of Jacob and the last words around Joseph bring the book of Genesis to a close.[87]

Outcome in Exodus–Numbers: Core of Israel's Experience

The Book of Exodus

In the present biblical text the accounts of the plagues are given in two clearly structured forms, and the forms are different.[88] Specifics vary; the different structures are clearly identifiable. The sequence of the plagues in each of these forms provides the backbone of what can be understood as two documentary sources.

---

86. Redford's comments on context and date may be noted. Context: "the Hebrew writer was not so well acquainted with Egypt as has often been imagined" (*Story of Joseph*, 241–42); date: "between the mid-seventh and mid-fifth centuries B.C." (ibid., 252).

87. According to tradition, Joseph's bones were buried at Shechem, in land that his father had bought (Josh 24:32); not unlike the burial of Abraham's family at Hebron, in land that Abraham had bought.

88. For a different approach, "neither sources nor editing," see Blum, *Studien*, 242–56. See also Werner H. Schmidt, "Die Intention der beiden Plagenerzählungen (Exodus 7–10) in ihrem Kontext," in *Studies in the Book of Exodus: Redaction–Reception–Interpretation*, ed. M. Vervenne, BETL 126 (Leuven: Leuven University Press, 1996), 225–43.

The preceding text (in Exod 3 and 6) provides two call narratives for Moses, one for each. In our judgment, it is not appropriate to take this duality back into Exod 1–2, where the texts have different roles to play (see below).

Within each plague, the forms noted are as follows:

> Form One: The Exodus Narrative (ExN)
> 1. God to Moses: tell Pharaoh to let my people go, under threat of plague. (Note: "my people" presupposes the relationship between God and Israel.)
> 2. Plague.
> 3. Pharaoh: departure offered
> 4. Plague stopped.
> 5. Pharaoh: heart hardened (root: *k-b-d*); departure denied.
>
> Form Two: The Sanctuary Narrative (SaN)
> 1. God to Moses: tell Aaron to inflict plague.
> 2. Plague.
> 3. Egyptian magicians.
> 4. Pharaoh: heart hardened (root: *ḥ-z-q*); did not listen.

Given this duality, two narrative sequences can be identified. On the analysis of details, differences of opinion exist.[89] The details of the verses are in appendix 4; by and large, we follow Noth (see Campbell and O'Brien, *Sources*). A continuous duality is fairly sure (i.e., the difference is identifiable); anything further is uncertain. Both forms take for granted the authority of Moses to negotiate with Pharaoh.

Exodus 1–2

With the Israelites on the point of making their exit from Egypt, the texts involved with this identifying moment in Israel's story need assessment. In our judgment, the two initial chapters (Exod 1–2) combine two functions. First, 1:1–14 may be seen as a bridge to the preceding text in Genesis, and 2:23–25 forges a link with the story of Exodus to come. Second, the stories of the midwives and the birth and flight of Moses are best treated as enrichments or expansions, at the disposal of the user, drawn from the pool of Israel's traditions.[90] The

---

89. Martin Noth, for example, oscillates between positions in his *Pentateuchal Traditions* and his later commentary (*Exodus*, OTL [Philadelphia: Westminster, 1962]). See Brevard S. Childs, *Exodus*, OTL (London: SCM, 1974), who claims to identify a highly fragmentary E (137–38), and John I. Durham, *Exodus*, WBC (Waco, TX: Word, 1987), 89–180. "There can hardly be any disputing the existence of separate traditions reporting the mighty acts designed to demonstrate Yahweh's powerful Presence and differences in detail between such separate traditions are inevitable" (Durham, ibid., 95). Detailed treatment is given by Fujiko Kohata, *Jahwist und Priesterschrift in Exodus 3–14*, BZAW 166 (Berlin: de Gruyter, 1986). In German recently, see J. C. Gertz, *Tradition und Redaktion*.

90. For a synchronic discussion and further literature, see Peter Weimar, "Exodus 1,1–2,10 als Eröffnungskomposition des Exodusbuches," in *Book of Exodus*, ed. M. Vervenne, 179–208.

structuring is skillful: (i) a concern for who were there in Egypt; (ii) the new situation, with regard to both Egypt (new king) and Israel (oppression); (iii) traditions concerning the leader who will deliver Israel from this oppression.

Several factors militate against giving Exod 1:1–7 an opening role in either narrative to follow. Concern for the sons of Jacob is highly understandable. As the exodus from Egypt became symbolic of something essential to Israel, it became essential that all Israel was understood to have been there. However, the "sons of Israel who came to Egypt with Jacob" is an odd formulation; from this verse one would not expect that Israel and Jacob were one and the same person. The later text of Exodus is unconcerned with the sons of Jacob; it does not use the phrase for the people of Israel ("house of Jacob" is used in 19:3). Jacob and the god of Jacob are mentioned; "sons of Jacob" are not. When the ancestral houses are named (6:14–25), after Reuben and Simeon the text focuses on the descendants of Levi; the rest of Jacob's sons are ignored. The references to Joseph (vv. 5–6) imply awareness of earlier traditions.

Exodus 1:8–14, with its "a new king arose over Egypt, who did not know Joseph," implies awareness of the exalted status claimed for Joseph in Egypt and does not make explicit the passage of an extended period of time. Nevertheless, the Israelites are described as "more numerous and more powerful than we" (v. 9); such affirmations are no more credible than those of Joseph's high favor.[91] Awareness of Joseph's status is assumed for the text's audience. Population growth such as is implied demands time.

Exodus 1:15–22 is a delightful story that would surely have been popular in the midwives' guild. Alas, it cannot be independent and, with only two midwives for all of the people, is hardly appropriate to a situation where it is alleged that the Hebrews are more numerous and powerful than the Egyptians and dreaded by them (v. 12). The episode can rightly be seen as part of the oppression; however, in the present context, it is a necessary preparation for the traditions of Moses.

Moses' birth story (Exod 2:1–10) is well known, as are the difficulties with it. Foremost among these is the contrast between the aspects of "the man born to be leader" (cf. the Sargon legend, *ANET*, 119) and the inarticulate and unwilling Moses of 4:10–13. Furthermore, anonymous as they may be, the Levite and his wife may be assumed to be newly married. The wife has a fine baby, but she also has an older daughter; later, Moses will have an older brother, Aaron aged eighty-three when Moses was eighty (Exod 7:7). Appeal to close relatives (ʾāḥ) rather than siblings is possible, but unlikely and unhelpful (cf. 6:20).[92] The story is beautiful and gets Moses into Pharaoh's household.

Problems, however, exist in Exod 2:11–25. The episode of murder and flight in 2:11–15a is in some tension with Moses' princely status. The story of Moses watering the flocks of the seven daughters of the priest of Midian and so coming

91. Note the different terminology for "taskmaster" in Exod 1:11 and 3:7; 5:6, 10, 13.

92. For Noth and Childs, the sister is embellishment of the narrative (Noth, *Exodus*, 25; Childs, *Exodus*, 18), which is possible but does not remove the tension; neither mentions Aaron. For Durham, Moses as firstborn is an "impression"; Aaron as Moses' brother is priestly pushiness (*Exodus*, 16).

to marry one of them is delightful; but it is a type scene (cf. Gen 24:15–27; 29:2–12) and all too easily introduced into the legend of a great leader figure. Fleeing into exile, Moses delivers seven daughters; returning from exile, he delivers his people. Verses 23–25 form a suitable transition from the enhancement to the following narrative; their function as a bridge from 1:14 to the following narrative is, of course, possible. The reference to God's covenant with Abraham, Isaac, and Jacob suggests a time when the preceding traditions of Genesis have moved toward final shape. It could be compatible with the SaN; no such reference is found in the ExN.

These two chapters may well enhance the story of Moses and the exodus of Israel from Egypt. It is unlikely, however, that they constituted the beginning of either narrative about this exodus. The call narrative has Moses in Midian, married to the priest's daughter. It is an abrupt beginning, as is also, for example, the first appearance of Aaron or Elijah (1 Kgs 17:1). Such a beginning invites legendary enhancement.

Out of Egypt

The text provides two call narratives for Moses, beginning with 3:1 and 6:2 respectively. The first opens with the famous episode of the burning bush, while Moses was shepherding Jethro's flock in Midian.[93] Distribution of its text across sources (traditionally J and E) is not necessary. The occurrences of *elohim*, usually attributed to E, can be accounted for as marking possibilities and options.

In 3:4b, for example, a possibility is offered that can be used either in place of v. 4a or in conjunction with it. Two options are on offer in v. 6: v. 6a emphasizes the ancestral relationship with God, whether spelled out or not (the three ancestral names are a probable enhancement); v. 6b introduces the option of behavior deemed by some appropriate before God, even for Moses.

In vv. 7–15, two parts are identifiable. A base text (vv. 7–10, using *yhwh*) has God order Moses to assemble the elders of Israel and with them go to Pharaoh. Verses 11–15 have Moses, very reasonably, raise two issues. First, what makes this acceptable to *me*? Who am I to do this, to take this leadership role? Second, what makes this acceptable to *them*?[94] If they ask, what do I say this god's name is?[95] The second part of the passage is freighted for many Bible readers with massive

---

93. Reflections on Exod 3–4 (with relevant literature)—significantly, with his KD beginning here and not in Genesis—are offered by Blum in "Die literarische Verbindung von Erzvätern und Exodus: Ein Gespräch mit neueren Endredaktionshypothesen," in *Abschied vom Jahwisten*, ed. J. C. Gertz et al., 119–56, esp. 123–33.

94. Cf. Durham, *Exodus*, 36–37; also Terence E. Fretheim, *Exodus*, Int (Louisville, KY: John Knox, 1991), 62–63; Childs, *Exodus*, 60–70.

95. It is most important at this point to hear the question correctly; so many do not (for example, for Propp, it is Moses' simple question: "What is his name?" [William H. C. Propp, *Exodus 1–18*, AB 2 {Garden City, NY: Doubleday, 1999}, 224]). The biblical text has Moses ask a quite different question: "If I come to the Israelites and say to them . . . and they ask me, 'What is his name?' what shall I say to them?" (Exod 3:13). Moses' question is not the simple "What is your name?"; instead, it is "What do I say to the Israelites that your name is?" It is wise to check the text closely before concluding "I think that Yahweh is simply being cagey" (Propp, 225).

overtones of emotion and sacredness, being regarded as the place of the revelation of God's name and its meaning.[96] It may not necessarily be so.

God's reply to the first issue is standard: "I will be with you" (v. 12); its formulation includes the explicit use of the verb "to be" in the first person: "*kî ʾehyeh ʿimmāk*" (v. 12). In Hos 1:9 this is used as the name of Israel's God: "I will not be *ʾehyeh* to you." The reason alleged to back up this assurance, "you [plural] shall worship God on this mountain," at first sight looks unhelpful. On reflection, its message is: "Who are you? You are to be the founder of Israel's worship on this mountain. That is who you are." It demands faith of Moses; it confirms faith in Moses among those who worship the God revealed on this mountain.

Moses presses the second issue; he expects to be asked. In the subsequent text (i.e., 4:29–31) he is *not* asked the question, which suggests that vv. 11–15 may be properly understood as no more than a possible enhancement. The complexity of God's reply has generated an enormous literature. But before the text's meaning is sought, a prior question needs clarification: What are these Israelites asking when they say, "What is his name?" (v. 13b)? Do they know the answer to their question (is it the equivalent of a password?), or is it to be a new revelation to them? At the moment, Moses is in Midian. When he returns, he may be greeted as a long-lost son or with the surly question, "Where did you come from?" The likelihood of his being recognized as a member of the Jewish community in Egypt is highly questionable. It might well be expected that he did not know the personal name of Israel's god; but the people of Israel would know the personal name of their god, so they could be expected to challenge the newcomer. Exodus 4:1 appears to assume that the Israelites knew the name of their god ("YHWH did not appear to you").

It is, of course, possible that the Israelites are portrayed not knowing YHWH as the personal name of God (cf. 6:2–3), and the accumulation of clauses here about the name may suggest something new and previously unknown. On the other hand, the two clauses in v. 14 are hardly helpful in the context; v. 15 echoes 3:6 and something of 6:2–3, so that it is not above suspicion.

As is well known, the text contains three answers: vv. 14a, 14b, and 15. The middle version—"Thus you shall say to the Israelites . . ." (v. 14b)—responds satisfactorily to the question: "What shall I say to them [the Israelites]?" (v. 13); "You shall say to the Israelites, *ʾehyeh* has sent me to you'" (v. 14b). It echoes something of the response already given in v. 12, with added weight coming from its use in Hos 1:9.

It is not appropriate here to undertake a full interpretation of what is unquestionably a contentious and difficult passage.[97] It is, however, the unsuitability of v. 14 to offer a new revelation that forces the reader to entertain the possibility

---

96. "This question has evoked such a long history of scholarly controversy and has been approached with so many oblique questions that it is extremely difficult to hear the text any longer within its present context" (Childs, *Exodus*, 74).

97. The traditional source-critical analysis of the text can distract rather than enlighten—but it is described by Werner Schmidt as a model example, "Musterbeispiel der Literarkritik" (*Exodus*, BKAT II/1, vol. 1: *Exodus 1–6* [Neukirchen: Neukirchener Verlag, 1988], 107). What is possible may

that the Israelites would know the answer to their question. Verse 15, to the contrary, is exactly the sort of answer that replies to the question asked in v. 13 (but can be understood as filling out v. 14b). Given Moses' claim, "The God of your ancestors has sent me to you," the question will be: "What is his name?" (v. 13). The answer: "YHWH, the God of your ancestors . . . has sent me to you" (v. 15a). However, two factors prevent v. 15 from being seen as obviously the original answer. First, the Hebrew text prefaces the sentence with the little adverb ʿôd (NRSV, "also").[98] The ʿôd implies that the sentence was not the first one there. Second, if v. 15 was the first sentence there, it is difficult to account for the later addition of v. 14. Why would someone in ancient Israel spoil a perfectly clear text by introducing a couple of difficult and obscure clauses in front of what was clear? Furthermore, the information contained in v. 15 recurs in v. 16, which contains an instruction that renders the question-and-answer sequence of vv. 11–15 unnecessary. Thus an enhancement is likely.

Verse 16's instruction ("assemble the elders") at first sight appears to conflict with v. 10's instruction (go to Pharaoh). The full text has God's concern for "my people" (3:7) and intention to deliver (3:8), sharpened and focused in vv. 9–10. What follows unfolds this: back in Egypt, the elders are assembled and acceptance is given by the people ("the people believed," 4:29–31); then Moses and Aaron meet with Pharaoh ("let my people go," 5:1).

Some passages, such as those that list the inhabitants of the land (e.g., 3:8*, 17*), may well be expansions from Deuteronomistic or other editing. There is little point in drawing attention to them here, if a significant contribution is not being made. Aaron is present at 4:13–16, 27–28, and 29–31. As a pair, Moses and Aaron occur frequently enough in this tradition later; any objection to their joint appearance at this point would be inappropriate.

At the end of ch. 3, vv. 18–22 offer a brief sketch of what might lie ahead: the request to Pharaoh (by Moses and elders, v. 18), the refusal from Pharaoh, the plagues from God, and Israel's departure from Egypt. The passage can be understood as an enhancement, allowing a storyteller to create a setting for what is to come.

In 4:1–5, the staff to be used by Moses (cf. Exod 7:15, 17; 9:23; 10:13) is not to be confused with the staff used by Aaron. It appears from 4:20 that Moses' staff came with him from Midian and may have been associated with the episode of the burning bush. Beyond 4:20, the only other occurrence of the "staff of God" in the Hebrew Scriptures is at Exod 17:9, the battle with the Amalekites (again involving Moses). Verse 5, abruptly resuming the divine discourse, may be treated

---

not be necessary and instead, by inviting to closure, may inhibit continued reflection. A further approach is opened up by Peter Weimar's concern for a deeper understanding of a name that was already known (e.g., "die dem schon bekannten Namen innewohnende Bedeutung" [*Die Berufung des Moses: Literaturwissenschaftliche Analyse von Exodus 2,23–5,5*, OBO 32 {Freiburg, Schweiz: Universitätsverlag, 1980}, 255–64, esp. 262]).

98. Note that in v. 14b, the NRSV has "He said further"; while this "further" might be translationally justifiable (representing the "and"), there is no specific word other than "and" in the Hebrew text, which reads simply "And he said." Cf. also 3:6.

as an enhancement. Rather than attribute v. 17 to another source,[99] it is possible to see it too as an enhancement, preparing for a particular understanding of v. 28 (i.e., Moses performed the signs). For vv. 18–26, see appendix 4; vv. 27–31 can be retained for the ExN.

The wretched plight of Israel is portrayed in 5:5–19; in their bitterness, the Israelite supervisors blame Moses and Aaron, and Moses in turn blames God (5:20–23). This allows the compiler of this text to introduce the beginning of the Sanctuary Narrative at this point. Moses and Aaron have put their request to Pharaoh and been dismissively rejected. As a result, life for Israel is portrayed as more oppressive, and despair is rampant, expressed by Moses to God. First, then, comes the response of the Exodus Narrative (6:1). Following it comes the response of the Sanctuary Narrative (6:2–9).[100] The narrative gives renewed encouragement to Moses and Aaron, and to its readers and listeners. This is "careful splicing of sources by a brilliant literary artist" (Robert Alter's words, in a different context).[101]

The Sanctuary Narrative (SaN), reflecting the twofold account of the plagues, begins at Exod 6:2, with what may be termed a second call narrative for Moses (in the present text, reaffirmation of Moses' call and renewed assurance to the people). Much is presupposed in 6:2–8. The *El Shaddai* tradition is in the background; the ancestors (in the sequence Abraham, Isaac, and Jacob) are taken for granted; the YHWH-Israel relationship is understood in terms of established covenant, related to the land; the sojourn in Canaan and the promise of the land are part of the past. Beyond these, elements such as "I am YHWH" (v. 2; cf. Gen 15:7; 28:13; then other occurrences), the "outstretched arm" (v. 6), the promise "you as my people . . . I as your God" (v. 7, here understood as relationship, articulated in vv. 4–5 as covenant), and the phrase, "lift up my hand to give" (v. 8, NRSV, "swore to give") are most unlikely to be early. This introduction dates the SaN in ways that are not so explicit in the following text. It is, however, a clear enough beginning and puts its stamp on what follows.

The SaN continues to the end of the initial demonstration of power before Pharaoh (7:13). The passage in 6:13–30 is easily understood as an enhancement, signaled by the address to Moses and Aaron in v. 13, reiterated in vv. 26–27. The address in the preceding text was to Moses, and in that sequence Aaron is not introduced until 7:1. Verses 28–30 modulate back into the narrative, interrupted at v. 12.

In the SaN's first encounter of Moses and Aaron with Pharaoh, God instructs Moses to tell Aaron to throw down his staff, which turns into a snake; the Egyptian magicians do the same. Pharaoh's heart is hardened (root: ḥ-z-q), and he does not listen.

Following this, the present text presents two plagues—the first, on the Nile and the waters of Egypt; the second, of frogs—drawing on both sources (ExN and SaN). Where the two shared plagues are concerned, the combination is achieved initially by first presenting God's instructions to Moses alone and then

99. Noth gives it to E because of the plural "signs" (*Exodus*, 47); also Childs (*Exodus*, 52).
100. We should note that the NRSV has in 6:2, "God also spoke to Moses" (perhaps translationally justifiable); the Hebrew has only, "And God spoke to Moses"—no "also."
101. *Art of Biblical Narrative*, 10.

including the version where Moses is to instruct Aaron. In the first case, Moses deals with the Nile while Aaron deals with the other waters of Egypt. When it comes to Pharaoh's refusal, the tendency is to draw first on the SaN (cf. 7:22; 8:3 [Heb.; NRSV 8:7]); some tidying up is achieved later (cf. 7:23–24 and the latter part of 8:11 [Heb.; NRSV 8:15]). Throughout, the hardening of Pharaoh's heart is noted consistently with two different Hebrew verbs, one for each source (for the ExN, root: *k-b-d*; for the SaN, root: *ḥ-z-q*).

The attribution of specific verses to each source for the plagues to come (prior to the death of the firstborn) is given in appendix 4. In global terms, it is straightforward and presents little difficulty.[102] The basic structural outline has been noted above.[103] According to the analysis followed here, after the two shared plagues just discussed, the others are presented in sequence: the plague of gnats is SaN; the plague of flies and the plague on livestock are ExN; the soot is SaN; the hail, locusts, and darkness are ExN. Finally, there is the death of the firstborn. All told, with the two shared plagues—the first one having the Nile and the waters merged into a single plague—the total (including the death of the firstborn) comes to ten. This is "careful splicing" at a thoughtful level. Assessed separately, in this analysis, the SaN has five plagues (including the firstborn) and the ExN has seven (excluding the firstborn).

The final plague or act of God, the killing of Egypt's firstborn, is treated in conjunction with the observance of the Passover meal. The structural patterns that distinguished the narratives in the preceding text no longer have the same force here. The initial text (11:4–8) follows directly on the dialogue between Pharaoh and Moses in the ExN's seventh plague, the plague of darkness. It is likely that 11:1–3 should be treated as an enhancement. It breaks the narrative sequence of the dialogue; v. 3b, concerning Moses, stands outside the narrative. The despoliation of the Egyptians is mentioned early, 3:21–22, and followed up at the actual time of Israel's departure, 12:35–36. Only in 3:22 (potentially) and 12:36 is the specific motif of plundering the Egyptians present (root: *n-ṣ-l*).

There is a certain delicacy in the use of language. In the enhancement (11:1), God speaks of bringing "one more plague" upon Egypt; its nature is not spelled out. Even in vv. 4–5, where it is Moses quoting God, God's action is to go out through the land; God is not named as the death-bringer. The echoes of 11:4–8 in 12:29–32 are clear.

The use of SaN terms (*môpēt* and *ḥ-z-q*) in 11:9–10 encapsulates the whole process of the plagues, although the final climactic act is still to come. The verses would perform this function well enough following 9:12, the fourth SaN plague; they are appropriately in place here, before the tenth in the present text.

---

102. It is neither necessary nor appropriate in a book such as this to go into detail on the analysis of the plague stories. Differences of detail do not affect the argument being presented.

103. Overall recently, see Childs, *Exodus*, 121–77, who retains fragments of an Elohist source (7:15b, 17b*, 20b, 23; 9:22–23a, 24a*, 25a, 35a; 10:12–13a, 15a*, 15b, 20, 21–23, 27; 11:1–3 [p. 131]). In some cases, we view the material as enhancement; in other cases, we would agree that it is possible, but do not believe it to be necessary. The issue of an Elohist source is, of course, much wider than these occurrences.

The present text puts the total process of the deliverance from Egypt within its setting, from misery (3:7) to deliverance (12:31). Within the ExN, there is the despoliation of the Egyptians (3:21–22 and 12:35–36). In the biblical text, it is not the first time that Egypt has been despoiled after plagues (Gen 12:20, "and all that he had," thanks to 12:16).

Within Exod 12, v. 37a ("The Israelites journeyed from Rameses to Succoth") is adequate for the ExN's report of departure from Egypt; vv. 37b–39 may be treated as an enhancement. For the SaN, it is likely that vv. 40–41a and 42–51 are to be treated as enhancement, which leaves only v. 41b for the report of Israel's departure ("on that very day, all the companies of the LORD went out from the land of Egypt").[104] Verse 41b, however, follows smoothly on the SaN's 12:28 (they did as commanded and that very day they went out); although terse, it too is an adequate report of the departure. The term translated "company" (ṣĕbā'ôt) occurs early (7:4) and again in the ritual for Passover (12:17); it is also at 6:26 and 12:51 (enhancements). Ritual regulations follow (13:1–16).[105]

Deliverance at the Sea

Continuing the narrative of Israel's deliverance (13:17–14:31), it is helpful to note Childs's observation that "the lack of unity in the account of the sea event has been recognized for well over a hundred years."[106] Two major sources are present, one operating with the east wind as God's instrument to push back the waters, the other with Moses' hand as God's instrument to divide the waters; there are several enhancements.[107]

Issues are here that lie beyond the scope of this study. The exodus from Egypt is complete; the deliverance at the Sea, therefore, is an independent story—at the disposal of users. The "east wind" version focuses on Israel's survival, escaping the Egyptian pursuit. The "Moses' hand" version focuses on God's glory, with Israel ordered back for the purpose (Exod 14:1–4). Two problems, however, present themselves for discussion here: (1) Can these stories be understood as continuing the plague sources? (2) How do we understand a source in which there is no crossing of the sea?[108]

The first problem arises from the disappearance of the pentateuchal sources. Where at least two sources, JE and P, were thought to extend from Genesis to Num-

---

104. For these enhancements in Exod 12:29–39 and 40–51, see appendix 4.
105. See Noth's comment: "The deuteronomistic section 13.1–16 is hardly all of a piece, but has apparently been inserted gradually" (*Exodus*, 101).
106. Childs, *Exodus*, 218.
107. For a full discussion of God's deliverance of Israel (Exod 13:17–14:31), see Campbell and O'Brien, *Sources*, 238–54; for the significance, see appendix 3, below.
108. We will discuss this briefly later, but it is not a new observation. Noth: "According to J, Israel did nothing during the decisive events. . . . J does not speak of a passage of Israel through the sea. Israel remained in their camp" (*Exodus*, 118). Childs: "There is no account of the crossing in J, or of any movement for that matter by the Israelites" (*Exodus*, 221). Durham (*Exodus*, 195–98) and Fretheim (*Exodus*, 156–61), and Propp (*Exodus 1–18*, 461–561, esp. 550–53) cover the matter with confusion. Kohata supports Noth (*Jahwist und Priesterschrift*, 281). Gertz agrees: no nonpriestly passage through the Sea (*Tradition und Redaktion*, 211, 231).

bers (with Deut 34:1a*, 7–9, or equivalent), there could be little room for doubt. The duality central to the text of the deliverance at the Sea (our avoidance of Red or Reed is deliberate; see below), coming after the plagues and the Passover, had to be distributed between these two sources. We, on the other hand, have asserted a basic duality in the plague narrative because of the presence of dual structures. Beyond that, we find room for doubt. The distribution of the two narratives regarding Passover is based on the probability of narrative sequence, following the final plague. The SaN continues on to the end of the book of Exodus; an account of the deliverance at the Sea, for the purpose of exalting God's glory, is understandable. A continuation of the ExN, on the other hand, is not to be found in the second half of the book; an ending for the ExN involving the deliverance at the Sea and its celebration in Exod 15:1–18 would be satisfying. But the "understandable" and the "satisfying" alone cannot be considered adequate evidence when interpreting text. Traditions are being made available to users, and users must put them to intelligent use.

At the Sea, in the traditions associated with Moses' hand, in 14:4, 17–18 the themes recur of God's hardening Pharaoh's heart (*h-z-q*; also v. 8) and getting glory and the Egyptians knowing that "I am YHWH." The Hebrew root *h-z-q* has been used throughout the SaN plague text for the hardening of Pharaoh's heart. The theme of God's getting glory does not occur before 14:4, but is not inconsistent with the preceding narrative. Finally, the theme of the Egyptians knowing that "I am YHWH" occurs within the SaN at 7:5. The corresponding theme for the ExN is that "you [the Israelites] may know that 'I am YHWH.'" At 7:3, God's hardening of Pharaoh's heart is spoken of, but a different Hebrew verb is used (root: *q-š-h*). In the circumstances of the respective contexts, it is a probable conclusion that these traditions continue the SaN.

For the ExN, the evidence is more tenuous. Pharaoh changes his mind in 14:5; he had done the same thing repeatedly earlier in the ExN (for example: 8:11, 28 [Heb.; NRSV 8:15, 32]; 9:7, 34).[109] As evidence, it is decidedly thin. Coupled with the "satisfying" nature of an ending involving the deliverance at the Sea and the celebration of it in Exod 15:1–18, it may have to do—it is at least a possibility. It is, of course, to be taken for granted that material of different origins may have been brought together to form a satisfactory narrative.

We come to the second problem: how do we understand a source in which there is no crossing of the Sea? The deliverance at the Sea is too significant a moment in Israel's theology to be left less clear than necessary. A few details will help. It is important to realize that nothing here is new. Noth and Childs agree that, in one source, there is no crossing of the Sea and no movement on the part of Israel—and no appeal to a gap in the text.[110] Before looking at the text more

---

109. See Noth, *Exodus*, 112.

110. For Wellhausen, in the Jehovist (J) the Egyptians cross the sea but Israel does not; the Egyptians, having succeeded in crossing the sea, "encounter the Hebrews on the eastern shore" (*Prolegomena*, 352; but cf. *Die Composition des Hexateuchs und der historischen Bücher des Alten Testaments* [cited from 4th unchanged printing; Berlin: de Gruyter, 1963; originals, 1876–78], where he extracts two crossings from the report of one: "die Hebräer zogen durch, die Ägypter hinterdrein," 76–77).

closely, it is important for interpreters to gird themselves for the task of scrutinizing the *text*, not searching for the *event*. This is a case where most interpreters are certain of what happened; but the text, unfortunately, is not—it is most uncertain. "Our chief and sole question must be that of the way in which J wished his own words to be understood; the historical question of what really happened is thus outside our scope."[111] It is significant that Noth in his commentary heads the section "The Miracle at the Sea"; for Childs, it is "The Deliverance at the Sea."

The *yam sûf* (literally: reed sea) is used in Hebrew to refer to both the Red Sea and the Reed Sea. The term occurs some twenty-four times in the Hebrew Scriptures. In 1 Kgs 9:26, the reference is unquestionably to the Gulf of Aqaba, between the Sinai peninsula and Saudi Arabia, at the head of the Red Sea. There are some eight other occurrences where the Red Sea proper (between Egypt and Saudi Arabia) is almost certainly meant (Exod 23:31; Num 14:25; 21:4; 33:10, 11; Deut 1:40; 2:1; and Judg 11:16). There are a couple of others where it is almost certain that a body of water much closer to Egypt is intended (Exod 10:19; 15:22). The rest refer to Israel's miraculous deliverance at the Sea, without being helpful in determining its location. Most modern scholarship takes for granted that the location was relatively close to Egypt and not east of Sinai. According to the biblical text, one important feature is clear: the Sea involved (*yam sûf*) was not an impassable obstacle. According to God's instructions in Exod 14:2, Israel was to "turn back" and camp "by the sea," presumably in preparation for crossing it under Moses' leadership. The difficulty was not in crossing the Sea; it was in escaping from the pursuing Egyptian chariot force (ExN) and getting glory for God (SaN).

While of all the names involved only Baal-zephon is relatively well identified, the broad outlines of what is envisaged by the east-wind text can be spelled out. The Israelites progressed to the eastern side of the "sea" under divine guidance by the pillar. They were followed by the Egyptian force. The pillar moved between the two camps, keeping them apart, and stayed there all night. Meanwhile, all night, God "drove the sea back by a strong east wind" so that the seabed was dry land (14:21). Just before dawn, "at the morning watch" (v. 24), God panicked the Egyptian force who fled westward toward Egypt, across the dry seabed. According to the text, the Egyptians fled to meet the sea (*liqrāʾtô* [significance overlooked by Noth]) and God "tossed" (root: *n-ʿ-r*) them into it (v. 27). All this happened while the Israelites remained in their camp; certainly, the text says nothing of their awareness until "Israel saw the Egyptians dead on the seashore" (v. 30).[112]

The creators of Israel's Scriptures have here taken two accounts of the deliverance at the Sea, one with a crossing and one without, and combined them to form a single text. As Noth has pointed out, the interweaving of two variants, pretty much in their totality, is an unusual procedure in the formation of the

---

111. Noth, *Exodus*, 116.
112. See Noth, *Exodus*, 118.

Hebrew Scriptures.[113] It is evident in the flood narrative and again here. As we have insisted: one *telling* of a story must choose between versions or options; one *text*, however, while offering one version can point to others. But why interweave two relatively complete versions in the one text? What does it say of Israel's theology that the significance here required the preservation in one text of these two contrasting traditions? What more does it say? What does it say of modern theology that sees only unity where contrast is evident? For more, see appendix 3.

One thing is clear: it is the deliverance that matters.

As we will see, there are few grounds in what follows to suggest the continuation of the ExN after the arrival east of the Sea. The evidence for the possibility of the ExN continuing through traces in Numbers to the plains of Moab will be discussed below. Although it is possible, in our judgment, it is a relatively remote possibility.

If there is no continuation of the ExN beyond this point, it is a reasonable possibility that the Song of Moses (Exod 15:1–18) was used to bring the narrative to closure. After the triumphant account of the deliverance at the Sea (15:1–12), the song goes on to bring the people to God's holy abode. Philistia, Edom, Moab, and Canaan are all mentioned (vv. 14–15). God's people enters into the mountain of God's own possession, the place of God's holy abode, God's sanctuary (v. 17).[114] As closure to the ExN, the Song is not unsuitable. It may be the best candidate available. Verses 19–21 may be understood as enhancements to its text. Verse 19 notes a variant (SaN) understanding of the deliverance; vv. 20–21 may well preserve an old tradition.

From Sea to Sinai

The text does not say whether Israel paused on the shore of the Sea to take stock; we, however, would be wise to do so. Prior to this, we have had Moses' call and the plagues, the Passover, and the deliverance at the Sea. The duality has been clear. The association of the two versions of the Sea deliverance with what preceded was fragile but plausible. In what is to come, duality is not immediately obvious; there is an itinerary—but only one—leading from the Sea to Sinai and the sanctuary to be constructed there. One thread (SaN) moves on from the Sea, via the wildernesses of Shur and Sin, to Sinai. The other narrative (ExN) is most likely to end at this point (technically, Exod 15:1–18).

To trace the thread of a journey through a compiled text, three steps are helpful: (i) to identify an itinerary; (ii) to clear away obstacles; (iii) to explore the track in relation to the stories (i.e., correlate the itinerary with the narrative). Traveling from the Sea to Sinai, we begin with the itinerary. Apparently, there is only one.[115]

---

113. Noth, *Pentateuchal Traditions*, 249–50.

114. For a succinct survey of the extensive literature on the Song, see Durham, *Exodus*, 202–5. "This magnificent poem has been much analyzed, dissected, scanned, and compared with an array of supposed precedent and counterpart works. It has been variously attributed and dated, and forced into a wide variety of forms and *Sitze im Leben*" (202).

115. It will come as no surprise that Childs should quote B. W. Bacon to the effect that this section provided "the most difficult problems hitherto met in the analysis" (*Exodus*, 264).

Between the Sea and Sinai, the present text has a total of five stations: Exod 15:22a (Marah, in the wilderness of Shur); 15:27 (Elim); 16:1 (wilderness of Sin); 17:1 (Rephidim); and 19:1–2a (Sinai). This itinerary text cannot be easily divided; perhaps it should not be divided at all.[116] It will help to have the key elements before us (in literal translation):

> 15:22 And Moses caused Israel to journey from Yam Suph and they went out to the wilderness of Shur
>
> 15:27 And they came to Elim . . . and they camped there
>
> 16:1 And they journeyed from Elim and the whole congregation of the people of Israel came [plur.] to the wilderness of Sin
>
> 17:1 And the whole congregation of the people of Israel journeyed [plur.] from the wilderness of Sin . . . and they camped at Rephidim
>
> 19:2 And they journeyed from Rephidim and they came to the wilderness of Sinai and they camped in the wilderness. (Israel camped [sing.] there in front of the mountain.)

References to the "whole congregation" point clearly to priestly circles and belong with the SaN, but there are only two such references. The phrase, "the whole congregation of" may possibly have been added to the phrase "the people of Israel," but it is unlikely. In such a hypothesis, one itinerary (without the "congregation") would have been put at the service of a second narrative (with the "congregation"); the evidence is not there for two itineraries.[117] The text is uneven and users are left uncertain.

Episodes before Sinai need to be examined for their contribution to a journey sequence. The most extensive, the Jethro episode (Exod 18:1–27) is easily accounted for. In the present telling of the story, it is widely regarded as an addition introduced at this point.[118] Naturally, if Jethro was to be given the initiating role, the episode needed to be put earlier than Sinai. From Sinai on, it would have seemed more proper for the initiative to have come from God (cf. Num 11).

---

116. A variety of views is listed by Durham (*Exodus*, 212). For Noth, for example, all of these itinerary texts are P (in the language of this book, SaN); none are J (*Exodus* [both font and comment], 127–29, 131, 138, 155). It should not be surprising that the wilderness wanderings do not receive extensive treatment in the biblical text. Childs observes that among Noth's five themes of the Pentateuch, the wilderness wandering is recognized "as a minor one in comparison with the others" (*Exodus*, 255). Van Seters correctly attributes these to "a unified itinerary chain" but fails to rebut the case for that chain belonging to P (*Life of Moses*, 154–56). Noth's own J text from the Sea to Sinai, minimal as it is, has no itinerary beyond the initial 15:22aβ (see Campbell and O'Brien, *Sources*, 144–45). For the assessment of these itinerary texts by Childs as P, see *Exodus*, 266, 275, 306, and perhaps 342 (for 19:1–2). Even if one concedes a beginning and an end (neither of which Childs claims), there is no middle for an early itinerary. It is not insuperable; it is a problem.

117. W. Johnstone notes that a pre-P version of this section "may have contained no more than Exod. 15,22abα; 19,2b" ("From the Sea to the Mountain: Exodus 15,22–19,2: A Case-Study in Editorial Techniques," in *Book of Exodus*, ed. M. Vervenne, 245–63, see p. 261). Apart from plural verbs in 15:22 and a singular verb in 19:2b, this would situate Sinai three days' journey from the Reed Sea—a view held by no one.

118. See Rolf Knierim, "Exodus 18 und die Neuordnung der Mosaischen Gerichtsbarkeit," *ZAW* 73 (1961): 146–71; also Childs, *Exodus*, 318–36; Durham, *Exodus*, 238–53.

In a different telling of Israel's story of the deliverance from Egypt, Moses' report of Israel's experience and Jethro's approval and confession could have had a place (Exod 18:5–11); they are distinct from vv. 13–27.[119] We may assume there were many such tellings. Details need not be discussed here.

Further episodes involve the incidents at Massah-Meribah (Exod 17:1–7) and the battle with Amalek (17:8–16). The itinerary is 17:1abα (i.e., as far as "they camped at Rephidim"). The Massah-Meribah episode involves journeying to Horeb rather than remaining at Rephidim; the battle with Amalek, however, is located at Rephidim. Without any report of a return to Rephidim, it seems likely that the text is offering alternative traditions: either water at Horeb (cf. 17:6) or war at Rephidim (cf. 17:8). With minor modification, a storyteller could employ both. The water story heightens the theme of "murmuring" introduced in 15:24—"to kill us and our children and livestock with thirst" (17:3);[120] it raises the central issue to which the SaN responds, "Is YHWH among us or not?" (17:7; cf. 25:8); it illustrates an impossible case: getting water from a rock; it underscores in symbolism the significance of Sinai/Horeb: source of water/life where none is expected. At this stage in the present text, the question surfaces that is to be central in later traditions of the SaN (appropriate to the desert and to the exile), that is, is God in Israel's midst or not? (17:7). In order to enable a strongly affirmative answer, God's sanctuary is commanded. "And have them make me a sanctuary, so that I may dwell among them" (25:8, cf. v. 22). The apparently isolated war tradition about Amalek completes the provision for Israel's needs in the desert: water, food, security from its enemies.[121] Since the episode with Amalek is located at Rephidim, of the two alternatives it may well have a primacy in the evocation of tradition.[122]

Of the episode at Marah (Exod 15:22–26), Childs remarks, "It is equally possible that the earlier source had elements of an itinerary."[123] It is instructive to observe what Noth must do to associate the sweetening of the water with that "earlier source" (i.e., J).[124] He begins his J text with Exod 15:22aβ, "and they went

---

119. Wellhausen, to his surprise ("ganz unmotivirte" and "sehr auffallende"), notes the different use of divine names (*Composition*, 80).

120. Much of the material on either side of Israel's stay at Sinai, the wilderness wandering, is built around the murmuring tradition. Childs distinguishes two patterns and comments, "The two patterns do not give the impression of being a literary creation, but stem from a particular situation already in the oral tradition" (*Exodus*, 258; see pp. 254–64). With the reassessment occurring here, renewed study of the murmuring tradition is needed.

121. Noth describes the victory over the Amalekites as "old narrative material" that "may derive from J" (*Exodus*, 141; cf. Childs, *Exodus*, 313).

122. Childs quotes from Reformed circles: "In vain shall Moses be upon the hill, if Joshua be not in the valley. Prayer without means is a mockery of God" (*Exodus*, 317). The Amalekite episode is a strange little tradition. In the present text, it has its place alongside the provision of water and food to provide the assurance of safety and security. In vv. 9–13, there is no mention of a location and no mention of God. Joshua and Hur are presupposed as known; so is Amalek. The emphasis is on Moses; reference to God occurs only in relation to the staff in Moses' hand (v. 9; cf. Exod 4:20). Verses 14–16 are an evident enhancement.

123. *Exodus*, 266.

124. Noth remarks that, while the phrases beginning and ending this Marah episode are from P, the material itself "does not display P's characteristic peculiarities" and "in all probability" is from J (*Exodus*, 127).

out into the wilderness of Shur." Technically, there is no subject for the verb "they went out." The subject in the immediate vicinity, the Israel led out by Moses (15:22aα), has been assigned to another source (P). A possible subject is "the people" in 14:31, but in the present text it is too far away. With certainty about the sources, such assumptions may be possible; in our present state, without such certainty, they appear rash. Furthermore, Noth's move is based on the MT; it is not possible with the Samaritan Pentateuch or the LXX, which both continue Moses' activity (see *BHS* apparatus; the LXX has "and he brought them into the wilderness of Sur"). In the light of this, to attribute the Marah episode to ExN (or J) is at best possible, but is highly unlikely. SaN is the more probable; in vv. 25b–26, an enhancement institutionalizes and extends the impact of the single event.[125]

The episode of the manna (Exod 16) has long been a battleground among interpreters.[126] Toward the end of the nineteenth century, Wellhausen respectfully disagreed with Abraham Kuenen's view that there was no trace of JE in Exod 16.[127] Childs comments that "the exact division into sources has never been satisfactorily accomplished."[128] For Wellhausen, the scant mention of manna in Num 11 presupposes a report earlier. With due respect, this is an understandable but egregious error, rather too common in biblical scholarship; to the contrary, more may have been known to ancient Israel than ever found its way into ancient Israel's Bible. An overview of the discussion of Exod 16 makes clear that what are attributed to an older source (JE) are not claimed to be more than fragments. If the Yahwist existed as an older source, an argument might be built on fragments; without the conviction that such a Yahwist existed, fragments hardly lead Israel to Sinai.

Paralleling Exod 16 and Num 11 is misleading, for the central difference needs to be recognized.[129] In Exod 16, both manna and quail are presented as God's gracious gift (cf. Exod 16:12). In Num 11, to the contrary, the Israelites are portrayed as deprived of meat and bored with manna (cf. Num 11:4–6); whatever might be thought of the quail, it was God's punishment (cf. Num 11:33). Furthermore, in Exod 16 the emphasis is on the manna, with the quail having a secondary role; in Num 11, the manna has a secondary role, and the emphasis is on the quail. Comparison from one passage to the other is precarious and unwise.

---

125. On v. 26, see Norbert Lohfink, "'I am Yahweh, your Physician' (Exodus 15:26): God, Society and Human Health in a Postexilic Revision of the Pentateuch (Exod. 15:2b, 26 [*sic*; original, Ex 15, 25b.26])," in Lohfink, *Theology of the Pentateuch: Themes of the Priestly Narrative and Deuteronomy* (Edinburgh: T & T Clark, 1994), 35–95. See also Childs, *Exodus*, 266–68.

126. For Noth "in Ex. 16 the language of P predominates"; J's contribution in Exod 16 is justified "from the occurrence of striking repetitions." But the contribution is meager, and the repetition far from striking. His claim that vv. 4–5 anticipate vv. 21–22 and that vv. 28–31 repeat what has been said before (*Exodus*, 131–32) are easily enough accounted for. They certainly do not point to the presence of a prior narrative trajectory.

127. *Composition*, 325–29. Oral tradition has it that Wellhausen had a high enough opinion of Kuenen's work that he learned Dutch in order to read it. The outcome of this reading can be found among the *Nachträge* to Wellhausen's *Composition*, 305–73.

128. *Exodus*, 274; see pp. 274–83.

129. Despite "some very obvious similarities" (see Philip J. Budd, *Numbers*, WBC [Waco, TX: Word Books, 1984], 124).

These passages have been discussed at some length because of their importance for our understanding of the place of Sinai in Israel's traditions. To summarize, it is certainly difficult to identify serious traces of a narrative trajectory
from the Sea to Sinai earlier than the texts of the Sanctuary Narrative (SaN). At
best, it is possible to claim that once there may have been one. The grounds for
source division are surprisingly frail.

Israel's progress from the Sea to Sinai is heavily laden with symbolism. Survival
is to the fore; it would hardly be fitting for departure from Egypt to be celebrated
by death in the desert (cf. 16:3). Whatever its origins, this progress is not merely a
historical event; its symbolism extends widely. After freedom from oppression, survival needs to be assured; water, food, and safety (victory over foes) give concrete
reality to survival. Israel in Egypt is God's people (3:7, ExN; 6:7, SaN). Israel is liberated from oppression in Egypt by God's action. Israel's survival in the desert is
portrayed as God's doing. Israel, as God's people, arrives at Sinai to be gifted with
God's Torah. If, after 19:1–2, the continuation of the SaN text is to found with
24:15, then on Israel's arrival the cloud of God's presence covers the mountain.

The text that is now between Exod 19:2 and 24:15 needs attention.[130] It is a
well-structured capsule, with an initial passage on covenant, then the preparation
for the theophany and gift of the law, followed by the Decalogue and the
Covenant Code, concluded with the covenant ceremony and the meal on the
mountain.[131] In relation to this Sinai capsule, two issues are important: the pri-
ority of relationship with regard to law, and the narrative context or independence of the capsule.

The issue of law and relationship is one that must be handled with care in discussing Sinai. The discussion should not reflect modern dogmatic theology, but
rather the present biblical text about Sinai. Where requirements (such as the
observance of law) are a precondition for relationship, by all human standards
the outcome is likely to be disastrous (e.g., "if you do what I ask, then I will love
you"). Where a relationship exists before any requirements are advanced, the outcome is more likely to be positive (e.g., "I love you; please do what I ask"). Where
a relationship continues to exist, even while requirements that are demanded are

---

130. At Sinai itself, Noth assigns to J part of the preparation in ch. 19 (shared with E) and part
of the covenant-making in ch. 34 (shared with "all sorts of secondary additions" [Noth]), with 34:1
following on from 19:20 and some part of 24:12–15a in the original J narrative (*Exodus*, 260). For
a helpful review of scholarship on Exod 34, see Childs, *Exodus*, 604–10; also Durham, *Exodus*,
458–60—note his "altogether too subjective . . . altogether too fragmentary" [459] about treatments
of Exod 34:10–28. Of the additional material in between, Decalogue and laws apart, the meal scene
(24:1, 9–11) is regarded as old; the covenant-making rite (24:3–8) that interrupts it is not. Furthermore, the occurrences for Sinai are significant: within the Pentateuch, Exod 13x, Lev 4x, Num 12x,
Deut 1x; outside the Pentateuch, 4x (Judg 5:5; Ps 68:9, 18 [Heb.; NRSV 68:8, 17]; Neh 9:13). For
Horeb: within, Exod 3x, Deut 9x; outside, 5x (1 Kgs 8:9; 19:8; Mal 3:22; Ps 106:19; 2 Chr 5:10).
It would seem that Torah matters; the place is less important.

131. Exod 20:18–21 is an enhancement, echoing what precedes the Decalogue and forming a
bridge to the Covenant Code that follows (cf. Deut 4:11; 5:22). Exod 24:12–14, concerned with the
tablets (with v. 14 an apparently independent tradition competing with Exod 18), is probably an
enhancement preparing for chs. 32–34.

not met, the relationship may be characterized as unconditional. Relationship implies appropriate trust; relationship involves appropriate boundaries. Both of these are essential; neither is a precondition or prior requirement.

In Egypt, at the beginning of the narratives, the relationship between Israel and God is emphasized as already in existence. "I have observed the misery of my people who are in Egypt" (3:7; cf. 3:10 [ExN])[132] and "I will take you as my people, and I will be your God. You shall know that I am the LORD your God who has freed you from the burdens of the Egyptians" (Exod 6:7; cf. 7:4 [SaN]). "My people" and "your God" are statements of relationship. In these texts, the relationship between God and Israel is in place well before Sinai. The Sinai capsule is not needed to establish this relationship.

Furthermore, on arrival at Sinai, the present text opens with Moses' first encounter with God and a proclamation that is clearly conditional (Exod 19:3–6).[133] "If you obey my voice and keep my covenant": the condition could scarcely be clearer. The consequences within the proclamation are significant: "you shall be my treasured possession . . . a priestly kingdom and a holy nation" (vv. 5–6). *Nothing is said about Israel being God's people, "my people"; that relationship has already been in place since Egypt at least.*[134] These three attributes, "treasured possession," "priestly kingdom," and "holy nation" offer a stage beyond simple relationship.[135] Their achievement is conditional on obedience and observance of the covenant (v. 5). The relationship itself is not expressed as dependent on such conditions; it is unconditional.[136] The proclamation prepares for the covenant. Beyond the already established relationship, it offers consequences of an even higher order flowing from observance of the Law. The Sinai covenant is about Israel's commitment to the Law.[137]

---

132. "Let my people go" is a leitmotiv of the ExN, cf. 5:1; 7:16, 26 (Heb.; NRSV 8:1); 8:16 (Heb.; NRSV 8:20); 9:1, 13; 10:3.

133. For many helpful details on this (postexilic) passage, see Jean Louis Ska, "Exode 19,3b–6 et l'identité de l'Israël postexilique," in *Book of Exodus*, ed. M. Vervenne, 289–317.

134. So Fretheim: "The issue is not how they might become God's people; Israel is the elect people already" (*Exodus*, 213).

135. This is the only occurrence of the three together; in this precise form, each occurs only here. For slight variations on "treasured possession" and "holy nation," see Deut 7:6; 14:2; 26:18–19.

136. See Rolf Rendtorff, "'Covenant' as a Structuring Concept in Genesis and Exodus," *JBL* 108 (1989): 385–93; Norbert Lohfink, *The Covenant Never Revoked: Biblical Reflections on Christian-Jewish Dialogue* (New York: Paulist, 1991). In our judgment, the *relationship* is primary; the *covenant* is an expression of it.

137. Agreement by the people to this proposal (19:8) and acceptance by the people of these laws (24:3, 7) frames this presentation. This is a nuance to be read into Childs (see *Exodus*, 367). The people's agreement (19:8) can only be to the proposal; under the proposal, the details of the Law are yet to come, to be accepted by the people in 24:3, 7. The "special relationship" (Childs, ibid.) is to be understood as the consequences special to this proposal; Israel's long-standing relationship with its God is already in place. This understanding is central to the formal and somewhat enigmatic passage in Deut 26:16–19. "This very day. . . . Today. . . . Today," what is known and long-standing has been affirmed: YHWH is Israel's God (26:17), and Israel is YHWH's people (26:18). As a consequence, Israel will observe the Law (26:17); as a consequence, YHWH will exalt Israel, God's people (26:18–19; cf. von Rad, *Old Testament Theology* 1:230–31). The framing signals, from early in Exod 19 to late in Deut 26, embrace the Law in its entirety.

If the relationship between God and Israel is already established and in place, the function of the Sinai capsule is to celebrate God's gift of the Law to Israel. It is not to establish the relationship; in the text, from the beginning of Exodus, the relationship is there. What then is the function of Exod 24:1–11? Verses 1–2 and 9–11 clearly constitute the "meal on the mountain" episode. Verse 2 introduces a nuanced specification; Moses is distinguished from the others in the party, and "the people" form a third element who are not privileged to come up the mountain. In vv. 1, 9–11, Moses and his party and seventy of the elders go up the mountain, see God, and eat and drink. Such a meal could celebrate the sealing of the relationship between God and Israel. However, with the relationship already established, this cannot be the passage's meaning. Instead, a new stage in the relationship is celebrated, a new stage in a long-standing association. At the end of the giving of Torah to the people, a formal celebration would certainly be in order.

Within Exod 24:1–11, vv. 3–8 report a covenantal liturgy, with reading from the book of the covenant and the "blood of the covenant" dashed against the altar (v. 6) and on the people (v. 8). In vv. 3–8, it is clear that a covenant is sealed. It is not a covenant that establishes the relationship between God and Israel; instead, it is a covenant to observe the requirements specified in the Torah. This is clear in the people's affirmation: "All that the LORD has spoken we will do, and we will be obedient" (v. 7). When relationship and law have been expressed within the notion of covenant, such a celebratory liturgy is appropriate. At one stage in Israel's religious development, the relationship with its God was strongly enough held to be assumed in language (e.g., "my people") and expressed unarticulated in liturgy (i.e., vv. 9–11). At another stage, Israel felt the need to articulate the relationship with its God in the language and ceremonies of covenant (vv. 3–8, běrît). The text of 24:1–11 holds together both.[138] The combination of the two can probably be interpreted in more than one way.[139] It is important, however, to recognize that the covenant ceremony is at the foot of the mountain (taḥat hāhār) and the meal is on the mountain; one had to precede the other. Verses 10–11 celebrate what is made explicit in the covenantal ceremony of vv. 3–8; it is the task of storyteller or user to come to terms with this.

The God-Israel relationship has clearly been in place since Egypt, at least. In the texts preceding the sanctuary, Sinai is about Torah.[140] The contrast in understanding between Exodus and Deuteronomy is illuminating. In Exodus, the emphasis is on Moses [singular] as mediator between God and people; the action is not between God and the people directly (the people's role is reduced to compliance, e.g., 19:8; cf. Exod 19:17, 20; 20:19, 21; note Deut 5:27). In Deuteronomy, the shift is from

---

138. An equivalent in modern mythology is the deal that once upon a time was concluded with a handshake and that nowadays is concluded with documents and batteries of lawyers.

139. See Childs, *Exodus*, 502; also E. W. Nicholson, "The Interpretation of Exodus XXIV 9–11," *VT* 24 (1974): 77–97; Durham, *Exodus*, 342–45; Fretheim, *Exodus*, 156–61.

140. To have a feel for what Torah meant to many in Israel, it helps to begin with Deut 4:5–8 or Ps 119.

"ancestors/them" [plural] in the past (despite the corrective in 5:5) to "us/you" [plural] in the present (cf. Deut 5:3). The people are directly involved. The covenantal context is more in evidence at Moab than at Sinai.

The second issue relating to this Sinai capsule (Exod 19:3–24:11) concerns its independence or its place in the narrative context. The capsule does not belong to the SaN. Without a viable continuation of the ExN from the Sea to Sinai, there is no narrative context for it to belong to. In our judgment, not unlike the book of Leviticus, it would have existed as an independent block of tradition in ancient Israel, prior to its present location. The aptness of the present location is evident from Exod 19:3–6. Israel is God's people. Beyond that, if "you obey my voice and keep my covenant" (19:5), you will be my "treasured possession," a "priestly kingdom," and a "holy nation" (19:5–6). With the sanctuary to come, God will dwell in Israel's midst: "Have them make me a sanctuary, so that I may dwell among them" (25:8; *wĕšākantî bĕtôkām*). The Jeremiah echo is hard to ignore (7:3, 7; cf. *BHS* and NRSV, etc.). The SaN is first and foremost about the relationship of God with Israel. That God should "dwell among them" is the height of intimacy and relatedness. Small wonder the text is so fussy about the details of construction.

When we look more closely at ch. 19, Noth's comment will not shock: "Of course it is no longer possible to make a smooth and satisfactory division of the whole between the two older sources [i.e., J and E]. This is not surprising, as it is easily understandable that the important central section of the tradition of the theophany on Sinai should frequently have been worked over and provided with expansions."[141] For Noth, the different names of God have to be used to separate these two older sources; in the approach advocated here, as we have seen, the names used of God may be differently interpreted.

Source critics famously (and illogically) divide 19:3 because of *elohim* in v. 3a and *yhwh* in v. 3b. Similarly, v. 17 has *elohim* and v. 18 *yhwh*; v. 19 has *elohim* and vv. 20–24 have *yhwh*. Clearly these occurrences could reflect sources, if such can be shown to have existed. However, there are also cases where the common noun for God (*elohim*) is possibly appropriate, that is, vv. 3a, 17, and 19, and cases where the proper name for Israel's God (*yhwh*) is then appropriate. Once the "foot of the mountain" (v. 17, *bĕtaḥtît hāhār*) is properly understood as the lower part of the mountain, it is no longer in sharp contradiction with "the mountain" in vv. 12–13 (*bāhār*). The remaining ground for source division is the attitude of the people who are terrified and ask Moses to act as their mediator (cf. 20:18–21 [E]) and the attitude of the people who have to be warned against coming too close (19:12–13 [J]).[142] The use of *elohim* in 20:19–20 may be an indication that here a variant understanding of the approach to God is being offered. The prohibition in 19:12 may be understood as relating to the time before the sound of the trumpet (v. 16); at the blast of the trumpet, the people may assemble on the base of the mountain (v. 17).

It is of major importance to recognize that the capsule Exod 19:3–24:11 is a single unit of text, with its introduction (19:3–25), central body (20:1–23:33),

141. *Exodus*, 154.
142. Noth, *Exodus*, 154.

and conclusion (24:1–11). The fundamental date of composition is uncertain (whatever of additions); discussion would not be in place here.[143]

The Sanctuary

With Exod 24:15, the cloud covers the mountain for six days, with the "glory of the LORD" settling on Mount Sinai; on the seventh day, Moses is summoned, enters the cloud, going up on the mountain, and is there for forty days and forty nights. Within the SaN, this material follows directly on 19:1–2. There is no trace of any SaN interest in between, and both the seven-day preparation and forty-day stay suggest a unit that is complete in itself.

A collection is to be taken up and a sanctuary made, "so that I may dwell among them" (25:8; *wĕšākantî bĕtôkām*). An ark is to be made too: "There I will meet with you (*wĕnôʿadtî lĕkā*; but cf. LXX "I will make myself known to you" [*wĕnôdaʿtî lĕkā*]) . . . I will deliver to you all my commands for the Israelites" (25:22). There is here a blending of presence (v. 8) and appearance (v. 22). At the end of it all, when the sanctuary has been completed, God does exactly that; God dwells among the Israelites: "the cloud covered the tent of meeting, and the glory of the LORD filled the tabernacle" (40:34). In the final three verses (40:36–38) there is the hint of a journey. No stages of the journey are named and no destination is given. One issue only is central: the guidance for the journey is given by God. When the cloud was taken up, Israel would set out; if the cloud was not taken up, Israel did not set out. All this was "before the eyes of all the house of Israel at each stage of their journey" (40:38).

Between chs. 25–31 and 35–40 is the triad, chs. 32–34. Once upon a time, the Yahwist Decalogue was extracted from Exod 34; the literature on this is extensive,[144] and it is not appropriate in this book to attempt a new analysis of the collection. The location of the chapters between the instructions for the sanctuary and its construction suggest that it is a later reflection looking back on the texts of Sinai.[145] If the approach we propose here is adopted, a fresh analysis will be in order.

The Sanctuary Narrative ends here, at Exod 40:38.[146] The book of Leviticus has its own integrity. There is no follow-up in the book of Numbers where one might expect it. A general verse (Num 10:12) speaks of departure from Sinai and

---

143. For further discussion, see Eckhart Otto, "Die nachpriesterschriftliche Pentateuchredaktion im Buch Exodus," in *Book of Exodus*, ed. M. Vervenne, 61–111, and Erich Zenger, "Wie und wozu die Tora zum Sinai kam: Literarische und theologische Beobachtungen zu Exodus 19–34," ibid., 265–88.

144. See, for example, Durham, *Exodus*, 458–59. Note Wellhausen, "Exod. 34 ist die Dekalogerzählung zur 'J'" (*Composition*, 334); the pages preceding this reveal just how artificial the process is.

145. Childs signals the lateness of the collection: "There are many signs which indicate that chs. 32–34 were structured into a compositional unit in one of the final stages of the development of the book of Exodus" (*Exodus*, 557). For a view of the "prepriestly" composition of Exod 32–34, see Blum, *Studien*, 54–75, esp. 73–75. But see also Otto: Exod 32–34 depends on Exod 19–24 ("Pentateuchredaktion," 83).

146. See in particular Thomas Römer, "Das Buch Numeri und das Ende des Jahwisten: Anfragen zur 'Quellenscheidung' im vierten Buch des Pentateuch," in *Abschied vom Jahwisten*, ed. J. C. Gertz et al., 215–31, esp. 216–18. In our judgment, Lev 8–9 are more properly at home in the book of Leviticus than in SaN. Blenkinsopp's insightful comment, "The place of worship is a scaled-down cosmos . . . the construction of the sanctuary is the completion of the work begun in creation" (*Pentateuch*, 218), does not necessitate one author for Genesis One and the SaN.

the cloud settling in the wilderness of Paran; what follows depicts the start but not the continuation of a journey. One verse notes the dismantling of the tabernacle and its move out at the start of the journey (Num 10:17), and one verse notes its potential reassembling (Num 10:21). There is no further mention of the tabernacle in relation to Israel's journey. Far more attention is paid to the places occupied by the standards of the camps in the vast and ordered procession envisaged (cf. 10:14–28)—after which there is no further mention of this deployment either. In this Numbers text, the sanctuary (tent and tabernacle) is not central, as it was in Exod 40:34–38. The cloud of the LORD is over Israel (Num 10:34), which is a change of imagery. The books of Exodus, Leviticus, and Numbers have been appropriately juxtaposed in the present text; they were largely independent documents originally, not a single document.[147]

Concerning the chapters about the sanctuary, the difficulty for a modern critic is in differentiating understandable later expansions from what may have been original; many suggestions are possible, but few are necessary. It is not appropriate to go into discussion of possible analyses in the context of this book.[148] Fortunately, it is not necessary, since the variants and expansions that have produced the present text may modify details but have not changed the basic meaning of the sanctuary: God's dwelling in Israel's midst, conceptualized as initially outside the land, not locked into any given place, but mobile and ready for whatever journey. For Noth, Exod 30–31 is secondary, dismissed in rather summary fashion.[149] On Exod 35–40, Childs remarks, "there is some evidence to suggest that a still further development of the traditions can be discerned in the redaction of these chapters."[150] The concept of the heavenly "pattern" (*tabnît*) occurs twice at the beginning of chs. 25–31 (25:9, 40). It does not recur in chs. 35–40. On the other hand, references to the Lord's command occur twenty-five times in chs. 35–40. The change is natural enough, but if the "pattern" were important, it would have been simple to introduce. As already noted by Childs, the concept of "meeting" (root: *y-ʿ-d*) occurs at five points in chs. 25–30 (25:22; 29:42, 43; 30:6, 36); it is not used in chs. 35–40.[151]

---

147. It is worth noting the frequency of occurrence of the three main terms—sanctuary, tabernacle, and tent of meeting—across these books.

Term	Exodus	Leviticus	Numbers
Sanctuary	2x	8x	5x
Tabernacle	55x	4x	35x
Tent of Meeting	33x	41x	54x

Ezekiel uses "sanctuary" 29x; Psalms use "tabernacle" 11x; other occurrences do not appear to be significant. The occurrences of "covenant" (*bĕrît*) between God and Israel in these books are worth noting: Exod 2:24; 6:4–5; 19:5; 23:32; 24:7–8; 31:16; 34 5x; Lev 2:13; 24:8; 26 6x; Num 5x, starting with 10:33.

148. For discussion of the analyses offered, see Childs, *Exodus*, 529–37, and Durham, *Exodus*, 350–53, 368–71, and 473–75. For the quasi-consensus view expressed by Noth earlier, see Campbell and O'Brien, *Sources*.

149. See Campbell and O'Brien, *Sources*, 50–52, particularly n. 58.

150. *Exodus*, 535.

151. While Moses speaks face to face with God, it is symbolically apt that God's presence to Israel should be almost invariably associated with the presence of the cloud. While Israel does not make use of the imagery of "the cloud of unknowing," the encounter with God is closely associated with the cloud. The symbolism is multifaceted and fitting.

The Book of Leviticus

Much that is important for understanding today's renewed interest in Leviticus may be found in the collection *The Book of Leviticus: Composition and Reception*.[152] Graeme Auld's comment catches something of Leviticus as a whole: "Accordingly Leviticus is the 'book' which can properly and simply conclude with the words, 'These are the commandments which the Lord commanded Moses for the people of Israel at Mt. Sinai.' Conceived admittedly as a supplement to Exodus, it is still a supplement which is complete in itself."[153] Baruch Levine speaks for many when he writes, "Most probably, it was a basic thrust of the priestly agenda to link the Tabernacle project to the Sinai theophany, and to embed Leviticus in the ongoing chronology of the wilderness period. In that traditional, priestly chronology, all that is recorded in the book of Leviticus took up one month's time. . . . We may assume that the Leviticus material was encased in a subsequently composed rubric, which began in Exodus 25 and concluded in Num 10:28, when the encampment set forth on the march. In Leviticus there is no movement."[154]

This needs to be complemented by Erhard Gerstenberger's description of Leviticus as "a fairly artificial excerpt from a larger narrative and legislative work, sewn together like a patchwork quilt from many different, individual pieces."[155] Both he and Martin Noth agree that "this book is one that particularly reveals something of the living variety and historical development of the whole system of worship in ancient Israel."[156]

The patchwork quilt, however, is fairly described as "complete in itself," embedded and encased in a later composition. There is something about it that makes it, in Gerstenberger's words, "the smallest and most awkward section within the Pentateuch."[157] Its unmoving focus on the life of the postexilic community gives Leviticus a unity of its own and withdraws it from the purview of the discussion here.

The Book of Numbers

In Martin Noth's view, "If we were to take the book of Numbers on its own, then we would think not so much of 'continuous sources' as of an unsystematic collection of innumerable pieces of tradition of very varied content, age and character."[158] Noth goes on to say, however, that, given the results of pentateuchal

152. Edited by R. Rendtorff and R. A. Kugler (Leiden: Brill, 2003).
153. "Leviticus: After Exodus and Before Numbers," in *Book of Leviticus*, ed. R. Rendtorff et al., 43.
154. "Leviticus: Its Literary History and Location in Biblical Literature," in *Book of Leviticus*, ed. R. Rendtorff et al., 23.
155. *Leviticus*, OTL (Louisville, KY: Westminster John Knox, 1996), 2.
156. Ibid.
157. *Leviticus*, 6.
158. Noth, *Numbers*, OTL (London: SCM, 1968), 4. Because the opening sentence of the English translation can be misunderstood on this important issue, it is worth pointing to the German: "Von einer Einheitlichkeit des 4. Mosebuches . . . kann keine Rede sein." As Römer notes, Noth's

analysis achieved elsewhere (i.e., in Genesis and Exodus), it is justifiable "to expect the continuing Pentateuchal 'sources' here, too, even if, as we have said, the situation in Numbers, of itself, does not exactly lead us to these results."[159] Without such "sources" earlier, we should dispense with them here.

The book of Numbers opens with a section (Num 1–10) that is not the continuation of either Exodus or Leviticus. God speaks to Moses in the tent of meeting (Num 1:1), whereas Exodus gave specific emphasis to the ark as the place where God would speak to Moses (Exod 25:22). The ark, of course, is in the tent of meeting (Exod 40:2); the earlier specific emphasis, however, is not repeated at Num 1:1. The date is specified in Num 1:1, but with a particular precision ("after they had come out of the land of Egypt") that is absent from Exod 40:2, 17. This precision suggests a new beginning. The "glory of the LORD" (cf. Exod 40:34–35; also Exod 16:7, 10; 24:16–17; and Lev 9:23) does not occur in this Numbers collection (the occurrences in Numbers are Num 14:10, 21; 16:19; 17:7 [Heb.; NRSV 16:42]). The "cloud" that was over the tent of meeting in Exod 40:34–35 does not occur in this Numbers collection until 9:15–10:34 where the language used is significantly different (but echoes Exod 40:36, where the cloud is over the tabernacle [*miškān*]; contrast vv. 34–35). Although these are minute details, they do not support a continuity with what precedes, for in this context minute details matter.

Rather than focusing on what the collection is not, it is more helpful to focus on what it is. It begins with the order to take a census of the whole congregation of Israelites, of all males over twenty able to go to war. These are then to be deployed by tribal groups, around the tent of meeting (*ʾōhel môʿēd*) at the center, itself entrusted to the Levites (2:17). There are four groups, each of three tribes, listed as east (Judah, Issachar, Zebulun), south (Reuben, Simeon, Gad), west (Ephraim, Manasseh, Benjamin), and north (Dan, Asher, Naphtali). When the departure is reported (Num 10:11–28), the deployment is observed, the eastern group heading out first (vv. 14–16), the second and third positions filled by the southern group (vv. 18–20) and the western group respectively (vv. 22–24), and the rear guard provided by the northern group (vv. 25–27). The tabernacle (*miškān*), entrusted to the Gershonites and Merarites, is placed between the first and second groups (v. 17); its equipment ("the holy things," literally *miqdāš*),

---

comment is frequently quoted these days—and recent study has found Noth's intuition right ("Das Buch Numeri," in *Abschied vom Jahwisten*, ed. J. C. Gertz et al., 215).

In ways that differ from the approach taken here, the "unsystematic" aspect of the collection has been addressed by Dennis Olson (*The Death of the Old and the Birth of the New* [Chico, CA: Scholars Press, 1985]—old and new) and Rolf Knierim and George Coats (*Numbers*, FOTL 4 [Grand Rapids: Eerdmans, 2005]—preparation and execution). Our basic observations are confirmed. The task of correlating origins and final text for this biblical book is far from finished.

159. Noth, *Numbers*, 5.

entrusted to the Kohathites, is placed between the second and third groups (v. 21).[160]

Both surprisingly and importantly, this whole complex, the deployment in camp and the order of march, is never heard of again (not in Numbers and not in Deuteronomy, not later)—it goes absolutely nowhere and is found absolutely nowhere.[161] Of course, this has implications for the sanctuary of Exod 25–31 and 35–40. If in the text there is no march involving this complex and this deployment, the sanctuary (constructed in Exod 25–40 and centered in the camp in Num 1–10) is not going anywhere either. It is not heard of again, and its meaning must be sought elsewhere.[162]

The collection in Num 1:1–10:28 has obviously undergone some degree of evolution. At no level is there any report of the march itself—beyond its first "setting out" (Num 10:12–28) but without a first "arrival" anywhere—or any mention of this elaborate camping order and marching order (10:12's reference to the "wilderness of Paran" is left hanging).[163] While these ten chapters contain much beyond the camping order and marching order, these elements—camping order and marching order—are central to the collection, and their meaning has to be found in something other than the march. Because there is no march reported in the text, the meaning of the collection—like that of the sanctuary—must be sought elsewhere.[164]

160. The Hebrew term rendered "group" here is *degel*. For Baruch Levine, the use of the term suggests "that what is projected in Numbers as the Israelite encampment of the wilderness period is really a mirror image of the Persian system of military colonies on the borders of the empire" ("Literary History and Location," 19).

161. Even in Num 33:1–49, neither camping order nor marching order is mentioned.

162. Of this sanctuary, Blenkinsopp says that it "is then established in the promised land after the conquest (Joshua 18–19)" (*Pentateuch*, 35; see also p. 185). Josh 18:1 has "the tent of meeting" set up at Shiloh, and 19:51 has the distribution of the land to seven tribes by lot take place "at the entrance of the tent of meeting." There is nothing reported to identify it with the sanctuary complex of Exod 25–40. If the Exodus complex was worth a dozen or so chapters, its establishment at Shiloh was worth more than an ambiguous verse or two. Such an identification is whimsy unless it is supported in the text (which it is not), because there is more than one concept of the tent of meeting (e.g., Exod 33:7; Num 11:16, 24, 26—outside the camp). Historically, such an identification is unreal. There is no trace of the tent's functioning at Shiloh, beyond this distribution of the land; to the contrary, see 1 Sam 3:3, which speaks of a temple there (*hêkal YHWH*) with the ark and no mention of the tent (but cf. 1 Sam 2:22, where however the issue of sexual abuse may be late). Thirdly, there is no trace in any text of the complex moving on (1 Kgs 8:4 is rightly suspect as late). Theoretically, of course, if the identification could be supported (which, in the present state of our knowledge, it cannot be), this location of the tent at Shiloh would be part of the "visionary construct" presented in Exodus.

163. Horst Seebass claims a satisfying consensus among critics that vv. 13–28 are an addition (*Numeri. Part Two: Numeri 10,11–22,1*, BKAT IV/2 [Neukirchen: Neukirchener Verlag, 2003], 7–8, but see vv. 9, 11–13; also, Noth, *Numbers*, 76–77); with or without vv. 13–28, there are no itinerary and no journey for the sanctuary and its camp.

164. Num 33:1–49 provides staging points, based on the present text of Numbers without discrimination. Surprisingly, elsewhere in Numbers beyond this there are scattered references rather than a systematic itinerary from Sinai to the plains of Moab (cf. Num 10:12, Sinai to Paran; 11:35, from Kibroth-hattaavah to Hazeroth; 12:16, from Hazeroth to Paran [cf. Kadesh, 13:26]; 20:1, came to Zin and stayed in Kadesh; 20:22, from Kadesh to Mount Hor; 21:4, from Mount Hor around Edom (with an itinerary, 21:10–20); 22:1, camped in the plains of Moab).

There are a dozen or more lists of the tribes of Israel.[165] The ordering in the lists is not random, although there are some apparently random differences. A specific disposition of the tribes is formally addressed in only two lists. Chapters 2, 7, and 10 in the book of Numbers represent one list; they alone have Judah named first. In Ezek 48, Judah occupies the prime position, next to the temple portion (*těrûmâ*)—but north of it. "This enormous final vision in the book presents . . . a counterpart to chapters 8–11. . . . In both, the whole section circles round the question, more or less clearly explicit, of the presence of the glory of Yahweh in the Jerusalem Temple."[166] Furthermore, "behind the present text there lies a lively process of growth and redaction."[167] The concern for "the presence of the glory of Yahweh in the Jerusalem Temple" echoes the concern of Exod 25–40, ending with "the glory of the LORD filled the tabernacle" (Exod 40:34–35). The "lively process of growth and redaction" speaks of intense interest among priestly circles, perhaps in Jerusalem.[168]

Just as the tabernacle of Exod 25–40 does not go anywhere in the text, and just as the camping order and marching order in Num 1–10 do not feature in any journey forward from Sinai, so the allotments in Ezek 48 "are made in complete disregard of historical reality."[169] Only in Num 1–10 and Ezek 48 is the tribe of Judah given a primacy or pride of place; otherwise, first place in the tribal lists is given to Reuben, the firstborn.[170] The possibility cannot be ignored that

---

165. For example, Gen 29–30; 35; 46; Exod 1; Num 1; 2; 7; 10; 13; 26; 34; Deut 33; Ezek 48; 1 Chr 2. The following are the more formally listed:

Gen 29–30	Exod 1	Num 1	Num 2/7/10	Num 13	Ezek 48
Reuben	Reuben	Reuben	Judah	Reuben	Dan
Simeon	Simeon	Simeon	Issachar	Simeon	Asher
Levi	Levi	Gad	Zebulun	Judah	Naphtali
Judah	Judah	Judah	Reuben	Issachar	Manasseh
Dan	Issachar	Issachar	Simeon	Ephraim	Ephraim
Naphtali	Zebulun	Zebulun	Gad	Benjamin	Reuben
Gad	Benjamin	Ephraim	Ephraim	Zebulun	Judah
Asher	Dan	Manasseh	Manasseh	Manasseh	Benjamin
Issachar	Naphtali	Benjamin	Benjamin	Dan	Simeon
Zebulun	Gad	Dan	Dan	Asher	Issachar
Joseph	Asher	Asher	Asher	Naphtali	Zebulun
(*Benjamin*)	Joseph*	Naphtali	Naphtali	Gad	Gad

166. Walther Zimmerli, *Ezekiel 2: A Commentary on the Book of the Prophet Ezekiel Chapters 25–48*, Hermeneia (German original, 1969; Philadelphia: Fortress, 1983), 327.

167. Zimmerli, *Ezekiel 2*, 328; see H. Gese, *Der Verfassungsentwurf des Ezechiel (Kap. 40–48) traditionsgeschichtlich untersucht*, BHT 25 (Tübingen: Mohr, 1957).

168. The disparate materials inserted into Num 1–10, beyond the concerns of the camping order and the marching order, need not detain us.

169. John W. Wevers, *Ezekiel*, NCB (London: Oliphants, 1969), 231; similarly Walther Eichrodt: "all other historical or geographical presuppositions about the settlement of the tribes are completely disregarded" (*Ezekiel*, OTL [London: SCM, 1970], 593).

170. Num 34:16–29 also has Judah in first place; Reuben is omitted. For Ezek 48, note Zimmerli: "The fact that Judah and Benjamin, the actual representative tribes of pre-exilic Judah, are given the places to the right and left of the ["holy portion"] is easily understood. What is remarkable here is the interchange between Judah and Benjamin in their geographical disposition" (541).

the tabernacle of Exod 25–40 and the camping order and marching order in Num 1–10 reflect a concern similar to that of the allotment of tribal lands in Ezek 48. The expression of such a concern, devoid of any realization in history but located in the realm of imagination, could only have been situated in the preconquest period or in an eschatological future. The placement of such a construct at Sinai is eminently understandable (using "construct" as a shorthand for "construct[ion] of reality," meaning a presentation of how things might be or ought to be).[171]

Such a construct could have had considerable and various meanings for the faith of an Israel that had suffered exile: (i) faith that God could be intimately present to Israel, despite failure (centuries of experience; but also Exod 15:24; 16:2–3, 12); (ii) faith that this presence of God could be experienced outside the land; (iii) faith that this presence of God did not have to be pinned down to any specific place, not to "the place that God will choose," not to Jerusalem, but could be understood as able to move with Israel; (iv) faith that any move was to be dependent on God's signal ("At the command of the LORD they would camp, and at the command of the LORD they would set out" [Num 9:23]). For the faith of exiled Israel, the theological possibilities are evident.

The journey to the plains of Moab requires careful scrutiny.[172] Does a journey narrative exist that might extend the ExN? At one stage in researching this book, recognizing the possibility of the ExN's bypassing Sinai, we expected that it might resume in Num 11 and continue on to the plains of Moab, but our expectation was disappointed.[173] As from the Sea to Sinai, the scrutiny will proceed in three stages: (i) itinerary; (ii) obstacles; (iii) story.

First, what might be thought of as itinerary notices in Numbers prove unhelpful. They can be listed.

171. Similarly, the Jubilee year in Lev 25.

172. Looking back, a parallel with the physical sciences helps. Richard Feynman writes that "in Newton's time, difficulties with a theory were dealt with briefly and glossed over—a different style from what we are used to in science today, where we point out the places where our own theory doesn't fit the observations of experiment" (*QED: The Strange Theory of Light and Matter* [Princeton, NJ: Princeton University Press, 1985], 23). It is our practice not to gloss over difficulties with the biblical text; we point them out in the quest for more accurate understanding.

173. Before the journey itself, there is a little collection of three traditions (Num 10:29–36). They appear in harmony with Israel's journey from Sinai; but they are in marked tension with what has preceded. In Exod 13:21–22, the pillar of cloud by day and the pillar of fire by night provide Israel with guidance. In Exod 40:36–38, both the cloud and fire are present, and the movement of the cloud is the signal for Israel to move. The same features return in Num 9:15–23, expanded by a theology insistent on waiting for YHWH. "Whether it was two days, or a month, or a longer time, that the cloud continued over the tabernacle, resting upon it, the Israelites would remain in camp and would not set out; but when it lifted they would set out. At the command of the LORD they would camp, and at the command of the LORD they would set out" (9:22–23). The cloud lifts in Num 10:11; "the command of the LORD" is mentioned in Num 10:13. All this appears to be ignored in 10:29–36. According to vv. 29–32, Hobab ben Reuel is to be their guide and "serve as eyes" for Israel. He will know where they should camp in the wilderness. But in 10:33–34, the ark of the covenant of YHWH (given this title here for the first time; in the Pentateuch, only at Num 10:33 and 14:44; Deut 10:8; 31:9, 25, 26) goes three days' journey before them "to seek out a resting place for them" (v. 33), the "fire" has vanished, and the "cloud" is "over them by day"—the language of "lifting" that was constantly present before has ceased. Finally, in vv. 35–36, the tradition reports sayings of Moses for when the ark started and stopped.

11:35 From Kibroth-hattaavah the people journeyed to Hazeroth.

12:16 After that the people set out from Hazeroth, and camped in the wilderness of Paran.

20:1   The Israelites, the whole congregation, came into the wilderness of Zin in the first month, and the people stayed in Kadesh.

20:22 They set out from Kadesh, and the Israelites, the whole congregation, came to Mount Hor.

21:4   From Mount Hor they set out . . . to go around the land of Edom.

22:1   The Israelites set out, and camped in the plains of Moab across the Jordan from Jericho.

Of these texts, the first two (11:35 and 12:16) frame the story of ch. 12 (and probably belong with it). The references to Mount Hor (in 20:22 and 21:4) frame the death of Aaron and a detour into the Negeb (21:1–3). It would be possible to isolate the people's stay in Kadesh (in 20:1), a move from Kadesh (in 20:22), and encampment in the plains of Moab (in 22:1). As an early itinerary for Israel's journey from Sinai to Moab, it is almost nonexistent.

Second, what might be termed "obstacles" are the texts of primary interest mainly to priestly circles. Concern for the "whole congregation" is already evident in the itinerary notices above. These texts are principally the conflict of Miriam and Aaron with Moses (Num 12); the rebellion of Korah, Dathan, and Abiram (framed by priestly concerns, 15:1–41; 16:1–50; 17:1–19:22); the death of Aaron (20:23–29); the episode of the bronze serpent (21:4–9), the little itinerary (21:10–20, Oboth to Moab), and the victories over Sihon and Og (21:21–35). The limits of space do not allow us to analyze these in detail, but none give grounds for belonging to an early narrative of Israel's journey to Moab.

Third, four passages along the narrative track are possible candidates for a journey sequence: (1) the story of the quail (Num 11); (2) the episode of the spies (Num 13–14); (3) the water from the rock (Num 20:2–13); and (4) the detour around Edom (Num 20:14–21).

1. The Quail The story of the quail—which mingles themes, emotions, and the unexplained—is deeply puzzling. The initial episode (11:1–3) with its own oddities is usually treated separately. The main story ends with God lavishing quail on the people and then, as they eat (the meat still between their teeth, v. 33), becoming angry and visiting them with plague (11:31–33). Within the core of the story, the rabble and the Israelites find the manna unsatisfactory, Moses is displeased with them, his spirit is shared out among seventy elders and more, the quail arrive, and shortly after that come plague and death. The "rabble" (NRSV; 11:4, *ʾăsapsūp*) is unique; it may reflect a tradition of elements that associated themselves with Israel's exodus (Exod 12:38). The tent of meeting, associated with the sharing of Moses' spirit in the enhancement, is clearly portrayed as being outside the camp (cf. vv. 16, 24, 26) as in Exod 33:7–11, in contrast to the tent in Leviticus and Num 1–10. Naturally, Eldad and Medad are unheard of elsewhere.

The change of theme within the story is dramatic and evident; no markers are needed. The first seam is visible between vv. 13 and 14. It is latent in v. 14's "I alone"; it is clear with the introduction of the seventy elders in v. 16. Verse 18 follows smoothly on v. 13 (assuming an introduction, as in v. 16). The second seam is evident when the theme of the elders recurs in vv. 24–30.[174] With v. 31, the story of the quail is back. An original story is, therefore, acceptable—with the theme of the sharing of Moses' spirit envisaged as an enhancement, reflecting the complexity of the concept of "burden" (*maśśā'*, vv. 11, 17). A further enhancement, however, needs to be allowed for in vv. 19–23, offering an alternative punishment to that of v. 33.[175]

It is appropriate to look to the story's place in any narrative sequence. There is no trace of the concerns (above all, of the camping order and marching order) of Num 1–10 or of the preceding Sanctuary Narrative. While this is obvious, what makes it obvious is worth spelling out. Despite the detailed departure of Num 10:12–28, there is no report of an arrival. There is no report of a signal to stop at the beginning of the passage, or of a signal to go at the end; there is no mention of Hobab, the ark, or the cloud. Aaron is not mentioned, and there is no sign of the tribal leaders or indication of organization by tribes; the image is rather of families at the entrance to their tents (v. 10). There is certainly no sign of any deployment in relation to the tent of meeting. Even the destructive divine fire is differently conceived here ("burned against"; root: *b-ʿ-r b-*) from Leviticus earlier (9:24; 10:2) and Num 16:35 a little later ("came out . . . and consumed"; roots: *y-ṣ-'* and *'-k-l*). All this is reinforced by the enhancement, with its tradition of the tent of meeting that is outside the camp and its different approach from Num 1:5–16 to the issue of assistance for Moses.

Two traditions of the relief of Moses' burden (regarding the feeding and the leading of the people) are nested within two traditions of God's destructive anger. The question is inevitable: what significance in this narrative caused it to be told in this way at this point? The story bears the marks of reflection on experience rather than the report of it; it is hardly a stage on a journey. Form-critically, an interpreter needs to know what sort of text is being interpreted.[176] The decision between report and story is a difficult form-critical decision. A report claims a direct correlation with events; matters are narrated in a report because they happened in the event—at least they are believed by the narrator to have happened in this way. A story's correlation with events is more complex; matters are narrated

---

174. Noth begins this section with v. 24b (*Numbers*, 83), probably unnecessarily. The necessary subject, Moses, is in v. 24a; if seventy elders are to move outside the camp, the people need to be told about it. Verse 24a is not needed later.

175. Num 11:12 is probably another small enhancement. The image of Moses carrying Israel as a child on his chest is paralleled by the image of God carrying Israel as a child (Deut 1:31); the promise of the land on oath to the ancestors, referred to in this verse, is primarily Deuteronomic/Deuteronomistic. The dtr interest in the issue of shared leadership is evident from Deut 1:9–18.

176. See Antony F. Campbell, "Form Criticism's Future," in *The Changing Face of Form Criticism for the Twenty-First Century*, ed. M. A. Sweeney and E. Ben Zvi (Grand Rapids: Eerdmans, 2003), 15–21.

in a story not so much because they may have happened, but because they are significant to the story's plot or symbolism.[177] As here, texts often do not yield lightly to the interpreter's inquiry whether they are report or story. As here, this distinction between report and story is often important.

2. The Spies   The episode of the spies sent into Canaan (Num 13–14) is relatively easily identified as an original story that has been expanded by two major enhancements. Its basic theme is the people's failure of nerve to go up and occupy the land (13:1–2a, 3a, 17b–33; 14:1b, 40, 44b–45). An extensive enhancement introduces Aaron and the congregation—in part in ch. 13 (esp. vv. 3b–17a) and much of ch. 14—with the penalty of exclusion for the wicked congregation (14:27, 35 only). The semblance of fragmentation in 14:1b, 40, 44b–45 may be only apparent.

Although the intricacies of the text would have been a challenge to any storyteller, certain possibilities can be sketched. Verse 36 can follow on 14:10. The whole congregation threatened to stone them (v. 10; "them": Moses and Aaron certainly, Joshua and Caleb probably). The "glory of the LORD" appears and intervenes, and the sinful spies die of plague "before the LORD" (v. 37). The inclusion of the divine speech—14:26–35 (in whatever stages) focusing on the death of the evil generation and exemplified in the death of the spies, vv. 36–38 (cf. v. 6)—requires as follow-up Moses' report to the people and their consequent mourning (v. 39), enabling a resumption of the story broken off at 14:1b. The minor enhancement in 14:41–44a reflects the growth of the chapter. Verse 45 ends the episode. The dtr-type contribution of Moses' dialogue with YHWH (14:11–25) is the second major enhancement. The pairing of Joshua and Caleb is rare (14:6, 30, 38). The text witnesses to the transformation of a tradition rather than the preservation of different traditions.[178] See appendix 4, pp. 154–55.

3. Water from the Rock   In the episode at Meribah, there is duality. But the earliest level appears to reflect priestly interests; the participants are Moses, Aaron, and the congregation (even 20:8).[179]

177. In a quite different context, but valuable for our own, Martin Krieger quotes an image from the great nineteenth-century physicist J. C. Maxwell: "In an ordinary belfry, each bell has one rope which comes down through a hole in the floor to the bellringer's room. But suppose that each rope, instead of acting on one bell, contributes to the motion of many pieces of machinery, and that the motion of each piece is determined not by the motion of one rope alone, but by that of several, and suppose, further, that all of this machinery is silent and utterly unknown to the men at the ropes, who can only see as far as the holes in the floor above them" (*Doing Physics: How Physicists Take Hold of the World* [Bloomington: Indiana University Press, 1992], x–xi). From a form-critical point of view, in a report, it is as if each bell has one rope, which acts directly on it; in a story, the link between bells and ropes may be more complex. In a story, the *text* is always in the bellringers' room; the *events* are in the room above.

178. Comparison with Deut 1–3 tends to confirm this analysis of Num 11 and 13–14. The dtr interest in the enhancement of ch. 11 has been noted (Deut 1:9–18); for the dtr spy story, see Deut 1:19–45. Associated further with the desert march are only the avoidance of strife with Edom and Moab and the dtr particularity of the defeats of Sihon and Og.

179. See Campbell and O'Brien, *Sources*, 86, esp. n.104.

4. Detour around Edom   There is duality in the episode concerning Edom; according to Noth, it is the first appearance of E in Numbers.[180] The passage does not help identify a trajectory for Israel from Sinai to the plains of Moab. Noth comments, "The lack of connection between the wilderness stories and the preparation for the conquest from east of the Jordan is also revealed by this quite unmotivated leap from Kadesh to Edom."[181]

All in all, these four stories do little to portray Israel's journey toward Canaan. The lack of connectedness at any early stage leaves Israel on the eastern shore of the Sea. Perhaps a further trajectory is possible, but in our view it is unlikely that the text preserves one.[182]

Our understanding of the latter part of Numbers (chs. 25–36) is that, overall, much of the reports, itineraries, laws, and so on, that later circles in Israel felt needed to be located within the Mosaic period has found its home here, after Israel's arrival at the plains of Moab and the stories of Balaam and before Moses' discourse in the plains of Moab (Deuteronomy).

Outcome in Deuteronomy: The Ideal for Israel

In this book we outline a possible alternative approach in the analysis of the Pentateuch. It is not a commentary on the five books, and Deuteronomy, with its principal concerns comprising exhortation, law, and covenant making, is not particularly in need of the insights we offer here.[183] Many things are recognized today, among them the difference between the law code and its framing introduction and conclusion, the further introduction (Deut 1–3 [4]) setting up the Deuteronomistic History (DH), with the possibility that a Josianic DH existed before the exile and a revised DH grappled with the issues of exile. Much is left uncertain and will probably remain that way.

We will restrict our task here to proposing an understanding of how Deuteronomy, as a whole, might be understood to function within the Pentateuch. We do not want to argue that its relationship to Genesis One was necessarily how it was understood in ancient Israel. We do want to argue that this is one legitimate way in which it may be understood today.

The Ideal: Genesis One and Deuteronomy

There may be more than one way of understanding Genesis One (i.e., Gen 1:1–2:4a). It may of course be understood as a creation account. It cannot be

---

180. See Campbell and O'Brien, *Sources*, 190 n.64; for Noth, J and E, no P (*Numbers*, 149); for a valuable survey of views, see Budd, *Numbers*, 222–24.

181. *Numbers*, 151.

182. Römer advocates a role for Numbers, late in the piece (postpriestly), as forming the connection (bridge) linking the already existing Gen–Lev and Deut ("Das Buch Numeri," esp. 220–24).

183. In our earlier presentation of the Deuteronomistic History (Campbell and O'Brien, *Unfolding*), we reckoned on the critical analysis of Deuteronomy as a minefield to be avoided. A footnote for each chapter (from chs. 6–26) summarized the positions of three competent scholars that were so

understood as *the* creation account, for there are too many others in the Bible that are different (e.g., Job 26:6–13 and 38:1–30; Ps 104; Prov 8:22–31; etc.). Having two conflicting accounts within the one narrative of Gen 1:1–2:25 is problematic. Resolution is needed; they are no longer the opening episodes of two separate sources. One possibility is to see a contrast between the ideal and the real. *Certainly*, Genesis One portrays an all-powerful God; God speaks and what God has said is done. *Certainly*, it portrays the ideal Israelite world in which six days of work are followed by a seventh day of rest. *Certainly*, there is a reassuring sense of order, with each created being in its right place at the right time. *Certainly*, there is a dignity given to humankind, male and female, made in the image and likeness of God. Viewed as an account of creation, Genesis One is majestic. Viewed as Israel's picture of an ideal world, Genesis One is unsurpassed.

At the other end of the Pentateuch, a version of the book of Deuteronomy (as we understand it today) most likely served as the image of the ideal to which the Deuteronomic reform and King Josiah and later generations aspired. According to today's judgment, Josiah's reform rested on the principles of the book of Deuteronomy, as did subsequent revisions of the Deuteronomistic History.

The challenge is there:

> See, I am setting before you today a blessing and a curse: the blessing, if you obey the commandments of the LORD your God that I am commanding you today; and the curse, if you do not obey the commandments of the LORD your God, but turn from the way that I am commanding you today, to follow other gods that you have not known. (Deut 11:26–28)

The guidance is there:

> Deuteronomy 12–26: the commandments of the Deuteronomic lawcode.

The ideal relationship with God is there:

> This very day the LORD your God is commanding you to observe these statutes and ordinances; so observe them diligently with all your heart and with all your soul. Today you have obtained the LORD's agreement: to be your God; and for you to walk in his ways, to keep his statutes, his commandments, and his ordinances, and to obey him. Today the LORD has obtained your agreement: to be his treasured people, as he promised you, and to keep his commandments; for him to set you high above all nations that he has made, in praise and in fame and in honor; and for you to be a people holy to the LORD your God, as he promised. (Deut 26:16–18)

The real possibility is there:

---

far apart as to make clear, as we put it, that "consensus in scholarship has been remarkable by its absence" (*Unfolding*, 41).

Surely, this commandment that I am commanding you today is not too hard for you, nor is it too far away. . . . No, the word is very near to you; it is in your mouth and in your heart for you to observe. (Deut 30:11–14)

The challenge is repeated:

See, I have set before you today life and prosperity, death and adversity. . . . Choose life so that you and your descendants may live, loving the LORD your God, obeying him, and holding fast to him; for that means life to you and length of days. (Deut 30:15, 19–20)

Following King Josiah, however, it did not work out that way. The ideal bowed to the real. The political entity of the people of Israel bowed to the political power of the people of Babylon. The hope of the Deuteronomic reform was followed by the near-despair of exile.

Political failure led to theological thought. The optimism of Josiah's time was replaced by a revised understanding, based on faith.

The commandments are given a faith-based evaluation:

When they hear all these statutes [the peoples] will say, "Surely this great nation is a wise and discerning people!" For what other great nation has a god so near to it as the LORD our God is whenever we call to him? And what other great nation has statutes and ordinances as just as this entire law that I am setting before you today? (Deut 4:6–8)

The need for faith to be fostered is spelled out:

But take care and watch yourselves closely, so as neither to forget the things that your eyes have seen nor to let them slip from your mind all the days of your life; make them known to your children and your children's children. (Deut 4:9)

Faith in God's action enables observance to be possible:

The LORD your God will circumcise your heart and the heart of your descendants, so that you will love the LORD your God with all your heart and with all your soul, in order that you may live. (Deut 30:6)

The ideal is encompassed within the mystery of faith:

The secret things belong to the LORD our God, but the revealed things belong to us and to our children forever, to observe all the words of this law. (Deut 29:29)

Among the "revealed things" is the ideal for the world that is articulated in Genesis One and to which Israel is exhorted in Deuteronomy. Among the "secret things" must remain the achievement of this ideal, whether by Israel or by the world. The Pentateuch may be understood to spell out the foundation on which Israel might build this ideal.

Outcome Overall

We have entitled the section Exodus–Numbers "the core of Israel's experience." At first sight, a more obvious heading is "the emergence of Israel." But Israel had emerged as a people by Exod 1:7–9 and did not emerge as a nation before David's time. The exodus from Egypt is central, but it does not include the traditions that follow. With the death of Moses, Israel has not yet emerged from the desert.

In Egypt, Israel experiences deliverance from political threat. In the desert, Israel experiences deliverance from natural threat. On the way, Israel experiences God's guidance. At Sinai, with the theophany, Israel experiences the gift of God's Law. At Sinai, with the sanctuary, Israel experiences the gift of God's presence. There is much more, but "the core of Israel's experience" is a suitable summary.

The nature and function of much of the priestly text around Sinai is illuminated by the realization that Leviticus is focused on the life of the postexilic community, appropriately projected back to Sinai—in the context of the sanctuary constructed before it (that is not heard of again), and the journey projected after it (that also is not heard of again). This does not detract from the reality of the life of the postexilic community.[184] It means, however, that for fuller understanding, the Sinai sanctuary and the deployment of the tribes in relation to it are to be envisaged as visionary constructs, on a par with the Jubilee program in Lev 25 or the land-allocation program in Ezek 48.

What precedes this "surreal" block is the arrangement of understandings that gave Israel existence and meaning. Its beginnings are a theological invitation to the ideal for humanity balanced by equally theological reflections on the reality of human life, and on that life in relationship with God (Gen 1–11). Following that are the archetypal images that gave identity to Israel at an ancestral level (Gen 12–36, 37–50); similarly, what follows are the archetypal images that gave Israel identity at a national level (Exodus–Numbers). With "all Israel" present in these texts where all Israel was clearly not, the generations of later Israel (the writers) have identified with the experiences articulated for the constitutive generations. Concluding the whole is the invitation or challenge to live out the ideal in the realm of reality (Deuteronomy). It is a massive, unwieldy, and enormously challenging achievement.

All of this gives identity, meaning, and a sense of destiny to a people. Individuals need reality and need vision. What do I eat? What do I dream? The Pentateuch, in its own untidy way, supplies both. Leviticus looks to what do I do and what do I eat,[185] with a construction of society that is permeated by the vision of

---

184. Should a reader find this baffling, which is not unlikely, it is not totally dissimilar to the bafflement engendered in the nonspecialist by theoretical physics, moving electrons and photons and the like back and forth in space and time in theory that conforms to the reality of the outcome of experiment (for example, Feynman, *QED*).

185. For example: "Which foods am I allowed to eat? When am I making myself impure, and thus unable to participate in worship? If the occasion arises, how do I perform sacrifices correctly? What expectations does Yahweh have with regard to my social deportment within my surroundings?" (Gerstenberger, *Leviticus*, 8–9).

the sanctuary and touched by the inner meaning of the dream of the tribal deployment. Israel's vision, in the wider Pentateuch, comes from its understanding of humanity and its own origins within that. Israel's hope is in its destiny to bring the ideal to fulfillment in the reality of life and so to bring blessing to all the families of the earth.

Chapter 4

Conclusion

It is a pleasure to have found others who have made observations ahead of us. It would be unnerving to have nobody else see what we have seen. The novelty of this book is that we bring many of these observations into a single responsible picture. The paradigm shift to a "user-base" approach, advocated at the beginning of this book, opens up wide-ranging vistas for the understanding of much biblical narrative. We propose it as a possibility worth serious consideration; its ramifications are far-reaching. The second paradigm shift, emerging during the course of the book, from Israel remembering its past to Israel pondering its present, also has wide-ranging implications, favoring a concern with theology (pondering) over history (remembering); for example: certainly for the early stories of humanity, the commands for the sanctuary, the construction of the sanctuary, the deployment for the march; probably for the triad Abraham-Isaac-Jacob.

One ramification may be that, with options and variants built into the biblical text as normal components, in much narrative text choices may be unavoidable, and "present-text" interpretation without such choices may, in principle, run counter to the nature of the text. The broad sweep of interpretation is always possible, but when close attention is given to certain texts, choices may be required. Such is the case when the text is judged to be evidently discordant.

Where close attention to rhetorical skills can identify a harmonious text, choice may not be necessary.

The Scriptures were not received as a single gift; they were received piece by piece in ancient Israel and the early Church and put together over the slow procession of generations. These Scriptures enabled our forebears in distant times to make selections and tell their stories as part of the search for understanding in their lives. We have received these Scriptures as a single gift, but that does not change their nature. We have received them so that we too might make our choices and tell our stories. The "user-base" approach, with its place for options and variants, often does not make any single text available for interpretation. Choices are required.

The "user-base" approach attends to the present biblical text. In the past, the focus of study was whatever lay behind the Pentateuch. The thinking and history reflected in hypothetical compositions was the holy grail of pentateuchal research. Many insights from this past endure. A new paradigm, however, has opened the way for us to recognize and rely on the skills of ancient users. A new paradigm has focused on the selections and expansions needed by the text. Attention to the text, facilitated by this paradigm, has revealed Israel pondering its present rather than remembering its past. All this comes from a sharpened focus on the present text.

While we have identified most of the elements that have gone to make up the text and have often identified ways in which substantial segments of the present text might have been composed, we have not attempted to describe a process for the composition of the final text from Gen 1 to Deut 34. It is not difficult to come up with a possible model, but to settle on any one model—without careful, painstaking, and exhaustive study—appears to us speculative and undesirable. Furthermore, we have not attempted an interpretation of this final text. At this stage in research, without publication and assessment from colleagues, such a venture seemed to us premature, even presumptuous. Beyond that, so significant an issue could not be dealt with in what is a little book.

Envoi

We are writing this envoi in February; the manuscript will go to its publisher in June. We are struggling with the full realization that the sanctuary (major Sinai section) and the camping order and marching order (major section at the start of Numbers, chs. 1–10) are isolated and not heard of again. The negative aspect of the book can be described as no J, no P, and—at least till late in the piece—no Sinai.[1] That last bit came as a shock.

If the outcome of this book scares the faith out of some people, we regret that, but we do not believe it need be the case. First, in some areas, we have traded dubious history for serious theology. That is surely a benefit. The Pentateuch is not so much the result of ancient Israel's remembering its past as of ancient Israel's pondering its present.[2] Second, the respect for the past—evident in the pondering—suggests tradition not invention, and tradition predates composition. Furthermore, as any good theologian knows, experience should precede theology. The sequence is from present experience to tradition (remembered experience, with all its selectivity) to theology (sustained reflection on both, with its essential subjectivity).

Third, any suggestion that a substantial part of Israel's Scripture emerged in "two or three generations" is pretentious and unfounded nonsense. The Scriptures

---

1. The gift of the law at Sinai (Exod 19–24) is clearly there; whatever of thematic aspects, there is equally clearly no surrounding and supporting narrative independent of the SaN (i.e., no pre-SaN itinerary).

2. The Pentateuch can be considered the originating myth of ancient Israel; for Israel, the Bible offers no other equivalent. An originating myth is the account that myth makers cause to be believed as to what constituted a people, giving them identity and destiny, their place and role in the world. Every nation has one, often more than one. An originating myth does not have to offer a historically balanced and factually accurate picture of a people's origins; it has to offer a plausible picture that gives meaning to the people it serves. An originating myth offers an answer to the question "Who are we?" often by reflecting the questions "What have we come out of?" and "What is the future we are going into?"

of Israel need not begin with the prophets. The composition of the initial Ark Narrative is situated by Miller and Roberts before David's major victories; the final version is situated by Campbell before Solomon's temple. The traditions available for the Story of David's Rise may in large part be blatant propaganda; blatant propaganda is seldom necessary long after the principal protagonist has left the scene. The Stories of David's Middle Years (2 Sam 11–20) are a mix of remarkable detail, involving David's brilliance as a strategist and his incompetence or ruthlessness as a politician; given the latter element, their composition cannot come from David's uncritical admirers, and, given the nature of the detail, it can hardly be too far from David's time. The Prophetic Record (a hypothesis based on so-far uncontested evidence) cannot have been put together much later than the end of the ninth century. At this point, we are verging on the forerunners to the Deuteronomistic History and two or three centuries have passed rather than two or three generations.

Faith may have come in for a bit of a shock; but it is of the essence of faith to be continually invited to thought and the exploration of experience. Ultimately, our finding God may matter as much as God's revealing God. Fascinating!

Appendix 1

Two Intensive Studies

Overview

This appendix provides the closely argued evidence for the position stated earlier (ch. 2) against the presence of P in Gen 1–11. Leaving aside Gen 5:1–2 (pp. 111–12), the two major conclusions are: (1) the account of creation in Genesis One (Gen 1:1–2:4a) *need not* be priestly; and (2) this creation account and the so-called P account of the flood most probably *cannot* have the same origin. The first study is straightforward; it is a simple vocabulary analysis. The second study is not for the fainthearted; having Hebrew helps. The evidence, however, is clear. It comes from an analysis of vocabulary, conceptualization, and more.

P and Genesis One

The following study is detailed and relatively demanding. Although its conclusion is scarcely surprising, it runs counter to the current almost automatic assumption that Genesis One is from P. The conclusion can be repeated here at the outset: from a study of its vocabulary, it is certainly *possible* that P composed Genesis One; it is certainly *not necessary* that P composed Genesis One.[1] This conclusion emerges from a vocabulary analysis that is not restricted to the Pentateuch but extends more broadly to the language of the Hebrew Bible.

1. Create   (ברא)

      Some 50 or so occurrences. Apart from Gen 6:7; Exod 34:10; Num 16:30; Amos 4:13; and Pss 89:12, 47; 104:30; 148:5, interesting issues are raised

---

1. The classical terminology of J and P is used in most of this chapter, which was once the first stage of the present book.

by Deut 4:32. Is there an association between the later revision of Deuteronomy and a text such as Genesis One?

2. Darkness   (חשֶׁךְ)

Some 98 occurrences. Apart from a wide range of texts, and Exod 10:21–22 and 14:20, there are again Deut 4:11 and also 5:23. Certainly nothing exclusive here.

3. Deep   (תהוֹם)

Some 36 occurrences. It is echoed in the flood, Gen 7:11 and 8:2; it recurs in Exod 15:5, 8 (Noth: nonsource). It is found in Deut 8:7 and 33:13. The "deep" occurs in association with the "heavens"—perhaps the extremities denoting the whole: see Gen 49:25; Deut 33:13; Pss 107:26; 135:6; Prov 8:27.

4. Separate   (בדל—hipꜥil)

Some 32 occurrences. Apart from the 8 occurrences in Leviticus, the verb is also found in Exod 26:33 and Num 8:14, both traditionally P texts. However, there are also Deut 4:41; 10:8; 19:2, 7; 29:21; see too 1 Kgs 8:53.

5. Dome   (רקיע)

Some 17 occurrences. Outside Gen 1 and Ezekiel, the term occurs only in Pss 19:2 (Heb.; NRSV, 19:1); 150:1; Dan 12:3. It does not occur in the flood story.

6. Gather together   (קוה—nipꜥal)

Only 2 occurrences: Gen 1:9 and Jer 3:17.

7. Dry land   (יבשׁה)

Some 14 occurrences. The term occurs 3x in the P text of the crossing of the Sea (Exod 14:16, 22, 29). It is also used in J text at Exod 4:9. The occurrences in Ps 66:6 and Jonah 1:9, 13; 2:10, as also Josh 4:22, combine to reinforce the denial of any exclusivity to P.

8. Gathering together   (מקוה—gathering/pool)

Some 4 occurrences. Only in Gen 1:10 does the word have the meaning "sea." The other 3 usages apply to something vastly more restricted (see Exod 7:19 [P]; Lev 11:36; Isa 22:11).

9. Vegetation   (דשׁא)

Some 16 occurrences. It is one of three or four words for grass or new growth that have a similar semantic range (see 2 Kgs 19:26). It occurs in Gen 1:11, 12; but also in Deut 32:2 and in Samuel and Kings, Isaiah and Jeremiah, Joel and Job, Psalms and Proverbs.

10. Plants   (עשׂב)

Some 38 occurrences. It too occurs in Gen 1:11–12 and again in vv. 29–30. It recurs in Gen 9:3. Any thought of exclusivity is banished by the occurrences in Gen 2:5 and 3:18. It is also in the J texts of the plagues of hail and locusts (Exod 9:22, 25; 10:12, 15). It is in both Deut 11:15 and 32:2. Also to be noted are 2 Kgs 19:26; Amos 7:2; and Ps 106:20.

11. Seed   (זרע—noun)

Some 230 occurrences. Occurring in Gen 1:11, 12, 29, it is also in Gen 3:15 (with the meaning of offspring); 4:25 (again "offspring"; for Noth: non-source); 7:3b (for Noth: J surprisingly); and 8:22 (J unquestionably). Exclusivity is out of the question, whether as seed to be sown or offspring to be born.

12. Kind   (מין)

Some 31 occurrences. Evident in Genesis One (1:11, 12, 21, 24, 25), it recurs in the P text of the flood (6:20; 7:14) and in the laws of Leviticus. Creating uncertainty, however, are 4 occurrences in Deut 14 (vv. 13, 14, 15, 18). Beyond these, there is only Ezek 47:10. Any conclusion is uncertain.

13. Light   (מאור)

Some 18 occurrences. It is used of the lights in the sky (Gen 1:14, 15, 16) and of the light/lamp in the sanctuary (10x in Exodus–Numbers)—all P texts. Its use in Pss 74:16 and 90:8 renders exclusivity impossible. See also Ezek 32:8.

14. Dominion   (ממשלה)

Some 17 occurrences. The use in Genesis One (1:16) is balanced by some 7 in the political sphere and a mixed bag of 5 in Psalms (103:22; 114:2; 136:8, 9; 145:13).

15. Swarm   (שׁרץ—both noun and verb)

Some 29 occurrences: noun 15x and verb 14x. The root is used in Genesis One (1:20–21) and also in the P text of the flood; the difference between Gen 1:28 (without it) and Gen 9:7 (with it, but without dominion [unemended Hebrew]) is important (cf. Exod 1:7). Among other occurrences, worth noting are the J text of the plague of frogs (Exod 8:3) as also Ps 105:30, and in the Deuteronomic list of the unclean (Deut 14:19). See also Ezek 47:9.

16. Living creatures   (נפשׁ חיה)

Some 13 occurrences. Despite the place of this term in Gen 1 and 9, any thought of exclusivity is excluded by Gen 2:7, 19. Of interest is also Ezek 47:9 and, while varying slightly in formulation, Job 12:10.

17. Sea monster   (תנין)

Some 14 occurrences. The sea monsters are created in Gen 1:21. As com-
batants in creation, the sea monsters figure in Job (7:12), a couple of passages in Isaiah (27:1; 51:9), and a couple of psalms (74:13; 148:7). Apart
from these, "tannin" signifies a rather less fearful snake or serpent, usually
land-based (Exod 7:9, 10, 12 [P]; Deut 32:33; Jer 51:34; Ezek 29:3; 32:2;
and Ps 91:13).

18. Creeping/moving   (רמש—both noun and verb)

Some 34 occurrences. While the root is well represented in Genesis One (vv.
21, 24, 25, 26, 28, 30), the P flood account (6:20; 7:8, 14, 21, 23; 8:17, 19;
9:2, 3), and the Leviticus laws (11:44, 46; 20:25), it is far from exclusive to
these. See, among others, Gen 6:7; Deut 4:18; 1 Kgs 5:13 (Heb.; NRSV
4:33); Hos 2:18; and Pss 69:35 (Heb.; NRSV 69:34); 104:20, 25 (creation);
148:10.

19. Wild animals   (חית הארץ)

Some 13 occurrences. David's taunt to the Philistine (1 Sam 17:46) puts to
flight any thought of exclusivity. Ps 79:2 is similar. There are also Job 5:22
and three occurrences in Ezekiel (29:5; 32:4; 34:28).

20. Image   (צלם)

Some 34 occurrences. The significance of Gen 1:26–27 can hardly be over-
rated; the significance of the language used certainly can. Apart from these
two, 5:3 and 9:6, the word for "image" has a wide range, starting with 1 Sam
6:5, 11 and including 2 Kgs 11:18 (2 Chr 23:17), Amos 5:26, a couple of
occurrences in psalms (39:7 [Heb.; NRSV 39:6]; 73:20), three in Ezekiel
(7:20; 16:17; 23:14), and 50 percent of the total in Daniel.

21. Likeness   (דמות)

Some 25 occurrences. Much the same as "image," "likeness" has three occurrences in Genesis (1:26; 5:1, 3) and a wide range elsewhere. Included are 2
Kgs 16:10, Ps 58:5 (Heb.; NRSV 58:4), Dan 10:16, a couple in Isaiah
(13:14; 40:18), and some 16 in Ezekiel. Gen 1:26 (human-divine) and 5:3
(inner human) are the only occurrences of the two together in one verse,
with inverse order in 5:3.

22. Fish   (דגה)

Some 15 occurrences. This term for "fish" occurs in Gen 1:26 and 28. It also
occurs in 3 J texts (Exod 7:18, 21; Num 11:5) and in Deut 4:18. Other
occurrences include Jon 2:1; Ps 105:29; Isa 50:2; and four in Ezekiel (29:4,
5; 47:9, 10).

23. Green   (ירק)

Some 11 occurrences. The 2 occurrences in P texts (Gen 1:30; 9:3) are followed by 2 in J texts (Exod 10:15; Num 22:4). Deuteronomy figures again (Deut 11:10). The breadth of potential use is probably underlined by the occurrence in Proverbs (15:17). Apart from these, there are Isa 15:6; 37:27; Ps 37:2; the Naboth story in 1 Kgs 21:2; and 2 Kgs 19:26.

24. Work   (מלאכה)

Some 166 occurrences. Beyond Gen 2:2–3, so common a word has a wide range of occurrences. Close by, in J texts, are Gen 33:14 and 39:11. There are many uses in the texts concerning sabbath, the sanctuary, and the cultic laws; there are many more elsewhere.

25. Rest   (שבת—verb)

Some 71 occurrences. Again the Gen 2:2–3 occurrences are balanced by the nearby J Gen 8:22. Exod 16:30 and 34:21 are both attributed to J. The range is wide. Proverbial usage is evidenced in Prov 18:18 and 22:10.

From this we conclude that the evidence of vocabulary indicating that P *must* have composed Genesis One is certainly *not* there. The evidence allowing the judgment that P *may* have composed Genesis One certainly *is* there. The language of Genesis One is not restricted to a small or exclusive group within the Hebrew-language community.

P and Genesis 1–11

Among the text that has usually been attributed to the Priestly Writer in Gen 1–11, genealogies, while long regarded as a sign of P, are not particularly helpful for language studies and have not necessarily been regarded as the Priestly Writer's own composition. When these genealogies are discounted (including contributions from the Toledoth Book), and with them Genesis One, text that has usually been attributed to the Priestly Writer in Gen 1–11 is restricted to Gen 5:1–2 and the so-called P account of the flood (i.e., within Gen 6:9–9:17). Comparison of Genesis One with these two texts is revealing. The conclusions can be repeated in advance: (1) Gen 5:1–2 is *not* an obvious continuation of the Genesis One creation account; and (2) the so-called P account of the flood most probably *cannot* have the same origin as Genesis One.

Genesis 5:1–2

Genesis 5:1–2 precedes the genealogy that, through ten generations, leads from Adam to Noah and the flood. It has an adequate opening sentence: "This is the list (*sēper tôlĕdōt*) of the descendants of Adam" (5:1). There follows a condensed account of creation, "when God created humankind," with four sentences at most: (1) humankind was made in the likeness of God, (2) was made male and female, (3) was blessed, and (4) was named. With that, the genealogy proper begins, leading to Noah (5:3–32).

This genealogy, with its own opening at creation, provides an adequate beginning for a study of the human relationship with God, centered on the story of the flood—God's commitment to a less-than-perfect world.[2] At the same time, its differences from Genesis One, minor though they are, are to be noted: (1) the creation is of humankind (*ʾādām*), rather than heavens and earth (v. 1); (2) the phrase "likeness of God" only is used, rather than Genesis One's image and likeness (5:1); (3) blessed and named are noted, not merely blessed (5:2). Likeness and image are used of Seth's relation to his father. These may be minor details, but as we noted above, in this context minor details matter.

Two further difficulties stand in the way of postulating a close association between Gen 5:1–2 and Genesis One. First, Gen 2:4a, the ending of Genesis One, has its own *toledoth* formula. Its juxtaposition with that of Gen 5:1 would be odd, even if 2:4a is merely editorial. Second, it is odd that the personal name "Adam" (cf. descendants of Adam) should be given to the man following Genesis One, where he is not named—he is first named in 4:25![3] As noted in Gen 5:1, humankind is made in the likeness of God; not until Seth comes along in 5:3 is use made of both the likeness and the image—and then it is in relation to his father. Finally, when humankind is created, they (plural in Hebrew) are blessed and named (5:2). In Genesis One, they are blessed but not named (1:28).

The conclusion from this is that Gen 5:1–2 is not an obvious continuation of Genesis One. Continuity between the two, however, is possible. Enough competent scholars have read one as the continuation of the other that it is evidently possible to do so. The juxtaposition of two previously independent texts to form a single composition is always a possibility. The discontinuity is minor enough to be overlooked, but evident enough that it should not be ignored.

The P Flood Account

Before exploring the flood narrative, it is worth being aware of its real importance. It is often read as a report of God's angry response to human wickedness. But it is vastly more important than that. The flood narrative is a theological response to two observations and a question. It says:

1. We are here.
2. We are no better than they were.

And it asks:

3. Where does that leave us in relation to God?

2. See Rendtorff, "Covenant," 386–87.
3. Noted by Wellhausen, *Prolegomena*, 309.

That "we are here" is obvious; that "we are no better than they were" should be equally obvious (see 8:21; 9:2–6). In any age, we may be more technologically or scientifically advanced than our forebears, but that advance is seldom accompanied by an advance in the quality of our humanity. Alas, we are just as cruel as they were, just as greedy, and just as inclined to function on the basis—to borrow from Thucydides, 2500 years ago—that the strong do what they have the power to do and the weak accept what they have to accept. The flood narrative holds together God's radical opposition to evil and God's tolerance of human living. It is one of the Bible's most remarkable theological claims. For more, see appendix 3.

Genesis One and the P flood story have more in common with each other than with the alternative J traditions of the flood. Both may be of relatively late date and have a similar theme: our world—in one, its creation; in the other, its destruction. The scope for repetition is considerable. In Genesis One, the creatures of sea, air, and land are brought into being (vv. 20–25) and situated within the creation (vv. 26–30); in the flood, representative creatures of land and air need to enter and leave the ark, while the rest perish. At this level, selections from 1:20–30 are available for comparison with 6:19–20; 7:14–16, 21; 8:17, 19; and 9:2–3 from the flood text (making due allowance for J [7:2, 3b, 22–23a] and later additions [7:3a, 8–9] and extending into 9:8–17).

Source of Waters

In the P account, the source of the waters of the flood is through the "windows of the heavens" and the "fountains of the great deep" (7:11; 8:2), and the mountains are a significant gauge of the flood waters' height (7:19–20; 8:4–5). When examined, however, Genesis One does not prepare for the flood. It has no mention of mountains (despite their presence in some creation texts), "windows" in the heavens (ʾărubbōt haššāmayim), "fountains" (maʿyān), or the "great deep" (těhôm rabbâ). The flood text has no mention at all of the "dome" (rāqîʿa, 1:6–8, 14–20).

We conclude: at a broad level, the picture is not the same.

Provision of Food

At the end of the flood story, "every moving thing" shall be food for humankind. In 9:3, God says: "just as I gave you the green plants" (yereq ʿēśeb); the Hebrew at the end of the verse is unclear, but the gift of "green plants" for human food seems certain. Genesis One, by comparison, has a different allocation of foodstuffs; humans will have for food "every plant yielding seed" and "every tree with seed in its fruit" (1:29). By contrast, the animals will have "every green plant for food" (1:30, yereq ʿēśeb)—that is, what was, according to 9:3, allocated to humankind in Genesis One.

We conclude: at the level of foodstuffs, the difference is notable.

Land Animals

Genesis One works with three zones of life—sea, air, and land—and uses a general term for life (living creatures) in the sea and on the land (nepeš ḥayyâ). On land, there are three logical subdivisions of the general term: wild (*ḥaytô ʾāreṣ*), domesticated (cattle: *bĕhēmâ*), and other (*remeś*; the classical and correct "creeping" has rather lugubrious overtones). These ordered categories are used in varying ways (see vv. 24, 25, 26, 28, 30).

The subdivisions in Genesis One—which seem peculiarly right (wild, domesticated, and creeping)—are, by contrast, not employed in the P flood narrative as systematically as one might expect. The trio that is found twice (6:20 and 8:17) is: birds, animals, and creeping/moving beings. The P flood narrative lacks the logic of the Genesis One subdivision, for example:

6:19–20	(initial)	all living, all flesh; birds–animals–creeping.
7:14	(entry)	wild–domesticated–creeping–bird, winged creature.
7:21	(death)	all flesh that creeps–birds–domesticated–wild–swarming–humans.
8:17	(exit I)	all living, all flesh–birds–animals–creeping.
8:19	(exit II)	all animals–creeping (noun)–birds–creeping (verb).
9:2	(food)	animals–birds–creeping–fish.

Translation is dependent on context for *bĕhēmâ* (animals or domesticated) and *ḥayyâ* (animals or wild); *remeś* has been rendered "creeping" here.

We conclude: unity of authorship is unlikely.

Birds

Birds feature in Genesis One as "birds" (2x), winged birds" (*kōl ʿôp kānāp;*), and "birds of the air" (*ʿôp haśśāmayim*; 3x). The P flood text has "birds" (6x) and "birds of the air" (*ʿôp haśśāmayim*; 1x). With one exception, both passages use the same terms, reversing the ratio of use by a precise factor of three (birds: 2x and 6x; birds of the air: 3x and 1x). (Note: for "winged birds," an equivalent exists in the P flood account, changing both the noun and the syntactical structure—*kōl ṣippôr kol kānāp* [7:14]; the phrase is not in the LXX, is not needed, and is certainly not "load-bearing.")

We conclude: the reversal of the ratio of use by a factor of three indicates at least a difference of preference, more probably a difference of origin.

All Flesh

In the P flood narrative, a global term, "all flesh" (*kol bāśār*), is used a dozen or so times, and includes humans (cf. 7:21). Genesis One uses a different term, "all life" (*kol nepeš haḥayyâ*), but tends to restrict it to one of the three life zones—sea, air, and land.

We conclude: while evidence against unity of authorship is not strong, evidence in favor of unity of authorship is not present at all.

Language in General

Comparison focuses on the land animals. The fish have no place in the flood narrative; quite literally, they are in their element. They are mentioned at 9:2, under the food chain. Genesis One's concern for the creation of the sea creatures does not belong in the P flood text. It is worth noting, however, that in God's proposal and its achievement (1:20–21), language is used that does not recur later. In v. 20, the waters are to swarm with "swarms of living creatures" (*šereṣ nepeš ḥayyâ*); in v. 21, there is a double specification: the great sea monsters (*hattannînîm haggĕdōlîm*) and every living creature that moves with which the waters swarm (*kol nepeš haḥayyâ hārōmeśet ʾăšer šārĕṣû hammayîm*). Both are peculiar to Genesis One. The verb "to swarm" (root *š-r-ṣ*) does not recur again in Genesis One; it is used differently in the P flood text. The difference regarding the birds is probably insignificant.

We conclude: while what evidence there is tilts against unity of authorship, it is not marked.

Review

Probably the least tendentious formulation of the conclusion emerging from this comparison is that although it is *possible* that both texts come from the same origin (individual or school), it is *unlikely*. It may be more tendentious to say it is *really quite unlikely*; on the other hand, it may be more accurate. We cannot demand obsessive regularity from any author, ancient or modern, yet the constant flow of minor differences makes the same origin for both texts unlikely. Creation and the salvation and destruction of the created are inevitably going to involve large-scale repetition.

To summarize, Genesis One is written in language shared with the rest of the ancient Hebrew community. It is *possible* that it was written by "the Priestly Writer," but it is equally *possible* that it was written by some other. On the other hand, while it is *not impossible* that Genesis One, Gen 5:1–2, and the P flood text were written by the same person or group, given the extent of the differences between them, such unity of authorship must be considered *highly unlikely*. The evidence does not justify claiming a P text or extensive P editing in Gen 1–11. Without the anchor of creation and flood at the beginning, it becomes difficult to make a case for a P document in Genesis. With certain texts as anchors, the existence of linking passages—no matter how bare—can be argued for and a source claimed; without the anchors, the "linking passages" have little function in terms of the source (see ch. 2).

One final note: the texts use two general terms for the living. "Living creatures" (*nepeš ḥayyâ*) is restricted to Genesis One. "All flesh" (*kol bāśār*) is found in P text within Gen 6:9–9:7. But both terms occur in Gen 9:8–17 (4x and 5x respectively—twice juxtaposed, vv. 15, 16—so it is hardly chance). This suggests that creation of the ideal (Genesis One) and destruction of the real (flood) are combined in the faith proclamation that life is to continue (cf. 8:22; 9:1, 7) without fear of destruction.

Appendix 2

Two Examples

Overview

The two examples discussed in this appendix illustrate how signals in the text that are perceived as difficulties by the modern interpreter may be perceived as opportunities for the ancient storyteller. The more difficult the text, the more the "user-base" approach comes into its own.

Genesis 12–13

Signals in the Text

    i. The command from God is to Abraham alone, but Lot features in 12:4–5, does not reappear until 13:1, and then is a full participant in the story of separation.

    ii. The Egypt story is a self-contained unit, devoid of context.

    iii. The story of separation has its start at the place between Bethel and Ai where Abraham had been before the story of separation and to which he returned.

    iv. The story of separation has a satisfactory conclusion in 13:12, with a comment from the narrator following the conclusion (v. 13). Verses 14–17 are an extended duplicate of a clause in 12:7.

    v. The itinerary from Shechem southward to Bethel/Ai begun in ch. 12 is completed in 13:18.

In the Present Text

Abraham family traditions (12:1–8, allowing for the mention of Lot and possessions in vv. 4–5; 13:18)

Egypt story   (12:10–20)

Abraham-Lot tradition   (13:2, 5–12 [13])

Enhancement   (13:14–17)

Blending   (12:9; 13:1, 3–4)

Discussion

In these two chapters, it is clear that the text combines three different components: (i) Abraham's journey to Canaan, ending at Hebron; (ii) the experience of Abraham and Sarah in Egypt; (iii) the separation of Lot from Abraham. Storytellers or users would have been free to select as needed.

Once these three components have been recognized, the verses involved in combining them into a single narrative are equally easily identified. To modulate to the Egypt story, 12:9 is needed; for the return from Egypt to Bethel, 13:1, 3–4 is needed.

The text of Gen 12–19 has a number of chapters involving traditions of Abraham and Lot, concluding with the destruction of Sodom and the origins of Moab and Ammon in ch. 19. The first of these traditions concerns Lot's establishment in the region of Sodom (ch. 13). Lot is named as Abraham's nephew (12:5), providing an association between Abraham and the Moabites and Ammonites. Preparation for this is allowed by including Lot with Abraham in the journey to Canaan and alluding to their wealth. The note concerning Lot in 13:1 is not strictly necessary; it may have served as a reminder to storytellers of different ways of handling Lot's presence in these traditions.

If Abraham is portrayed as unrestrictedly generous to Lot (13:9), God's benevolence to Abraham is unfolded, in turn, in the divine speech of vv. 14–17. Abraham's journey to Canaan is brought to a close with 13:18.

The sequence of the final text is scarcely straightforward. Abraham arrives between Bethel and Ai, moves to the south bypassing Hebron, because of famine sojourns in Egypt, then returns north to the same place between Bethel and Ai where he had been before, separates from Lot, and finally journeys south to Hebron. A straight-line sequence would have had Abraham's separation from Lot take place before the Egypt episode, avoiding the deep detour, and resulting in the following: Canaan, separation at Bethel, Egypt, journey north to Hebron. In the present text, following God's command and promise in 12:1–3, experience of a famine is clearly a challenge (to Abraham and to today's interpreter). Humanly speaking, obedience to God's command and trust in God's promise has led Abraham to the disaster of famine. From a narrative point of view, it appears that the Egypt story had an importance that required its telling as soon as Abraham had reached Canaan, before anything else. The duplicates of this story at 20:1–18 and 26:1–11 may be pointers to an importance that eludes us. Genesis 20:1–18 is at the start of Abraham's life in the land without Lot; Gen 26:1–11 is at the start of Isaac's life on his own in a foreign land. It may be that, while multiple aspects are present, all three passages are witness to the belief that, called by God into the danger of the new and the unfamiliar, the ancestral couple are better protected and cared for than they realized. Despite Abraham's failure—failure to trust God and failure to trust the foreigner—they were taken care of.

Genesis 18–19

Signals in the Text

i. While YHWH appears to Abraham in v. 1 and Abraham sees three men in v. 2, Abraham himself is not named until v. 6.

ii. The use of singular and plural varies. At the beginning of ch. 18, the singular and plural alternate irregularly, with vv. 1 and 3 using the singular and the others using the plural. In what follows, text featuring YHWH principally has the singular (e.g., 18:10–15, 17–21, 23–33); text featuring principally the *malʾākîm* (Hebrew; angels or messengers or both) has the plural (above all, 19:1–18). The singular returns at 19:19, with a degree of ambiguity in 19:18.

iii. While 18:16 and 18:22 almost constitute a doublet, occurring between them are vv. 17–19, which contain a proposal (in the form of a question) that prepares for vv. 23–33, but the proposal is not communicated to Abraham—unless vv. 20–21 are understood to do this.

iv. The timing around Sodom's fate is unclear: is it yet to be determined (18:20–21), or has it been already determined (19:13)? Genesis 18:20–21 speaks of YHWH's "going down" to verify the outcry against Sodom and Gomorrah; even if understood as a communication to Abraham, the "visitation" is not carried out in the text. In 19:13, Sodom's destruction is reported as having been previously determined—its destruction is the mission of the two *malʾākîm*. In conjunction with this, it may be noted that while the *malʾākîm* may have been sent to destroy Sodom, the text reverts to the singular at 19:19, and it is YHWH who rains sulfur and fire on Sodom and Gomorrah (19:24–25).

In the Present Text

Abraham Family Traditions   (18:1, 3, 9–15) The beginning of the text here has been interwoven with the Abraham-Lot traditions associated with Sodom, affecting particularly vv. 1–9. Verse 1, with the mention of YHWH, is appropriate for the announcement of Sarah's son. As they stand, vv. 3 and 9 facilitate the transition to the family story; v. 3 preserves the singular, while v. 9 retains the plural. Such fluctuations in a unitary text are the bane of a source critic's life; for a storyteller, they open the way to needed flexibility and point to choices that may be made. As a final product to be pondered, these verses are unhelpfully complex. As a base text, for a user to expand or select from, they hold together the major elements that are important to a storyteller or theologian.

Abraham-Lot Tradition   (18:2, 4–8; 18:23–19:38) Intermeshed, as discussed, with the Abraham family traditions at the beginning; the use of the plural in vv. 4–8 suggests their attribution to the Abraham-Lot tradition.

Blending   (18:16–22) The blending is not so much a matter of combining traditions as of including options.

Discussion

The complexity of this text is renowned: one visitation, two missions (to Sarah, to Sodom); three men together or one God with two angels (*mal^ʾākîm*); destruction of Sodom by the angels or by God. Von Rad's comment is typical: "many traditions are collected which were originally independent of one another" but that have an "inner unity"; he later concludes, "the succession of narratives in chs. 18 and 19 is unusually compact."[1] Traditions belonging within the Abraham family traditions have been combined with Abraham-Lot traditions. The combined text, as we have it now, can be seen as offering a series of options to its users.

YHWH's announcement of a son to be born to Sarah belongs within the Abraham family traditions. Traditions belonging within the Abraham-Lot collection have been interwoven with the beginning of this Sarah tradition. One divine visit has been used for two purposes. A twofold complication is associated with the motif of Sodom's destruction. First, the text involves references to a destruction by God and a destruction by the two *mal^ʾākîm*. Second, the text contains scenes from before and after the destruction itself. Before it is the famous scene of Abraham's intercession; after it is the scene with Lot's daughters. Meshed into the end of the destruction story is the sparing of Lot. There is much to invite the exercise of a storyteller's skills.

Abraham's name does not feature until 18:6. Usually in Hebrew narrative, the preceding verses would depend on the occurrence of the name earlier. The closest earlier mention of Abraham by his tent at Mamre was Gen 13:18; it is hardly satisfying, but it may be better than emending the present text.[2] Two areas of the text can be understood as offering storytellers possible options. Verses 16–21 constitute one of these, offering two options: option one, Abraham's intercession, is taken up in the text; the other, YHWH's visit to pass judgment on Sodom, is not. The second area with options, 19:1–25, following Abraham's intercession, also offers at least two options. In one option, the *mal^ʾākîm* have been sent to destroy the city (see v. 13); enmeshed in their mission is the scandalous episode with the men of Sodom. In the other, the destroyer of Sodom is a figure in the singular (v. 19), shortly to be clearly identified as YHWH (vv. 24–25)—not to be involved in any scandalous episode.

---

1. G. von Rad, *Genesis*, 204 and 225.
2. C. Westermann's comment is not helpful: "The heading does not mention Abraham, who is first named in v. 6; this is indicative of the stage of redaction which presupposes a coherent Abraham story. V. 1a, therefore, . . . is a later addition" (*Genesis 12–36*, 277). Verse 1a, of course, includes the mention of YHWH, specifying that there is a God among the three visitors.

The complexity of the final text can be attributed, as it has been by past scholars, to the preservation of multiple traditions. It is a shift of emphasis to see in this preservation the offering of options to storytellers, well skilled in adapting traditions appropriately for their audiences. Holding so much, the present text is unusually complex; ancient users would have made their selections.

Appendix 3

Two Exceptions

Overview

The point of this appendix is to draw attention to two passages whose remarkable significance is usually overlooked. In Martin Noth's view, both are exceptions to the normal pattern of combining sources, because both are relatively complete. The *fact* is easily established: the major variants in both passages are relatively complete. Although brief, the versions combined in both passages each have a beginning, a middle, and an end. The *significance*, however, requires attention, because it comes not from the completeness but rather from the paradoxes presented by both passages.

In both versions of the flood, God first determines to destroy life and afterward, with no improvement in humankind, decides never to destroy all life again. God is portrayed as reconciled with human depravity. In both versions of the deliverance at the Sea, Israel is delivered, and the Egyptians perish in the sea. In one version, however, Israel crosses the sea; in the other version, Israel does not. Faith in deliverance is portrayed; ignorance as to the manner of deliverance—the "how"—is revealed.

The biblical story of the flood (Gen 6–9) is a text of extraordinary theological depth. The story of Israel's deliverance at the Sea (Exod 14) offers valuable insight into the nature of biblical text. The complete texts for both passages, as analyzed by Martin Noth, are found in Campbell and O'Brien, *Sources of the Pentateuch*, pp. 211–23 (for the flood) and pp. 238–54 (for the deliverance at the Sea).

Flood Text (Genesis 6–9)

One story has seven pairs of clean animals and goes on to the sacrifice at the end; without the seven pairs at the beginning, the sacrifice at the end would have been an ecological disaster. In between, it has 40-day blocks and rain from above; it has no account of the building of the ark nor the debarkation from it. The other story has one pair of all animals and fortunately no sacrifice; in between, it has 150-day blocks and water from the heavens above and the depths below. The first ends with humankind perceived as evil (8:21a), God's decision not to destroy again (8:21b), and God's promise that life will continue (8:22). The second ends implying evil in humankind's future (9:2–6, fear and dread, murder and the death penalty), with God's command for life to go on (9:1, 7), and with God's everlasting covenant never to repeat the flood (9:8–17). It is an astounding—and comforting—paradox.

It is clear why the two flood stories had to be interwoven with each other. Each account ends with a divine commitment never to destroy again. Placed in sequence, with one after the other, the second would subvert the first. The first would end with God's promise not to destroy; the second would then begin with God again destroying. Beyond that, the interweaving is essential for the key differences throughout the two versions: number of animals, duration of flood, source of waters, sacrifice or not.

The theological depth is remarkable. Whether as separate variants or combined present text, an all-holy God is committed to a less-than-holy humankind. Genesis 6:5–7 is followed by 8:21–22; Gen 6:11–13 is followed by 9:2–6 with 9:1, 7, and 8–17. At the beginning, a world is to be destroyed because it is evil; at the end, even though evil, even because it is evil, the world is never to be destroyed. Both accounts in this text affirm faith in God's capacity to coexist with human evil—a massively comforting faith.

Sea Text (Exodus 14)

The duality of the account in Exodus 14 is clear enough. In one account God works through the agency of Moses' hand, in the other account God works through the agency of a strong wind. Harmonization has been tried; it fails. The duality is not surprising; immediately before, duality is evident in the stories of the plagues and the Passover. Taken together, the three—plagues, Passover, Sea—portray the birth of a nation, and a birth can happen only once. Despite their brevity, the completeness of both versions highlights their difference.

In one account (God's agent: Moses' hand) the Israelites cross the sea; by contrast in the other account (God's agent: the wind) the Israelites remain beside the sea all night.

Attentive readers will notice that the simplest understanding of the account with the wind from God has Israel already camped on the east side of the sea. An encampment on the west side would require a storyteller to explain why the panicked Egyptians fled away from home into the seabed. The Egyptians, therefore, after rounding the sea to come up with the Israelites, are separated from the Israelite force by the pillar, and camp there all night (v. 20), until in the morning watch (before dawn) they are panicked by God from the pillar (v. 24), take flight across the seabed westward toward Egypt, and are overwhelmed by the returning waters.[1] In the second account (with Moses' hand), Israel gains the eastern shore only after passing through the divided sea, pursued by the Egyptians—who followed them into the sea and were swamped.

The ancient compilers who put this passage together had at their disposal at least two accounts of Israel's deliverance at the Sea. In one account, Israel crossed through the sea from west to east, pursued by the Egyptians. In the other, protected by the pillar, Israel camped all night on the (eastern) shore, from which the Egyptians, panicked by God at the end of the night, fled into the returning waters.

The present text invites to faith in God's deliverance of Israel from the Egyptian pursuit. It affirms a deliverance, but equally—by including two contradictory accounts—it affirms ignorance as to precisely how the deliverance happened. The present text insists on the sharp differences in the ways in which that deliverance was told in tradition.

1. The body of water envisaged here (*yam sûf*: Sea of Reeds/Red Sea) is relatively close to Egypt and of limited extent; it can be gone around (cf. 14:2). It is not the Gulf of Aqaba.

Appendix 4

Analysis of the Text

Overview

This appendix lists the entire biblical text for Genesis 1 to Exodus 40 and Numbers 1–24, by chapter and verse, indicating the origin and function of each component. Under the "analysis" rubric, the text is presented in its linear biblical sequence; under "discussion," decisions are explained unit by unit.

It is important to remember that the letters "a" and "b" indicate the two major divisions of a verse, marked by punctuation in Hebrew (following the sense); when necessary, Greek symbols (α, β, γ = alpha, beta, gamma) indicate subdivisions within these two, again marked by punctuation in Hebrew (following the sense). Where it seems simpler and sufficient, the asterisk (*) is used to denote part of a verse.

The abbreviations used are easy to grasp.

adj   adjustment = a word or two that needs adjustment if a particular variant is chosen
alt   alternative = a tradition available as an option
bl   blending = a verse or two that facilitates the merging of text
br   bridging = a verse or two that links two blocks of text
en   enhancement = options or variants that are noted within a text
ex   expansion = material that adds to a text without notably enhancing it

The Past in the Present

A Cautionary Note

In preparing listings such as these, we are well aware of places where editorial intervention has been advocated, putting forward suggestions that we have not accepted in these pages. As a rule, the suggestions of intervention in one form or another have been considered and deemed unnecessary on grounds of the approaches that are proposed in this book; discussion is not always possible within the scope of the book. Readers need to know this and reflect for themselves when they encounter possible cases.

As noted at the beginning of this book, it is important to keep an open mind about the manner of Israel's knowledge of its past. We use formulas like "Abraham family traditions," "tradition pool" (the wealth of traditions shaping Israel's perceptions of its past), and so on. Whether any of these were written documents, fixed traditions, or fluctuating memories are questions that here we prescind from. In some cases, it is possible to mount arguments for one position or another. Within the limited scope of this book, we have not judged it appropriate to do so.

STORIES OF HUMANITY

Theme	*GENESIS ONE*	*HUMANITY I*	*NOAH STORY*	*HUMANITY II*
TEXT	**Gen** 1:1–2:4a;	2:4b–4:26;	5:1–10:32;	11:1–9.

Without attending to details, it is helpful to see the structural sweep of Gen 1:1–11:9. Genesis One is well known, but more as creation than as ideal. A narrative of the stability of human existence (the flood, with God's guarantee never again to destroy) is flanked by two sets of story exemplifying why life should not be so stable—human unwillingness to find fullness of life within the limits of human living. A sketch of the ideal world (Genesis One) is followed by sketches of the real world with, at their core, a faith statement of God's decision not to toss in the towel and abandon the project, that is, the decision not to destroy. The Pentateuch to come will place before Israel the possibility of restoring that first ideal.

Genesis One

Analysis

Theme	*GENESIS ONE*
TEXT	**Gen** 1:1–2:4a.

Discussion

GENESIS ONE
  Gen 1:1–2:4a
  Content:
    An account of creation in six days and the hallowing of the seventh.

Comment
  In the Bible, creation texts abound, but this text, with its stately progress through six days, ending in the hallowing of the seventh, is without parallel in

the Hebrew Bible. Its meaning can be sought in the presentation of creation, in which case it is one among many—for example, Gen 2:4b–25; Ps 104; Prov 8:22–31; Job 26:6–13; 38:4–38; and other creation texts. Alternatively, its meaning can be sought in the reflection of what is created, the stateliness of the process, and the perfection of the product, in which case it is in a class of its own. The process covers the whole majestic movement of creation in its unfolding without any sign of struggle or any significant gaps. The product can be said to be perfect in that everything is in its place, as willed by God, human beings are in God's image and likeness, and the crown of creation is the seventh-day rest. The text, Gen 1:1–2:4a, can be seen as an image of the ideal, how our world might be envisaged coming from the hands of a creator God.

The text is structured in three major sections: the chaos before creation (1:1–2); the goodness of the world in creation (1:3–31); the sabbath rest of God after creation (2:1–3). A six-day creation and a seventh-day Sabbath evoke the historical reality of Israel.

Stories of Humanity I

Analysis

Theme	*THE GARDEN*	*CAIN*	*LAMECH*
TEXT	**Gen 2:4b–3:24;**	4:1–16;	4:17–24 (25–26).
Options	*bl: 2:4b*; en: 2:9b*; 3:22–24*		*br: 25–26*

Abbreviations:		
bl = blending	br = bridging	en = enhancement

Discussion

These three stories—of the Garden, Cain, and Lamech—could clearly be told independently. Equally clearly, in the present text they are not independent. "The man knew his wife, Eve" (4:1); her name was given in 3:20. "Cain knew his wife" (4:17). Practically speaking, the sentence is identical with the start of 4:1; some introduction would be desirable for Cain in an independent story. An adequate appreciation of the text has to take into account both the potential independence of the three stories and the actual blending of the three into one in the present composition.

THE STORY OF THE GARDEN
Genesis 2:4b–3:24

Content:
The story of the Garden: its creation and that of man and woman and all else within it, coupled with the command, its transgression, and consequences.

Enhancement/expansion:

> Within 2:4b–25. Verse 9b* introduces the tree of life to offer the option of an alternative version of the story at the end of ch. 3.

> Within 3:1–24. Verses 22–24 offer a pointer to an alternative version of the story, centered on the tree of life rather than the tree of the knowledge of good and evil. Its language speaks of "the man," not of the couple. Banishment from the garden is not presented as a punishment for eating the fruit but as a means of preventing him from eating of the tree of life.

Blending:

> The story needs an introductory temporal clause (such as 2:4b). "The heavens," however, have no place in the story; it is possible that the word was introduced into v. 4b to facilitate combination with Genesis One.

Comment

The Garden Story, the first of four stories of The Beginning, portrays the creation of a human couple in their environment, their complementarity, and their transgression that led to their exclusion from the garden. The presence of two trees (2:9) and the description of one as "the tree that is in the middle of the garden" (3:3) are problematic. The focus on the tree of life (3:22–24) allows for variant versions where the story is told in relation to the tree of life, or the tree of the knowledge of good and evil, or more fully involving both. It is possible that a version of the story (without the tree of life) ended with 3:21, without the couple portrayed as expelled from the garden.

THE STORY OF CAIN
Genesis 4:1–16

Content:

> The apparent inequality before God of Cain, the agriculturalist, and Abel, the pastoralist, leads Cain to kill Abel. Elimination of the other proves not to be an adaptive coping mechanism. Cain is alienated from earth and others.

Comment

> Their mother is named as Eve (cf. 3:20); 4:16 is an ending.

THE STORY OF LAMECH
Genesis 4:17–24 (25–26)

Content:

> Cain built a city. Three notes of cultural advance: tents and livestock; lyre and pipe; bronze and iron. In the seventh generation (from the beginning), Lamech is capable of disproportionate violence.

Bridging:

> Adam, as proper name, occurs for the first time; Cain and Abel are mentioned in v. 25, but do not appear in what follows. Seth replaces the mur-

dered Abel, and Cain apparently lives on. Seth provides the bridge from the stories of Cain and Lamech to the genealogy of Gen 5.

The Noah Story

Analysis

Theme   *THE STORY OF NOAH*

   Text A: 6:9–22; 7:6, 11, 13–16a, 18–21, 24; 8:1–2a, 3b–5, 13a, 14–19; 9:1–17

   Text B: 6:5–8; 7:1–2, 3b–5, 7a*b, 10, 12, 16b, 17b, 22–23; 8:2b–3a, 6, 8–12, 13b, 20–22

                                          |

TEXT   **Gen 5:1–32**   **[6:1–4]**   **6:5–9:17**   **[9:18–29]**   **10:1–32**
                  | | | | |
Options   *en: 24, 29* | | | *en: 8–19, 21, 24–30*
                               ex | *ex*
                        en: 7:3a, 7a*, 8–9, 17a; 8:7

Abbreviations:
en = enhancement   ex = expansion

Discussion

THE NOAH STORY

Text:

   Gen 5:1–32; 6:1–4; 6:5–9:17; 9:18–29; 10:1–32.

Content:

   A genealogy from Adam to Noah; the generation of Nephilim, not known after the flood; the account of the flood; a curse flowing from Noah's first hangover; a genealogy from Noah's sons, spread abroad on the earth after the flood.

   For Texts A and B, see *Comment*, below.

Enhancement:

   Within 5:1–32. Verse 24, the little note on Enoch, is outside the genealogical structure; it adds traditions about his going. Verse 29 is also outside the genealogical structure, giving an explanation for the name Noah. Appeal to the text of Gen 3:17 runs into *yhwh* here and *yhwh elohim* there; association with the tradition of 9:20 is possible.

   Within 6:5–9:17. Texts A and B will be discussed below (see *Comment*). The enhancements listed note minor adjustments. In ch. 7, v. 3a includes the birds, but with "seven pairs" reflecting Text B and "male and female" reflecting Text A; v. 7a* includes sons and wives within Text B when they were previously a Text A concern (cf. 6:18); vv. 8–9 include clean, unclean, and the birds (with clean-unclean as B and two and two, male and female as A); v. 17a notes the length of the flood before its end; in ch. 8, v. 7 (lacking a subject) points to the option of the raven. In text B, Noth locates 8:2b–3a between 8:6a ("At the end of forty days") and 8:6b. Within 10:1–32. (i) Verses 8–19 interrupt the sequence from v. 7 to v. 20; (ii) v. 21 anticipates v. 22; (iii) vv. 24–30 take off from the name Arpachshad, and the matter of vv. 22–23 is not completed until v. 31. Three categories of tradition are combined in 10:1–32; first, the main genealogy attending to all three of Noah's sons; second, expansions of this by blocks of further information within the major genealogy; third, two pieces of additional information (vv. 9, 21).

Expansion:

The strange little episode of 6:1–4 has to be where it is. There is no mention of the Nephilim in the flood account and no role for them after the flood (even with Num 13:33). While interpreters tend to be shocked at this divine-human miscegenation, initiated by the "sons of God" (Westermann: "this scandal," *Genesis 1–11*, 382), the penalty is slight (although 120 years of life is substantially less than the 969 years of Methuselah), and the offspring were "warriors of renown" (literally, men of the name; Heb. *ʾanšê haššēm*). The fragment may be ancient; it certainly is not clear—and can safely be described as "marginal" (Brueggemann, *Genesis*, 73).

The episode of 9:18–27 is also where it needs to be; earlier, it would not have sat well with Noah's reputation for righteousness, and, naturally, it had to precede the report of his death (9:28–29). At the same time, overreaction is unnecessary. As the first vintner, he can hardly be blamed for not knowing the potency of his product. Westermann is restrained when he remarks, "The structure of 9:20–27 is markedly contrived" ["ein stark zusammengesetzter Charakter"] (*Genesis 1–11*, 483). To lay a curse on the absent Canaan for the indiscretion of his father Ham is troubling (see Westermann, *Genesis 1–11*, 483–84).

Comment

In the Flood account, Text A uses *elohim*, while Text B uses *yhwh*. The analysis of the text follows Noth, with minor variations. For the full text and discussion of the flood text, see Campbell and O'Brien, *Sources*, 211–23.

As is well known, the *elohim* narrative is complete; the *yhwh* narrative is not (at least two gaps exist: the building of the ark and the disembarkation from it). Precisely how the combined text is to be understood is not clear; there are numerous differences of detail, such as the length of time, number of animals, the origin of the waters. Enough details are preserved to allow for the telling of at least two versions, but it is far from sure that this was the goal of the compilation. What is clear in the present text is God's change from destruction at the start to nondestruction at the end (see appendix 3). The goal of the compilation may have been to combine witnesses to this change.

The meaning of the text is puzzling. If, as has long been assumed, it seeks to preserve two accounts of the event, the two gaps (building and disembarkation) are pointers to inadequacy. The desire to preserve evidence of two accounts is possible, given the significance of the divine decision. Other possibilities may yet be elaborated.

Stories of Humanity II

Theme   *THE STORY OF BABEL*

TEXT   Gen 11:1–9

THE STORY OF BABEL
Genesis 11:1–9

Content:

The earth has one language and an (unspecified) group comes from the east, settles in Shinar, and undertakes the task of building a city and a tower, with the intention of making a name for themselves. Their plans are frustrated by God. The place was called Babel.

Interpretation:

It is not unusual to identify the presence of two stories here, separating city and tower, on the one hand, and confusion and scattering, on the other. Some such duality appears imposed by the reporting of YHWH's descent (v. 5), on the one hand, and the formulation of a proposal by the gods (v. 7, "let us go down") on the other. An abruptness in the sequence from v. 7 to v. 8 seems to support this duality.

Without intolerable fragmentation, the text cannot be analyzed in such a way as to separate two versions (cf. Westermann, *Genesis 1–11*, 531–57, esp. 540); nevertheless, two versions would certainly be within the possibilities of any storyteller. It is simplest, however, to understand the present text as presenting a single story, while allowing for further possibilities. In this view, YHWH's descent in v. 5 is a preliminary reconnoitering of the scene, with its outcome in v. 6. No return to heaven is noted; it can be assumed. Subsequently, in v. 7 the proposal for divine action is formulated. The language is to be confused (v. 7), and then the group is to be scattered (v. 8). The difficulty of YHWH in vv. 5–6 and 8–9, while the gods are plural in v. 7, would not have been foreign to Hebrew storytellers (cf., for example, Gen 1:26; 3:22).

A skilled storyteller would have little difficulty weaving this disparateness into a single story; equally, a skilled storyteller would have little difficulty spinning a rich story around one or the other element.

Comment

The single group with a single language is clearly independent of the narrative that precedes it. Sequentially, it is out of place (cf. 10:31); imaginatively, it is in the appropriate place. As a portrayal of an attempt to transcend the boundary of human existence, it returns to Gen 2:4b–3:24, vividly exemplifying the rightness of 8:21's "the inclination of the human heart is evil from youth." It is a story that the people of Abraham will reverse: they come out of the east; they find a unity in Israel; rather than make a great name for themselves, a great name will be made for them by God. As story, it is a fitting prelude to the journey that will end on the plains of Moab.

STORIES OF ISRAEL'S ANCESTORS

The Abraham Cycle

The Abraham cycle is a complex collection; no other Genesis text is quite like it. The final text cannot be metamorphosed into a product of single origin, for it is a blend. When its ingredients are labeled, it is seen to flow remarkably well.

Analysis

Origins	*TP*	*AFT*	*AT*	*A-L*	*AFT*	*A-L*
TEXT	Gen 11:10–32,	12:1–9,	10–20;	13:1–17,	18;	14:1–24;
Options		*en: 5a br: 9*		*br: 1, 3–4; en: 14–17*		

Origins	*AT*	*AFT*	*ES*	*AFT*	*A-L*	*AFT*	*A-L*	*AFT*
TEXT	Gen 15:1–21;	16:1–16;	17:1–27;	18:1,	2,	3,	4–8,	9–15,
Options	*en: 13–16*	*en: 10–14*						

Origins	*A-L*	*AT*	*AFT/ES (?)*	*AFT*	*AT*
TEXT	Gen 18:16–19:38;	20:1–18;	21:1–7,	8–21,	22–34;
Options	*bl: 18:16–22 (alt: 18:20–21)*		*en: 6–7*		*bridging*

Origins	*AT*	*TP*	*ES*	*RBK*
TEXT	Gen 22:1–19,	20–24;	23:1–20;	24:1–67;
Options	*en: 15–18*	*ex: 23a [RBK]*	*en: 3–18*	*en: 7, 25, 30, 40b, 61, 62b*

Origins	*TP*	*ES*	*ES*
	|	|	|
TEXT	Gen 25:1–6,	7–11,	12–18.
			|
Options			*en: 17*

Identifications:

AFT = Abraham family traditions   *AT* = Abraham tradition

A-L = Abraham-Lot collection   *ES* = *El-Shaddai* tradition

RBK = Rebekah tradition   *TP* = Tradition pool

Abbreviations:

alt = alternative   bl = blending   br = bridging

en = enhancement   ex = expansion

Discussion

THE ABRAHAM FAMILY TRADITIONS   (*AFT*)

Text:

Genesis 12:1–8; 13:18; 16:1–16; 18:1, 3, 9–15; 21:1–7, 8–21.

Content:

Divine command and promise, report of compliance with command (= journey into Canaan), flight of Hagar, promise of a son to Sarah, birth of Isaac, Isaac and Ishmael.

Enhancement/expansion:

Within 12:1–8. Verse 5a ("and all the possessions they had gathered together, and the persons whom they had acquired in Haran") includes the possessions needed in Canaan for the story of separation (cf. 13:6–7). Sarah's presence allows for 12:10–20. Verse 4b is often included here unnecessarily; within an ancestral narrative Abraham's age is appropriate.

Within 16:1–16. Verses 10–14 include the future of Hagar's offspring and nature of Hagar's encounter, enhancing the Hagar story with details of Ishmael's destiny.

Within 21:1–21. As noted (ch. 3 [pp. 33–34]), attribution within vv. 1–5 is extremely uncertain. Aspects of chs. 17 and 18 may be reflected. Verses 6–7 may well echo 18:12–15 and 17:17 respectively.

THE ABRAHAM-LOT COLLECTION   (*A-L*)

Text:

Genesis 13:2–17; 14:1–24; 18:2, 4–8; 18:16–19:38.

Content:

Separation of Abraham and Lot; rescue of Lot; Sodom and Gomorrah, Moab and Ammon.

Blending and Alternative:

> Within 18:16–19:38. Verses 16–19 of ch. 18 allow for the telling of the bargaining story in vv. 23–33; to this extent, they are blending verses. Verses 20–21 then offer a variant version of a divine visitation of Sodom and Gomorrah (not actualized) as another way of telling much the same Sodom and Gomorrah story (see Appendix 2).

Enhancement/expansion:

> Within 13:2–17. Verses 14–17 add the dimension of God's generosity to Abraham surpassing Abraham's generosity to Lot; they allow for further reflection on God's promise of the land and descendants.

ABRAHAM TRADITION   (*AT*)

Text:

> Genesis 12:10–20; 15:1–21; 20:1–18; 22:1–19.

Content:

> Episode in Egypt; first covenant with Abraham; episode at Gerar; sacrifice (binding) of Isaac.

Enhancement/expansion:

> Within 15:1–21. Verses 13–16 include a divine promise beyond the ritual, applying the account of the covenant more exactly to the history of the people.
>
> Within 22:1–19. Verses 15–18 offering a variant interpretation of the sacrifice of Isaac.

EL SHADDAI TRADITION   (*ES*)

Text:

> Genesis 17:1–27; 21:1–5 (?); 23:1–20; 25:7–11, 12–18.

Content:

> Second covenant with Abraham; circumcision of Isaac (?); Sarah's age, death, and burial including the specification "Kiriath-arba [that is Hebron] in the land of Canaan" (cf. Gen 35:27); death and burial of Abraham; descendants and length of the life of Ishmael.

Comment:

> As noted above (and in ch. 3 [pp. 33–34]), the analysis of 21:1–5 is extremely uncertain. Verse 4's concern for circumcision reflects *El Shaddai* concerns in ch. 17. Genesis 25:11b might well relate to 24:62; source-critical analysis seems unnecessary. Genesis 25:12–18 is included in the *El Shaddai* tradition because of the association between 17:20 and 25:16.

Enhancement/expansion:

> Within 23:1–20. Verses 3–18 include details of the purchase of the ancestral grave.
>
> Within 25:12–18. Verse 17 notes the length of the life of Ishmael, between the list of his sons (vv. 12–16) and the place of Ishmaelite settlement (v. 18)—twelve "princes" mentioned nowhere else.

REBEKAH TEXT   (*RBK*)
>Text:
>>Genesis 24:1–67.

>Content:
>>Marriage of Rebekah

>Enhancement/expansion:
>>Within 24:1–67. Verses 7, 25, 30, 40b, 61, 62b offer enhancements to the story of Rebekah's coming as bride for Isaac. Note that in 22:20–24, verse 23a prepares for Rebekah.

TRADITION POOL   (*TP*)
>Text:
>>Genesis 11:10–32; 22:20–24; 25:1–6.

>Content:
>>Abraham's lineage; children to Abraham's brother, Nahor; descendants of Abraham's second wife (indicative of Abraham's fidelity and Sarah's sterility).

>Enhancement/expansion:
>>Within 22:20–24. Verse 23a offers an expansion ensuring Rebekah's place as family.

BLENDING, BRIDGING   (*bl, br*)
>Text:
>>Genesis 12:9; 13:1, 3–4; 21:22–34

>Function:
>>12:9; 13:1, 3–4. Enable the incorporation of Abraham and Sarah's journey to and from Egypt.
>>21:22–34. Contributes to the bridge between the Abraham complex and the Jacob complex.

The Jacob Cycle

Analysis

Origins	*JFT*	*JFT*	*RBK*	*JFT*	
	|	|	|	|	
TEXT	**Gen 25:**19–20,	21–27,	28,	29–34;	
	|	|			
Options	*RBK revision: 20**	*en: 26b*			

Origins	*IT*	*IT*	*ES*	*RBK*	*ES*
	|	|	|	|	|
TEXT	**Gen 26:**1–11,	12–33;	26:34–35;	27:1–45,	46–**28:**9;
	| |	|		|	
Options	*br: 1aβ* |	*ex: 15, 18, 24–25*		*br: 42–45*	
	en: 3–5				

Origins	*JFT*	*JFT/RBK*	*JFT*	*JFT*
TEXT	Gen 28:10–22;	29:1–14,	15–30;	29:31–30:24;
Options	*en: 13–15*	*RBK revisions in:*		*br: 30:21*
	adj: 16 [YHWH]	*vv. 10, 12, 13*		
	adj: 21 [YHWH]			

Origins	*JFT*	*JFT*
TEXT	Gen 30:25–43,	31:1–32:3 (Heb.; NRSV 32:2)
Options		*en: 19b, 24, 29–30, 32–35, 37, 42b, 45–53*
		ex: 18aβb [ES]; 32:2b–3 (Heb.; NRSV 32:1b–2)

Origins	*JFT*	*JFT*
TEXT	Gen 32:4–22 (Heb.; NRSV 32:3–21)	32:23–33 (Heb.; NRSV 32:22–32);
Options	*en: 10*[RBK]*	
	alt: 14b–22	

Origins	*JFT*	*TP/ES*	*ES*
TEXT	Gen 33:1–20;	34:1–31;	35:1–29;
Options	*alt: 4–5, 8–11*		*ex: 8, 22*
	en: 18[ES]		

Origins	*TP/ES*	*TP/ES*	*TP/ES*	*TP/ES*	*TP/ES*
TEXT	Gen 36:1–8,	9–14,	15–19,	20–30,	31–42.
Options	*br: 6–8*				

Identifications:
  JFT = Jacob family traditions   *IT* = Isaac tradition
  ES = El-Shaddai tradition   *RBK* = Rebekah text
  TP = Tradition pool
Abbreviations:
  adj = adjustment   alt = alternative   br = bridging
  en = enhancement   ex = expansion

Discussion

THE JACOB FAMILY TRADITIONS *(JFT)*

Text:

Genesis 25:19–20, 21–27, 29–34; 28:10–22; 29:1–14, 15–30; 29:31–30:24; 30:25–43; 31:1–32:3 (Heb.; NRSV 32:2); 32:4–22 (Heb.; NRSV 32:3–21); 32:23–33 (Heb.; NRSV 32:22–32); 33:1–20.

Content:

Lineage and marriage, birth oracle, birth, barter of birthright, Bethel dream, arrival at Laban's, marriages to Leah and Rachel, children of Jacob, wages of Jacob, flight from Laban, fear of Esau, wrestling at the Jabbok, encounter with Esau, settlement at Succoth and camp at Shechem.

Alternatives:

Within 32:4–22 (Heb.; NRSV 32:3–21). Verses 14b–22 (Heb.; NRSV vv. 13b–21) provide an alternative version of the approach to Esau, differing from the embassy in 32:4–6 (Heb.; NRSV 32:3–5) and the strategy in 32:8–9 (Heb.; NRSV 32:7–8). The references to spending the night smoothly bracket the alternative (cf. vv. 14a and 22b [Heb.; NRSV 13a, 21b]).

Within 33:1–20. Verses 4–5 and 8–11 add a more emotional quality to the meeting, with Esau running to meet his brother and reference to the gift of 32:14b–22 (Heb.; NRSV 32:13b–21).

Enhancement/expansion:

Within 25:19–20. In v. 20, it is possible (and no more) that Rebekah's kinship is an insertion (i.e., 20*: "daughter of Bethuel the Aramean of Paddan-aram, sister of Laban the Aramean").

Within 25:21–27. Verse 26b adds the detail of Isaac's age at the birth of his sons.

Within 28:10–22. Verses 13–15 offer the YHWH-speech as a potential enhancement. If this enhancement is not used, adjustments from *yhwh* to *elohim* in vv. 16 and 21 are required.

Within 31:1–32:3 (Heb.; NRSV 32:2).

For discussion of the enhancement verses, see ch. 3 (pp. 42–44).

Verse 18* ("all the property . . . land of Canaan") adds detail to the blunt "all his livestock," in line with 30:43, and emphasizes the family-centered nature of Jacob's journeying (although when Jacob left Isaac some twenty years earlier [cf. 31:38, 41] the aged Isaac was near his end). A geographical location both for what has happened (the accord) and for what is to come is given at the end of the passage, 32:2b–3 (Heb.; NRSV 32:1b–2).

Within 33:1–20. Verse 18 assures Jacob's return to Canaan, west of the Jordan.

THE ISAAC TRADITION   (*IT*)
Text:

Genesis 26:1–11, 12–33

Content:

The story of Isaac and Rebekah at Gerar; Isaac's dealings with Abimelech.
Enhancement/expansion:

Within 26:1–11. Verses 3–5 provide Isaac with God's promise of land,
descendants, and universal blessing, in a Deuteronomistic formulation.
Verse 2 can remain with the original story, with a less expansive promise
than v. 3.

Within 26:12–33. Verses 15, 18, and 24–25 are expansions of the Isaac
text, appealing back to Abraham traditions.

THE REBEKAH TEXT   (*RBK*)
Text:

Genesis 25: 20*, 28; 27:1–45; [29:1–14]

Content:

Isaac married to Rebekah (see above); relationship of parents to sons; blessing deceitfully acquired for Jacob; association of Laban with Rebekah (possible revisions in 29:10, 12, 13).

EL SHADDAI TRADITION   (*ES*)
Text:

Genesis 26:34–35; 27:46–28:9; 35:1–29

Content:

Esau's marriages outside the clan; Isaac's sending Jacob back to Paddan-
aram to marry within the clan; Esau's marriage to the daughter of Ishmael.
Jacob's passage from Shechem via Bethel (where he does not settle) to
Hebron.
Expansion:

Within 35:1–29. Verses 8 and 22 add two pieces of information that
are not integral to the narrative thread: the death of Deborah, Rebekah's nurse (v. 8), and Reuben's incestuous intercourse with Bilhah
(v. 22).

TRADITION POOL   (*TP*)
Text:

Genesis 34:1–31; 36:1–8, 9–14, 15–19, 20–30, 31–42

Content:

The rape of Dinah; the descendants of Esau. These two stories have been
associated by us with the *El Shaddai* material (i.e., TP/ES). In the first case,

the issue of circumcision is central. In the second, the links are less evident but the outsider (i.e., Ishmael) and his descendants give weight to such links as are there: the anomalous separation parallel with Lot (13:5–7, with vv. 8–12, and 36:6–8) and the concern for marriage within the family (26:34–35 and 27:46–28:9).

Comment

Commentators (e.g., Gunkel, Noth, Westermann, even Seebass) have tended to break up ch. 34. The justification given for these analyses does not thoroughly satisfy. Westermann, after painstaking analysis, concludes to the formation of "a new narrative out of two at hand [tribal and family]" (*Genesis 12–36*, 536). Probing behind the present text of this "new narrative" seems to us to be unduly speculative. Hard evidence is not adduced. In v. 30, Jacob upbraids Simeon and Levi, which is appropriate; they are the principal figures, killers of "all the males" (v. 25) including Hamor and Shechem (v. 26). "The [other] sons of Jacob" (v. 27) are responsible for plunder, not killing; in the context, the NRSV's "other" is scarcely special pleading, despite Gunkel—certainly not beyond a storyteller's skill, if needed. In our judgment, other minor discrepancies may be left to storytellers to iron out. The respective roles of Hamor and Shechem are not problematic. Noth suggests vv. 4, 6, 8–10, 15–17, 20–23, 27, 28 (and Hamor's presence in vv. 13a, 18, 24, 26) as "a series of additions which . . . apparently depend upon the basic material of the chapter" (*Pentateuchal Traditions*, 30 n.99); Seebass, on the other hand, claims a core in vv. 1–4, 7–8, 10–13a, 14–25a, 26, 27aα, 29b and dismisses anything further as "too hypothetical" (*Genesis II/2*, 418–35, esp. 432). With respect, we find the various analyses rather too hypothetical; we do not find the evidence compelling.

BLENDING, BRIDGING   (*bl, br*)

Text:

Genesis 26:1aβ; 27:42–45; 30:21; 36:6–8

Function:

26:1aβ. The little bridge ("besides the former famine that had occurred in the days of Abraham") enables the story of 26:1–11 to be introduced into the narrative, distinguishing it from the former famine of Gen 12:10–20.

27:42–45. These verses form the bridge from the story of the stolen blessing to the story of Isaac's sending Jacob to Haran.

30:21. It possibly qualifies as a bridging verse preparing for ch. 34. It is devoid of almost all the features of the other entries.

36:6–8. These verses create the bridge from Esau in Canaan to his descendants in the hill country of Seir. The situation alleged echoes that of Abraham and Lot and is not compatible with Gen 33.

THE JOSEPH STORY

Analysis

Origins	*Joseph*		*TP*		Joseph
TEXT	**Gen** 37:1–36;		38:1–30;		39:1–23;
Options	*bl: 1–2aα en: 22b, 28aα, 29–30*				*Potential alt: see ch. 3*
	alt: 36				

Origins	*Joseph*	*Joseph*
TEXT	**Gen** 40:1–23	41:1–57;
Options	*Potential alt: see ch. 3*	
	bl: 3*, 5*	

Origins	*Joseph*		*Joseph*		*TP*
TEXT	**Gen** 42:1–45:15;		45:16–46:7;		46:8–50:26
Options	*en: 42:22, 27–28aα, 37*		*en: 45:16–24*		*See ch. 3*
	en: 44:1b, 2aβ		*en: 46:1*–5a*		

> Identifications:
>   *Joseph* = Joseph story   *TP* = Tradition pool
> Abbreviations:
>   alt = alternative   bl = blending   en = enhancement

Discussion

THE JOSEPH STORY   (*Joseph*)
    Text:
        Genesis 37:1–36; 39:1–46:7

    Content:
        Joseph in Canaan falls foul of his brothers; Joseph in Egypt finds favor with
        Pharaoh, through maltreatment of his brothers reaches reconciliation,
        finally has his father and family come down into Egypt.
    Alternatives:
        Within 37:1–36. Verse 36 points to the possibility of an alternative version
            in which the Midianites do not sell Joseph to the Ishmaelites (v. 28) but
            to Potiphar in Egypt (see Campbell and O'Brien, *Sources*, 227, 235–37).

Concerning 37:36–40:5, beyond ch. 38, the potential for alternative presentations has been discussed in ch. 3 (pp. 65–66).

Enhancement/expansion:

Within Gen 37:1–36. Verses 22b, 28aα, 29–30 are enhancements allowing a more acceptable stance to Reuben (see ch. 3 [pp. 64–65]).

Within Gen 42:1–45:15. (i) Genesis 42:22 and 37 can enhance the narrative by heightening tension or allow here for an alternative version more favorable to Reuben. (ii) Genesis 42:27–28aα allows a storyteller to emphasize that the brothers knew about the money (in one sack) before they reached Canaan. (iii) Genesis 44:1b, 2aβ allows for development of the story along the lines of 42:25–28, 35—a possibility the text here does not exploit.

Within Gen 45:16–46:7. (i) In 45:16–24, the elaborate goodwill of Pharaoh suggests a less-than-sober expansion. (ii) Genesis 46:1*–5a forms an enhancement (bracketed by the references to Beer-sheba) reflecting the concerns of Gen 26:23–25.

TRADITION POOL   (*TP*)

Text:

Genesis 38:1–30; 46:8–50:26

Content:

The Judah-Tamar episode (see ch. 3 [pp. 63–64]). Various traditions relating to the sojourn of the Israelites in Egypt and distinct from the Joseph story proper, which may have had its ending in 46:1–7* with the arrival in Egypt of Jacob and his family. Even Westermann was dismissive where the final chapters are concerned: much of ch. 46 is "a continuation of the patriarchal story of Gen. 25–36" (*Genesis 37–50*, 154); the concluding chapters, Gen 46–50, are an insertion, as was the very beginning of ch. 37 (ibid.). Genesis 48:1–7 (blessing of Manasseh and Ephraim); 49:1a, 29–33 (instructions for Jacob's burial) come from the *El Shaddai* circle (see ch. 3 [p. 52]).

BLENDING, BRIDGING   (*bl, br*)

Text:

Genesis 37:1–2aα

Function:

37:1–2aα—allows the Joseph story to be blended into the overarching cycle of Jacob (ending with: "the family of Jacob"); v. 2aγ (= "he was a helper to the sons of Bilhah and Zilpah, his father's wives") is integral to the story (cf. Westermann, *Genesis 37–50*, 36). Verse 1's "lived as an alien" (*māgôr*) is an unusual expression (see Gen 17:8; 28:4; 36:7; 37:1; 47:9; Exod 6:4; and four others).

THE BOOK OF EXODUS

Analysis

Origins	*TP*	*TP*	*TP*
TEXT	Exod 1:1–14,	1:15–2:22,	23–25;
Options	*bridging*	*en: 2:4, 7–10aα*	*bridging*
	en: 8–12		

Origins	*ExN*	*ExN*	*SaN*
TEXT	Exod 3:1–4:31;	5:1–6:1,	6:2–7:13,
Options	*en: 3:1bβ*, 4b, 6, 11–15, 16*, 18–22*	*en: 4*	*en: 13–30*
	en: 4:5, 17, 19, 21–23		

Origins	*Shared–1st plague: Nile and waters of Egypt*	*Shared–2nd plague: frogs**
	ExN: 14–18, 20aβ–21a, 23–24	*ExN: 7:25–8:4, 8–15a*
	SaN: 19–20aα, 21b–22	*SaN: 8:5–7, 15b*
TEXT	Exod 7:14–24,	7:25–8:11 (Heb.; NRSV 8:15)

Origins	*SaN–3rd plague: gnats*	*ExN–4th plague: flies*
TEXT	Exod 8:12–15 (Heb.; NRSV 8:16–19),	8:16–28 (Heb.; NRSV 8:20–32);

Origins	*ExN–5th plague: on livestock*	*SaN–6th plague: soot*	*ExN–7th plague: hail*
TEXT	Exod 9:1–7,	9:8–12,	9:13–35;
Options			*en: 14–16, 31–32, 35*

Origins	*ExN–8th plague: locusts*	*ExN–9th plague: darkness*	*ExN–Warning of final plague*
TEXT	Exod 10:1–20,	10:21–29;	11:1–8,
Options	*en: 1b–2, 20*	*en: 27*	*en: 1–3*

*NRSV numbering used.

	Shared—Passover		
Origins	*ExN: 12:21–23, 27b*		
	SaN: 11:9–12:20, 28	*ExN–Firstborn and departure*	*SaN*
	|	|	|
TEXT	Exod 11:9–12:28,	12:29–39,	12:40–51;
	|	|	|
Options	*en: 12:24–27a*	*en: 37b–39*	*en: 40–41a, 42–51*

	Shared–Deliverance at the Sea	
Origins	*ExN: 13:20–22, 14:5b–7, 9aα, 10bα, 13–14, 19b-20, 21aβ, 24, 25b, 27aβb, 30–31*	
	TP *SaN: 14:1–4, 8, 9aβ–10a, 10bβ, 15–18, 21aαb, 22–23, 26–27aα, 28–29*	
	|	|
TEXT	Exod 13:1–16,	13:17–14:31;
		|
Options	*en: 13:17–19; 14:5a, 11–12, 19a, 25a.*	

Origins	*ExN*	*SaN–itinerary*	*SaN*
	|	|	|
TEXT	Exod 15:1–21,	15:22a,	15:22b–27;
	|		|
Options	*ex: 19, 20–21*		*ex: 25b–26*

Origins	*SaN–itinerary*	*SaN*	*SaN–itinerary*	*TP*
	|	|	|	|
TEXT	Exod 16:1,	16:2–36;	17:1,	17:2–16;
		|	|	|
Options		*en: 8, 35b*	*br: 1bβ*	*Alternative traditions:*
		ex: 4bβ, 28, 36		*Water: 2–7*
				Amalek: 8–13 (ex: 14–16)

Origins	*TP*	*SaN*	*TP*	*TP*
	|	|	|	|
TEXT	Exod 18:1–27;	19:1–2,	19:3–25;	20:1–23:33;
			|	|
Options			*en: 9, 12–13, 16a*–17, 19*	*analysis not given here*

Origins	*TP*	*TP*
	|	|
TEXT	Exod 24:1–11,	24:12–14,
		|
Options		*analysis not given here*

Origins	*SaN*	*TP*	*SaN*
TEXT	Exod 25:15–31:18;	32:1–34:35;	35:1–40:38
Options	*analysis not given here*	*analysis not given here*	*analysis not given here*

Identifications:
  ExN = Exodus narrative   *SaN* = Sanctuary Narrative
  TP = Tradition pool
Abbreviations:
  br = bridging   en = enhancement   ex = expansion

Discussion

THE EXODUS NARRATIVE   (*ExN*)
  Text: (in these listings, the asterisk [*] before a passage indicates shared origin; numbering from NRSV)
    Exodus 3:1–4:31; 5:1–6:1; *7:14–8:15; 8:20–9:7; 9:13–11:8; *11:9–12:28; 12:29–39; *13:17–14:31; 15:1–21. (End of ExN)

Content:
  Call and commission of Moses, oppression of Israel, plague of Nile and waters of Egypt, plague of frogs, plague of flies, plague on livestock, plague of hail, plague of locusts, plague of darkness, warning of firstborn, Passover, death of Egypt's firstborn and Israel's departure, deliverance at the Sea.
Comment:
  Noth claims additions in both verses of 9:24–25 (*Pentateuchal Traditions*, 30); the evidence is stronger in v. 24 than v. 25 (see Campbell and O'Brien, *Sources*, 139 n.114). There are thunder, hail, and lightning (fire) in v. 23; thunder and hail recur in vv. 33–34. Where there is thunder, there is likely to be lightning; formatting the fire in v. 24 as enhancement seems unnecessary.
Enhancement/expansion:
  Within 3:1–22. Verse 1bβ* ("Horeb," the last word of the verse) identifies "the mountain of God" in Midian as Mount Horeb. The name "Horeb" is overwhelmingly from Deuteronomy (9x); it does not occur in reference to the mountain in Exod 4:27 (nor in Exod 18:5 and 24:13 [but there the location, Sinai, has already been given, 19:1–2]). It is probably added here to claim the mountain as Horeb/Sinai; its form with the final *hê* is unique. Verses 4b, 6, 11–15, 16* offer an enhancement of the narrative, indicated in the main by the use of *elohim* (see the discussion in ch. 3 [pp. 71–73]). Verses 11–15 have been the object of intense attention and study as the revelation of the divine name (see ch. 2). Within

v. 16, the triple enumeration of the ancestors can be seen as an enhancement. Verses 18–22, as enhancement, offer the storyteller the opportunity for an overview of the exodus narrative to come.

Within 4:1–31. For vv. 5 and 17, see ch. 3 (pp. 73–74). Verses 18 and 19 come from different speakers (Jethro and God) and address different motivations (the living and the dead). It is not surprising that the narrative has Moses act with appropriate courtesy and inform his father-in-law before leaving with his wife and sons, Jethro's daughter and grandsons (so vv. 18 and 20a). Verse 19 may be viewed as an enhancement; it repeats the whereabouts of Moses, "in Midian," unnecessarily, but puts the narrative more immediately under God's direction. Verses 21–23 cover both ends of the spectrum: they look back to God's instructions in 4:1–9; they look ahead to the killing of the firstborn. As an anticipation, it may well be enhancement here, functioning for the encouragement of Moses (as well as users of the narrative); v. 21 uses some of the language of the SaN (*môpēt* and *ḥ-z-q*). The verses that follow (vv. 24–26)—with God's attempt on the life of Moses and Zipporah's saving her husband with the blood of circumcision—are included in the text simply because it would be hubris to omit them. They may quite possibly be viewed as an enhancement. It remains true, however, that their meaning escapes us, whether in the original narrative or as enhancement of it.

Within 5:1–6:1. While most commonly used in apposition to Pharaoh, the term "king of Egypt" is used frequently enough independently. However, its use in 5:4 may be a hermeneutical tag alerting users to an enhancement of the text; "Pharaoh" in v. 5 is uncomfortably close. The king addresses Moses and Aaron by name, which is most unusual; syntactically, the back-to-work order could apply to the people or, more probably, to Moses and Aaron, which, again, would be most unusual. Verse 4 gives an explicit answer to v. 3's request, which v. 5 does not; v. 2 has Pharaoh contemptuous of Israel's God, and v. 4 has him contemptuous of Israel's leaders. An enhancement is likely.

Within 9:13–35. Verses 14–16 introduce a new theme, God's incomparability, power, and name, not mentioned in what follows until v. 29b (which may inspire it). Verses 31–32 interrupt the narrative flow and provide supplementary information. As such, they may be understood as enhancement, without necessarily being secondary.

Concerning 9:35; 10:20, 27. These three verses use the SaN term for the hardening of Pharaoh's heart, occurring, however, in ExN contexts. All three introduce the notion of not letting Israel go (using the *piʿel* of the root *š-l-ḥ*). Apart from the firstborn, these are the last three plagues, following the SaN plague of soot. In each case, an enhancement in the combined text is likely. Without 10:20 and 27, the narrative in both contexts lacks the hardening of Pharaoh's heart; perhaps that is as it should be.

Within 10:1–20. As in the case of 9:14–16, vv. 1b–2 introduce a new theme (catechesis) that is not present in what follows. Enhancement is appropriate. For 10:20, see above.

Within 11:1–8. Despite Noth's fluctuations (see Campbell and O'Brien, *Sources*, 141 n.121), it is probably best to view vv. 1–3 as an enhancement (see Childs, *Exodus*, 161—for whom they are E, p. 131). They interrupt the narrative sequence where 11:4 follows closely on 10:29. The theme of despoliation was introduced at 3:21–22 and will be brought to completion with 12:35–36. A storyteller has the freedom to judge how the theme is best used in this context, if desired.

Within Exodus 11:9–12:28. 12:24–27a has an obvious association with the children's question in Deuteronomy. Verse 27a resumes v. 23; v. 27b provides the continuation. It is likely here to be an enhancement, coming from dtr circles.

Within 12:29–39. Verses 37b–39 are puzzling in the extreme. Verse 37b anticipates the census in Numbers, although its clearest echo is Num 11:21. Verse 38's "mixed crowd" (*ʿēreb rab*)—puzzling enough in itself (cf. Noth, *Exodus*, 99)—may echo something of Num 11:4; it is not certain. The presence of "livestock in great numbers" is not mentioned later and is hardly compatible with the stories of manna and quail. Similarly, verse 39 with its "unleavened cakes" sits uncomfortably with the need for the manna. However, precisely these serious difficulties make it impossible to account for the inclusion of vv. 37b–39 by competent authors or editors. They have a place in the tradition that is at present unknown to us.

Within 13:17–14:31. For a fuller discussion, see appendix 3. It is not always clear whether enhancements were located within the ExN, the SaN, or the combined text; where it is not clear, it is seldom of importance. (i) Exodus 13:17–19 fits smoothly enough before 13:20–22, but whether as the ExN alone or as part of the combined text is uncertain. In the present text, however, 13:17–19 interrupts the sequence from 12:37a to 13:20. Carrying Joseph's bones (13:19) reflects Gen 50:25. (ii) Exodus 14:5a has the term "king of Egypt"; it is used across the sources (see Campbell and O'Brien, *Sources*, 185 n.53). It is found in apposition, "Pharaoh, king of Egypt" (Exod 6:11, 13, 27, 29; 14:8). Outside the appropriate use in apposition, it is possible that it is used to signal the addition of material. As enhancement, it provides a reason for the change of heart in v. 5b. (iii) The angel of God (14:19a), as enhancement, offers an alternative to the pillar of cloud and fire. (iv) Verse 25a can be understood as an enhancement to v. 24, offering a particular understanding of how the Egyptians were panicked by God; the use of a quite different word for chariot (*merkābâ*) suggests that another tradition is being drawn on. While these enhancements may have been drawn from whatever sources or origins in Israel's traditions, they are not to be looked on as remnants of earlier continuous narratives. They are placed in the text here to be at the storyteller's disposition.

Within 15:1–21. For vv. 19, 20–21, see ch. 3 (p. 79). For vv. 20–21, issues of age and relation to vv. 1–18 are matters of contention.

THE SANCTUARY NARRATIVE   (*SaN*)

Text: (in these listings, the asterisk [*] before a passage indicates shared origin; numbering from NRSV)

Exodus 6:2–7:13; *7:14–8:15; 8:16–19; 9:8–12; *11:9–12:28; 12:40–51; *13:17–14:31; 15:22–17:1; 19:1–2; 24:15–31:18; 35:1–40:38. (End of SaN)

Content:

Call of Moses, demonstration of power, plague of Nile and waters of Egypt, plague of frogs, plague of gnats, plague of soot, Passover, departure (12:41b), deliverance at the Sea, provision of water, provision of manna, arrival at Sinai, instructions for sanctuary, construction of sanctuary.

Comment:

8:11b (Heb.; NRSV 8:15b). This verse is given to the SaN. Note the refrain "just as the LORD had said" (7:13, 22; 8:15 [Heb.; NRSV 8:19]; 9:12) here appropriately placed at the end of the report of this plague; the first half of the refrain, "Pharaoh's heart was hardened," may have been omitted in the blending process.

24:15. It has long been traditional to begin this section with v. 15b, because v. 18 repeats that Moses "went up on the mountain." With this understanding, however, it is almost impossible to account for the presence of v. 15a, in which Joshua is not mentioned. It may be wiser to begin the section at v. 15a, with the understanding that in v. 18, after entering the cloud, Moses continued his ascent within it.

Enhancement/expansion:

Within 6:2–7:13. An enhancement in 6:13–30 includes the list of the heads of the ancestral houses of Reuben and Simeon and the names of the descendants of Levi, involving both Moses and Aaron and ending with Phinehas (cf. Num 25:6–15). It begins in v. 13, which refers to both Moses and Aaron; the preceding text has mentioned only Moses. The importance of Moses and Aaron to this enhancement is clear from vv. 26–27. Verses 28–30 modulate back into the narrative interrupted at v. 12.

Within 12:40–51. Two reasons suggest that vv. 40–41a (the 430-year stay) may be an enhancement. First, v. 41b ("on that very day") follows more smoothly on 12:28 than do vv. 40–41a. The day is emphasized in 12:14; the language of v. 41b echoes that of 12:17. Second, the little verb *wayhî* (JPS: "and it came to pass"; not represented in the NRSV) occurs twice in v. 41—unnecessarily, unless the repetition signals an enhancement. A survey of the period of time involved is a concern elsewhere (e.g., Gen

15:13; 1 Kgs 6:1); it is understandable that it should have a place here, but it smacks of a globalizing overview absent from the preceding text. The three little passages, 12:42, 43–49, and 50–51, are probably also enhancements. The first two stipulate aspects of the Passover ritual; v. 42 with its concern for the national observance of the Passover ritual ("a night of vigil . . . by all the Israelites throughout their generations"), and vv. 43–49 spelling out details of the Passover ritual, beyond what has been said above, envisaging conditions inappropriate for Israelites in Egypt. Verses 50–51 wrap up the enhancement by rejoining v. 41b; they pick up what was said at 12:28 for the action of Israel, along with Moses and Aaron, and at 12:17 for the action of God. Note that v. 42's "observance" (Heb., *šimmūrîm*; NRSV "vigil") occurs nowhere else in the Hebrew Scriptures.

Within 13:17–14:31. (i) Verses 11–12 articulate a familiar theme (see Num 14:2; 16:13; 21:5); an enhancement within the SaN is likely. A smoothly flowing narrative here challenges the storyteller's skills.

Within 15:22b–27. As Lohfink notes, postexilic verses 25b–26 may well be appropriate at the outset of the first narrative of the wilderness period ("Your Physician," 92).

Within 16:2–36. (i) Verse 8 draws on what precedes and what follows to fill out the response in vv. 6–7. (ii) Verse 35b is a slightly different formulation from v. 35a and here specifies that the "habitable land" is to be understood as Canaan. (iii) Verse 4bβ, along with v. 28, echoes the same concern for the law as 15:25b–26; continuity from v. 27 to v. 29 is unsatisfactory—with v. 28 included, it is an improvement but is not problem free. (iv) Verse 36 is a straightforward antiquarian note; "verse 36 is a gloss and can hardly be assigned to a source with certainty" (Childs, *Exodus*, 275).

TRADITION POOL   (*TP*)

Text:

Exodus 1:15–2:22

Content:

The traditions in these verses form an expansion of the ExN or of a combination of the ExN and the SaN. The story of the midwives prepares for the birth of Moses; the story around the birth holds the significant detail of his Egyptian upbringing ("as her son," 2:10); the story of conflict and flight to Midian prepares for Moses' call (1:15–2:22). While there are three units here (1:15–22; 2:1–10; 2:11–22), they can be focused together under the single head of the origins of Moses.

Enhancement/expansion:

Within Exod 2:1–10. Verses 4, 7–10a* (as far as: "to Pharaoh's daughter") may signal an optional alternative.

Bridging texts:
>For Exod 1:1–14 and 2:23–25, see below under BLENDING, BRIDGING.

Text:
>Exodus 17:2–16

Content:
>Two traditions are represented; see ch. 3 (p. 81).

Enhancement/expansion:
>Verses 14–16 appear to go beyond the battle story itself; tensions with regard to memorial (written in a book), remembrance (utterly blotted out), and future war (from generation to generation) point to various options. YHWH is more involved than in vv. 8–13.

Text:
>Exodus 19:3–25

Content:
>Several fragments of tradition prepare for the gift of the law and, therefore, are part of a passage of importance to Israel that has been worked over intensely. Whatever the origin of these traditions, reflection is needed on their placement in the present text. (i) Verse 3a, with its opening *elohim*, can be understood as a wide-ranging headline: what follows is about Moses going up to (encountering, meeting with) God. The sentence is not discursive; simply and tersely: subject, verb, predicate. (ii) Verse 3b introduces a special fragment of tradition, vv. 4–8, concerning the consequences of observance of the law (see ch. 3 [p. 84]). The people give their assent (v. 8a); their words are reported to YHWH by Moses twice (vv. 8b and 9b). Verse 9a, between the two, is to be understood as an enhancement, with v. 9b as resuming v. 8b. (iii) The next tradition concerns the people's purification (vv. 10–15) before the theophany and the gift of the law. The purification is ordered in vv. 10–11 and carried out in vv. 14–15. Once again, the intervening verses (vv. 12–13) can be understood as an enhancement. (iv) The final fragment (vv. 16–25) depicts YHWH's coming down on the mountain, with concern about the contact of priests or people with the mountain (v. 24). An enhancement is present in vv. 16a*–17 (from: "there was thunder") and v. 19.

Enhancement/expansion:
>Verse 9 provides an understanding of the association of dense cloud with God's presence. This is not spelled out elsewhere. It appears clumsily here, but users can be expected to know how to integrate it.
>
>Verses 12–13 deal with the issue of keeping the people clear of the mountain until the trumpet (*yōbēl*) sounds, involving the death penalty (v. 12b) and an unusually specific ruling on the penalty's execution.
>
>Verses 16a*–17 (from: "there was thunder") and 19 portray a theophany with thunder and lightning, thick cloud, and the blast of the trumpet (*šōpār*). Moses' dialogue with God (v. 19) is "at the foot of the mountain" (v. 17). *Elohim* is used.

Text:

Exodus 20:1–23:33

Content:

The Decalogue (20:1–17), with a fragment on the people's attitude (vv. 18–21), and a legal collection, the Book of the Covenant (20:22–23:33).

Text:

Exodus 24:1–11

Content:

The "meal on the mountain" (vv. 1–2, 9–11) with the covenant ceremony at the foot of the mountain (vv. 3–8); see ch. 3 (pp. 85–86).

Text:

Exodus 24:12–14

Content:

These verses may prepare for ch. 32 (see Noth, *Exodus*, 199; also Childs, *Exodus*, 507–8). Verse 14 appears to be an enhancement, reflecting another tradition. Joshua appears in 32:17; Hur is not mentioned again (he figures in the Amalek episode, Exod 17:10, 12).

Text:

Exodus 32:1–34:35

Content:

These three chapters contain the lengthy episode of the golden calf (ch. 32), traditions associated with the journey to the promised land and the status of Moses, and finally the covenant and its requirements (34:10–35).

For Noth, the material is mainly old. "The theme of the tables, broken (ch. 32) and then renewed (ch. 34), holds the whole together, whereas ch. 33 is a further independent development of the subordinate theme of the departure from Sinai which appears at the end of ch. 32. Apart from small additions in the style of the P narrative, in chs. 32–34 we are once again dealing with old Pentateuchal narrative material" (*Exodus*, 243).

For Childs, on the contrary, the composition is among the final stages of the book of Exodus. The difference between these two positions is evident; but it should not be exaggerated. Childs goes on: "The achieving of this compositional unity appears to stem from the hand of a literary redactor, who composed his story. Of course, he made much use of older sources, but it is important to recognize that his task was far wider in scope than simply piecing together parallel accounts from the J and E sources. Indeed, it is the decisive role of the redactor in the formation of chs. 32–34 which distinguishes the character of this section from that of Ex. 19–24" (*Exodus*, 558).

Because of the uncertainty surrounding Exod 19–24 (see above), to say nothing of the texts preceding it, in our judgment it has seemed wiser to refrain from detailed analysis of Exod 32–34. In all probability, there is old tradition here as there is in the earlier gift of the law. Whatever their past, these chapters may well form, as Durham affirms, "a marvelous literary unity" (*Exodus*, 418). As with traditions of the gift of the law at Sinai, so here it seems likely to us that we are dealing with material from Israel's pool of traditions that, at the present time, we are not in a position to situate with more precision.

BLENDING, BRIDGING   (*bl, br*)
>Text:
>>Exodus 1:1–14; 2:23–25

>Function:
>>The bridging texts here link forward and back. Exodus 1:1–14 lists those Israelites coming into Egypt and reports their oppression; 2:23–25 allows the narrative to move from Israel's oppression to the call of Moses and Israel's deliverance. Verse 24, at least, echoes the language of the SaN. Within Exod 1:1–14, vv. 8–12 reflect the present Joseph story; it is possible that they form an enhancement relating to it.

>Text:
>>Exodus 17:1bβ

>Function:
>>The bridging text ("but there was no water for the people to drink") allows the little tradition about water from the rock to be associated here with Rephidim.

THE BOOK OF NUMBERS

Chapters 1–24

Analysis

Origins	*TP*	*TP*	
	|	|	
TEXT	Num 1:1–10:36;	11:1–35;	
	|	|	
Options	*analysis not given here*	*en: 14–17, 19–23, 24–30*	

Origins	*TP*	*TP*	*TP*
	|	|	|
TEXT	Num 12:1–16;	13:1–14:45;	15:1–18:32;
		|	|
Options		*en: 13:2b, 3b–17a, 26*	*analysis not given here*
		14:1a, 2–10, 11–25, 26–39, 41–44a	

Origins	*TP*	*TP*	*TP*	*TP*
	|	|	|	|
TEXT	Num 19:1–22;	20:1–13,	14–21,	22–29;

Origins	*TP*	*TP*	*TP*
TEXT	Num 21:1–3,	4–9,	10–20,

Origins	*TP–Sihon*	*TP–Og*	*TP*
TEXT	Num 21:21–32,	33–35;	22:1–24:25.

> Identifications:
>   *TP* = Tradition Pool
> Abbreviations:
>   *en* = enhancement

Discussion

TRADITION POOL   (*TP*)

Text:
        Numbers 1:1–10:36; 11:1–35; 12:1–16; 13:1–14:45; 15:1–18:32; 19:1–22; 20:1–13, 14–21, 22–29; 21:1–3, 4–9, 10–20, 21–32, 33–35; 22:1–24:25.

Content:
        Preparations for the journey; the Taberah episode, followed by the easing of Moses' burden by the provision both of meat (quail) and of the aid of seventy elders; God's anger kindled against the people and the place named Kibroth-hattaavah (graves of the craving); Miriam and Aaron in conflict with Moses; the episode of the spies and the failure to occupy the land at this stage; the revolt of Korah, Dathan, and Abiram and surrounding laws; further laws; waters of Meribah; passage through Edom refused; death of Aaron; detour north into the Negeb; the bronze serpent; the little itinerary; Sihon; Og; arrival at the plains of Moab and the Balaam stories.

Enhancement/expansion:
        Within Num 11:1–35. Three passages may be classed as enhancement, two concerning the elders (vv. 14–17 and 24–30); the third offers possible variants within the story of the quail (vv. 19–23). See discussion in ch. 3 (pp. 94–96).
        Within Num 13:1–14:45. The enhancement here is considerable, with a concern for the congregation of Israel and its leaders (Moses and Aaron) being involved (13:2b, 3b–17a, 26), the motif of the failed generation that died in the wilderness, exemplified in the deaths of the spies, and the disastrous attempt to take the land without God (14:1a, 2–10, 11–25, 26–39, 41–44a). In the midst of this is the well-known dtr-influenced insertion (here, despite Noth, reckoned as 14:11–25) with

God's will to disinherit Israel and Moses' intercession on Israel's behalf (Noth: vv. 11b–23a, *Numbers*, 108–9; cf. Exod 32:7–14). Verse 22 speaks of "these ten times" that Israel has tested God, implying experience of a more extensive period than any understanding of the desert sojourn might justify.

Bibliography

Alter, Robert. *The Art of Biblical Narrative.* New York: Basic Books, 1981.

Astruc, Jean. *Conjectures sur les mémoires originaux dont il paroit que Moyse s'est servi pour composer le livre de la Genese; avec des remarques, qui appuient ou qui éclaircissent ces conjectures.* Brussels: Fricx, 1753.

Auld, Graeme. "Leviticus: After Exodus and Before Numbers." In *Book of Leviticus*, ed. R. Rendtorff and R. A. Kugler, 41–54.

Bartlett, J. R. "Edom." In *ABD* 2:287–95.

Blenkinsopp, Joseph. *The Pentateuch: An Introduction to the First Five Books of the Bible.* London: SCM, 1992.

Blum, Erhard. "Genesis 33,12–20: Die Wege trennen sich." In *Jacob*, ed. J.-D. Macchi and T. Römer, 227–38.

———. *Die Komposition der Vätergeschichte.* WMANT 57. Neukirchen-Vluyn: Neukirchener Verlag, 1984.

———. "Die literarische Verbindung von Erzvätern und Exodus: Ein Gespräch mit neueren Endredaktionshypothesen." In *Abschied vom Jahwisten*, ed. J. C. Gertz et al., 119–56.

———. *Studien zur Komposition des Pentateuch.* BZAW 189. Berlin: de Gruyter, 1990.

Blum, E., C. Macholz, and E. Stegemann, eds. *Die Hebräische Bibel und ihre zweifache Nachgeschichte: Festschrift für Rolf Rendtorff zum 65. Geburtstag.* Neukirchen-Vluyn: Neukirchener Verlag, 1990.

Boadt, Lawrence. *Reading the Old Testament: An Introduction.* New York: Paulist, 1984.

Boorer, Suzanne. *The Promise of the Land as Oath: A Key to the Formation of the Pentateuch.* BZAW 205. Berlin: de Gruyter, 1992.

Brodie, Thomas L. *Genesis as Dialogue: A Literary, Historical, and Theological Commentary.* New York: Oxford University Press, 2001.

Brueggemann, Walter. *Genesis.* Int. Atlanta: John Knox, 1982.

Budd, Philip J. *Numbers.* WBC. Waco, TX: Word Books, 1984.

Campbell, Antony F. "Form Criticism's Future." In *The Changing Face of Form Criticism for the Twenty-First Century*, ed. M. A. Sweeney and E. Ben Zvi, 15–21. Grand Rapids: Eerdmans, 2003.

———. *Joshua to Chronicles: An Introduction.* Louisville, KY: Westminster John Knox, 2004.

———. *Of Prophets and Kings: A Late Ninth-Century Document (1 Samuel 1–2 Kings 10)*. CBQMS 17. Washington, DC: CBA, 1986.

———. "The Priestly Text: Redaction or Source?" In *Biblische Theologie und gesellschaftlicher Wandel: Für Norbert Lohfink SJ*, ed. G. Braulik, W. Groß, and S. McEvenue, 32–47. Freiburg im Breisgau: Herder, 1993.

———. *1 Samuel*. FOTL 7. Grand Rapids: Eerdmans, 2003.

———. *2 Samuel*. FOTL 8. Grand Rapids: Eerdmans, 2005.

———. "The Storyteller's Role: Reported Story and Biblical Text." *CBQ* 64 (2002): 427–41.

Campbell, Antony F., and Mark A. O'Brien. "1–2 Samuel." In *The International Bible Commentary*, ed. W. R. Farmer, 572–607.

———. *Sources of the Pentateuch: Texts, Introductions, Annotations*. Minneapolis: Fortress, 1993.

———. *Unfolding the Deuteronomistic History: Origins, Upgrades, Present Text*. Minneapolis: Fortress, 2000.

Carr, David M. *Reading the Fractures of Genesis: Historical and Literary Approaches*. Louisville, KY: Westminster John Knox, 1996.

Childs, Brevard S. *Exodus*. OTL. London: SCM, 1974.

Clanchy, M. T. *From Memory to Written Record: England 1066–1307*. London: Edward Arnold, 1979.

Coats, George W. *From Canaan to Egypt: Structural and Theological Context for the Joseph Story*. CBQMS 4. Washington, DC: CBA, 1976.

———. *Genesis: With an Introduction to Narrative Literature*. FOTL 1. Grand Rapids: Eerdmans, 1983.

Dalley, Stephanie. *Myths from Mesopotamia: Creation, the Flood, Gilgamesh and Others*. Oxford: Oxford University Press, 1989.

Dicou, Bert. *Edom, Israel's Brother and Antagonist: The Role of Edom in Biblical Prophecy and Story*. JSOTSup 169. Sheffield: Sheffield Academic Press, 1994.

Diebner, B., and H. Schult. "Alter und geschichtlicher Hintergrund von Gen 24." *DBAT* 10 (1975): 10–17.

Durham, John I. *Exodus*. WBC. Waco, TX: Word, 1987.

Eichrodt, Walther. *Ezekiel*. OTL. London: SCM, 1970.

Ellis, Peter F. *The Yahwist: The Bible's First Theologian*. Notre Dame, IN: Fides, 1968.

Farmer, William R., ed. *The International Bible Commentary: A Catholic and Ecumenical Commentary for the Twenty-First Century*. Collegeville, MN: Liturgical Press, 1998.

Feynman, Richard. *QED: The Strange Theory of Light and Matter*. Princeton, NJ: Princeton University Press, 1985.

Fretheim, Terence E. *Exodus*. Interpretation. Louisville, KY: John Knox, 1991.

Frye, Northrop. *The Great Code: The Bible and Literature*. New York: Harcourt Brace Jovanovich, 1982.

Gerstenberger, Erhard. *Leviticus*. OTL. Louisville, KY: Westminster John Knox, 1996.

Gertz, Jan Christian. *Tradition und Redaktion in der Exoduserzählung: Untersuchungen zur Endredaktion des Pentateuch*. FRLANT 186. Göttingen: Vandenhoeck & Ruprecht, 2000.

Gertz, J. C., K. Schmid, and M. Witte, eds. *Abschied vom Jahwisten: Die Komposition des Hexateuch in der jüngsten Discussion*. BZAW 315. Berlin: de Gruyter, 2002.

Gese, H. *Der Verfassungsentwurf des Ezechiel (Kap. 40–48) traditionsgeschichtlich untersucht*. BHT 25. Tübingen: Mohr, 1957.

Greene, Brian. *The Elegant Universe: Superstrings, Hidden Dimensions, and the Quest for the Ultimate Theory*. New York: Norton, 2003.

Gunkel, Hermann. *Genesis*. German original: 3rd ed., 1910. Macon, GA: Mercer University Press, 1997.

Ha, John. *Genesis 15: A Theological Compendium of Pentateuchal History*. BZAW 181. Berlin: de Gruyter, 1989.

Hahn, Herbert F. *The Old Testament in Modern Research*. With a survey of recent literature by H. D. Hummel. Philadelphia: Fortress, 1966.

Hyatt, J. P. *Exodus*. NCB. London: Oliphants, 1971.

Johnstone, W. "From the Sea to the Mountain: Exodus 15,22–19,2: A Case-Study in Editorial Techniques." In *Book of Exodus*, ed. M. Vervenne, 245–63.

Kitchen, Kenneth A. *On the Reliability of the Old Testament*. Grand Rapids: Eerdmans, 2003.

Knierim, Rolf. "Exodus 18 und die Neuordnung der Mosaischen Gerichtsbarkeit." *ZAW* 73 (1961): 146–71.

Knierim, Rolf, and George Coats. *Numbers*. FOTL 4. Grand Rapids: Eerdmans, 2005.

Knight, Douglas A. "The Pentateuch." In *The Hebrew Bible and Its Modern Interpreters*, ed. D. A. Knight and G. M. Tucker, 263–96. Philadelphia: Fortress, 1985.

Kohata, Fujiko. *Jahwist und Priesterschrift in Exodus 3–14*. BZAW 166. Berlin: de Gruyter, 1986.

Kratz, Reinhard G. *Die Komposition der erzählenden Bücher des Alten Testaments*. UTB 2157. Göttingen: Vandenhoeck & Ruprecht, 2000.

Kraus, H. J. *Geschichte der historisch-kritischen Erforschung des Alten Testaments*. 2nd ed. Neukirchen-Vluyn: Neukirchener Verlag, 1956/69.

Krieger, Martin. *Doing Physics: How Physicists Take Hold of the World*. Bloomington: Indiana University Press, 1992.

Kuhn, Thomas S. *The Structure of Scientific Revolutions*. 1st ed., 1962. 3rd ed., Chicago: University of Chicago Press, 1996.

Lemaire, André. "Schools and Literacy in Ancient Israel and Early Judaism." In *The Blackwell Companion to the Hebrew Bible*, ed. L. G. Perdue, 207–17. Oxford: Blackwell, 2001.

Levenson, Jon D. "The Hebrew Bible, the Old Testament, and Historical Criticism." In *The Future of Biblical Studies: The Hebrew Scriptures*, ed. R. E. Friedman and H. G. M. Williamson, 19–59. Atlanta: Scholars Press, 1987.

———. "Why Jews Are Not Interested in Biblical Theology." In *Judaic Perspectives on Ancient Israel*, ed. J. Neusner, B. A. Levine, and E. S. Frerichs, 281–307. Philadelphia: Fortress, 1987.

Levin, Christoph. *Der Jahwist*. Göttingen: Vandenhoeck & Ruprecht, 1993.

Levine, Baruch. "Leviticus: Its Literary History and Location in Biblical Literature." In *Book of Leviticus*, ed. R. Rendtorff and R. A. Kugler, 11–23.

Lohfink, Norbert. *The Covenant Never Revoked: Biblical Reflections on Christian–Jewish Dialogue*. New York: Paulist, 1991.

———. "'I am Yahweh, your Physician' (Exodus 15:26): God, Society and Human Health in a Postexilic Revision of the Pentateuch (Exod. 15:2b, 26 [*sic;* original, Ex 15, 25b.26])." In *Theology of the Pentateuch: Themes of the Priestly Narrative and Deuteronomy*, by Norbert Lohfink, 35–95. Edinburgh: T & T Clark, 1994.

———. *Die Väter Israel's in Deuteronomium. Mit einer Stellungnahme von Thomas Römer*. OBO 111. Freiburg, Schweiz: Universitätsverlag, 1991.

Macchi, J.-D., and T. Römer, eds. *Jacob: Commentaire á plusieurs voix de Gen 25–36*. MdB 44. Geneva: Labor et Fides, 2001.

Marx, Alfred. "Genèse 26,1–14A." In *Jacob*, ed. J.-D. Macchi and T. Römer, 25–36.

Mayes, A. D. H. *Deuteronomy*. NCB. London: Oliphants, 1979.

Mays, J. L. *Amos*. OTL. London: SCM, 1969.

Meinhold, A. "Die Gattung der Josephsgeschichte und des Estherbuches: Diasporanovelle I." *ZAW* 87 (1975): 306–24.

———. "Die Gattung der Josephsgeschichte und des Estherbuches: Diasporanovelle II." *ZAW* 88 (1976): 72–93.

Nicholson, Ernest W. "The Interpretation of Exodus XXIV 9–11." *VT* 24 (1974): 77–97.
———. *The Pentateuch in the Twentieth Century: The Legacy of Julius Wellhausen*. Oxford: Clarendon Press, 1998.
Niditch, Susan. *Oral World and Written Word: Ancient Israelite Literature*. Library of Ancient Israel. Louisville, KY: Westminster John Knox, 1996.
Noth, Martin. *Exodus*. OTL. Philadelphia: Westminster, 1962.
———. *A History of Pentateuchal Traditions*. German original, 1948. Chico, CA: Scholars Press, 1981.
———. *Könige I. 1–16*. BKAT 9/1. Neukirchen-Vluyn: Neukirchener Verlag, 1968.
O'Brien, Mark A., and Antony F. Campbell. "1–2 Kings." In *The International Bible Commentary*, ed. W. R. Farmer, 608–43.
Olson, Dennis T. *The Death of the Old and the Birth of the New: The Framework of the Book of Numbers and the Pentateuch*. BJS 71. Chico, CA: Scholars Press, 1985.
Otto, Eckhart. "Die nachpriesterschriftliche Pentateuchredaktion im Buch Exodus." In *Book of Exodus*, ed. M. Vervenne, 61–111.
Propp, William H. C. *Exodus 1–18*. AB 2. Garden City, NY: Doubleday, 1999.
Pury, Albert de. "La tradition patriarcale in Gen 12–35." In *Le Pentateuch en question: Les origines et la composition des cinq premiers livres de la Bible à la lumière des recherches récentes*, ed. A. de Pury, 259–70. Geneva: Labor et Fides, 1989.
Rad, Gerhard von. *Old Testament Theology*. Vol. 1: *The Theology of Israel's Historical Traditions*. Edinburgh: Oliver & Boyd, 1962.
Redford, Donald B. *A Study of the Biblical Story of Joseph (Genesis 37–50)*. VTSup 20. Leiden: Brill, 1970.
Rendsburg, Gary A. "Some False Leads in the Identification of Late Biblical Hebrew Texts: The Cases of Genesis 24 and 1 Samuel 2:27–36." *JBL* 121 (2002): 23–46.
Rendtorff, Rolf. "'Covenant' as a Structuring Concept in Genesis and Exodus." *JBL* 108 (1989): 385–93.
———. *The Problem of the Process of Transmission in the Pentateuch*. JSOTSup 89. German original, 1977. Sheffield: JSOT, 1990.
Rendtorff, R., and R. A. Kugler, eds. *The Book of Leviticus: Composition and Reception*. Leiden: Brill, 2003.
Ricoeur, Paul. *The Symbolism of Evil*. Boston: Beacon Press, 1967.
Rofé, Alexander. "An Enquiry into the Betrothal of Rebekah." In *Hebräische Bibel*, ed. E. Blum et al., 27–39. Neukirchen-Vluyn: Neukirchener Verlag, 1990.
Rogerson, John. *Old Testament Criticism in the Nineteenth Century: England and Germany*. London: SPCK, 1984.
Römer, Thomas. "Das Buch Numeri und das Ende des Jahwisten: Anfragen zur 'Quellenscheidung' im vierten Buch des Pentateuch." In *Abschied vom Jahwisten*, ed. J. C. Gertz et al., 215–31.
———. "The Form-Critical Problem of the So-Called Deuteronomistic History." In *Changing Face of Form Criticism*, ed. M. A. Sweeney and E. Ben Zvi, 240–52.
———. *Israels Väter: Untersuchungen zur Väterthematik im Deuteronomium und in der deuteronomistischen Tradition*. OBO 99. Freiburg, Schweiz: Universitätsverlag, 1990.
———. "Recherches actuelles sur le cycle d'Abraham." In *Book of Genesis*, ed. A. Wénin, 179–211.
Sandmel, S. "The Haggada within Scripture." *JBL* 80 (1961): 105–22.
Schama, Simon. *A History of Britain: At the Edge of the World? 3000BC–AD1603*. London: BBC, 2000.
Schmid, Hans Heinrich. *Der sogenannte Jahwist: Beobachtungen und Fragen zur Pentateuchforschung*. Zurich: Theologischer Verlag, 1976.
Schmid, Konrad. *Erzväter und Exodus: Untersuchungen zur doppelten Begründung der Ursprünge Israels innerhalb der Geschichtsbücher des Alten Testaments*. WMANT 81. Neukirchen: Neukirchener Verlag, 1999.

————. "Die Josephsgeschichte im Pentateuch." In *Abschied vom Jahwisten*, ed. J. C. Gertz et al., 83–118.

————. "Die Versöhnung zwischen Jakob and Esau (Genesis 33,1–11)." In *Jacob*, ed. J.-D. Macchi and T. Römer, 211–26.

Schmidt, Werner H. *Exodus*. BKAT II/1, vol. 1: *Exodus 1–6*. Neukirchen-Vluyn: Neukirchener Verlag, 1988.

————. "Die Intention der beiden Plagenerzählungen (Exodus 7–10) in ihrem Kontext." In *Studies in the Book of Exodus: Redaction-Reception—Interpretation*, ed. M. Vervenne, 225–43.

Schmitt, Hans Christoph. *Die nichtpriesterliche Josephsgeschichte: Ein Beitrag zur neuesten Pentateuchkritik*. BZAW 154. Berlin: de Gruyter, 1980.

Scullion, John J. *Genesis: A Commentary for Students, Teachers, and Preachers*. Collegeville, MN: Liturgical Press, 1992.

Seebass, Horst. *Genesis I: Urgeschichte (1,1–11,26)*. Neukirchen-Vluyn: Neukirchener Verlag, 1996.

————. *Genesis II: Vätergeschichte II (23,1–36,43)*. Neukirchen-Vluyn: Neukirchener Verlag, 1999.

————. *Numeri*. Part Two: *Numeri 10,11–22,1*. BKAT IV/2. Neukirchen-Vluyn: Neukirchener Verlag, 2003.

Simon, Richard, Prêtre de la Congregation de l'Oratoire. *Histoire Critique du Vieux Testament*. Nouvelle Edition, & qui est la premiere imprimée sur la Copie de Paris, augmentée d'une Apologie generale & de plusieurs Remarques Critiques. Rotterdam: Reinier Leers, 1685. Reprinted, Geneva: Slatkine, 1971.

Ska, Jean Louis. "Exode 19,3b-6 et l'identité de l'Israël postexilique." In *Book of Exodus*, ed. M. Vervenne, 289–317.

————. "Genèse 25,19–34—Ouverture du cycle de Jacob." In *Jacob*, ed. J.-D. Macchi and T. Römer, 11–21.

————. "The Yahwist, a Hero with a Thousand Faces: A Chapter in the History of Modern Exegesis." In *Abschied vom Jahwisten*, ed. J. C. Gertz et al., 1–23.

Soggin, J. Alberto. *Das Buch Genesis*. Darmstadt: Wissenschaftliche Buchgesellschaft, 1997.

————. *Introduction to the Old Testament: From Its Origins to the Closing of the Alexandrian Canon*. Philadelphia: Westminster, 1976.

Sweeney, Marvin A., and E. Ben Zvi, eds. *The Changing Face of Form Criticism for the Twenty-first Century*. Grand Rapids: Eerdmans, 2003.

Talmon, Shemaryahu. "The Textual Study of the Bible—A New Outlook." In *Qumran and the History of the Biblical Text*, ed. F. M. Cross and S. Talmon, 321–400. Cambridge: Harvard University Press, 1975.

Van Seters, John. *Abraham in History and Tradition*. New Haven, CT: Yale University Press, 1975.

————. *The Life of Moses: The Yahwist as Historian in Exodus-Numbers*. Louisville, KY: Westminster/John Knox, 1994.

————. *The Pentateuch: A Social-Science Commentary*. Sheffield: Sheffield Academic Press, 1999.

————. *Prologue to History: The Yahwist as Historian in Genesis*. Louisville, KY: Westminster/John Knox, 1992.

Vervenne, Marc, ed. *Studies in the Book of Exodus: Redaction–Reception–Interpretation*. BETL 126. Leuven: Leuven University Press, 1996.

Weimar, Peter. *Die Berufung des Moses: Literaturwissenschaftliche Analyse von Exodus 2,23–5,5*. OBO 32. Freiburg, Schweiz: Universitätsverlag, 1980.

————. "Exodus 1,1–2,10 als Eröffnungskomposition des Exodusbuches." In *Book of Exodus*, ed. M. Vervenne, 179–208.

Wellhausen, Julius. *Die Composition des Hexateuchs und der historischen Bücher des Alten*

Testaments. Cited from 4th unchanged printing. Originals, 1876–78. Berlin: de Gruyter, 1963.

———. *Prolegomena to the History of Ancient Israel.* German original, 1883. Meridian Books. Cleveland: World Publishing, 1957.

Wénin, A., ed. *Studies in the Book of Genesis: Literature, Redaction and History.* BETL 155. Leuven: Leuven University Press, 2001.

Westermann, Claus. *Genesis 1–11.* Minneapolis: Augsburg, 1984.

———. *Genesis 12–36.* Minneapolis: Augsburg, 1985.

———. *Genesis 37–50.* Minneapolis: Augsburg, 1986.

Wevers, John W. *Ezekiel.* NCB. London: Oliphants, 1969.

Whybray, R. N. *The Making of the Pentateuch: A Methodological Study.* JSOTSup 53. Sheffield: Sheffield Academic Press, 1987.

Wilson, Robert. "Genealogy, Genealogies." *ABD* 2:929–32.

———. *Genealogy and History in the Biblical World.* New Haven, CT: Yale University Press, 1977.

Winnett, F. V. "Re-examining the Foundations." *JBL* 84 (1965): 1–19.

Witte, Markus. *Die biblische Urgeschichte: Redaktions- und theologiegeschichtliche Beobachtungen zu Genesis 1,1–11,26.* BZAW 265. Berlin: de Gruyter, 1998.

Wolff, H. W. *Joel and Amos.* Hermeneia. Philadelphia: Fortress Press, 1977.

Wynn-Williams, Damian J. *The State of the Pentateuch: A Comparison of the Approaches of M. Noth and E. Blum.* BZAW 249. Berlin: de Gruyter, 1997.

Zenger, Erich. "Wie und wozu die Tora zum Sinai kam: Literarische und theologische Beobachtungen zu Exodus 19–34." In *Book of Exodus,* ed. M. Vervenne, 265–88.

Zimmerli, Walther. *Ezekiel 2: A Commentary on the Book of the Prophet Ezekiel Chapters 25–48.* German original, 1969. Hermeneia. Philadelphia: Fortress, 1983.

Scripture Index

The asterisk (*) denotes less than a half-verse.
Comparative references only are indexed from appendix 4 (pp. 127–55).

Genesis				
Gen 1–Exod 40	7	1:25	109, 110, 114	5	31
Gen 1–Deut 34	104	1:26	110, 114, 133	5–10	8, 28, 30
Gen 1	109	1:26–27	110	5:1	110, 111
1–11	xiv, 11, 12, 14,	1:28	109, 110, 111, 114	5:1–2	11, 12, 28, 107,
	30, 100, 107,	1:29	109, 113		111, 115
	111, 115	1:29–30	109	5:2	111
1:1	26	1:30	110, 111, 113	5:3	110, 111
1:1–2:4a	2, 8, 11, 12,	2	29	5:3–32	28, 111
	24, 26, 27,	2–3	24, 28	6–9	123
	97, 107	2–4	8, 30	6:1–4	29
1:1–2:25	98	2:2–3	111	6:5–9:17	2, 24
1:1–11:9	40	2:4b–25	26, 27	6:5	29
1:3	27	2:4b–3:24	134	6:5–7	124
1:6–8	113	2:4b–4:24	2, 27, 28	6:6	28, 29
1:9	108	2:4b–11:9	24	6:7	107, 110
1:10	108	2:4	53	6:9–9:7	115
1:11	108, 109	2:4a	111	6:9–9:17	111
1:11–12	109	2:4b	26	6:9	53
1:12	108, 109	2:5	109	6:11	29
1:14	109	2:7	109	6:11–13	124
1:14–20	113	2:16–17	28	6:19–20	113, 114
1:15	109	2:19	109	6:20	109, 110, 114
1:16	109	3:15	109	7:2	113
1:20–21	109, 115	3:18	109	7:3a	113
1:20–25	113	3:22	29, 133	7:3b	109, 113
1:20–30	113	4:14	28	7:8	110
1:21	109, 110	4:23–24	28	7:8–9	113
1:24	109, 110, 114	4:25	109, 111	7:11	108, 113
		4:25–26	28	7:14	109, 110, 114

163

Genesis (*continued*)

7:14–16	113
7:19–20	113
7:21	110, 113, 114
7:22–23a	113
7:23	110
8:2	108, 113
8:4–5	113
8:17	110, 113, 114
8:19	110, 113, 114
8:20–22	29
8:21	29, 112, 124
8:21–22	124
8:22	29, 109, 111, 115, 124
9	29, 109
9:1	115, 124
9:1–7	29
9:2	29, 110, 114
9:2–3	113
9:2–6	112, 124
9:3	110, 111, 113
9:5	29
9:6	29, 110, 124
9:7	109, 115
9:8–17	29, 113, 115, 124
9:15	115
9:16	115
10	29
10:1	53
10:21–31	29
10:31	133
11	29
11:1–9	8, 24, 28, 29
11:10	53
11:10–32	31
11:10–25:18	31, 40
11:27	53
12	117
12–13	xiv, 14, 117
12–19	118
12–25	21, 31
12–36	21, 30, 31, 100
12–50	12
12:1	31, 43
12:1–3	31, 32, 35, 118
12:1–8	117
12:2	30
12:4	31
12:4–5	117
12:5	118
12:5a	31
12:7	117

12:9	118
12:10	62
12:10–20	31, 32, 35, 36, 118
12:16	76
12:20	76
13	33, 35, 118
13:1	118
13:2	118
13:3–4	118
13:5–12	118, 141
13:6	45, 48, 52
13:9	118
13:12	117
13:13	117, 118
13:14–17	31, 32, 118, 118
13:16	39
13:17	31
13:18	31, 117, 118, 120
14	32, 35
14:6	45
15	2, 32, 33, 35
15:1–21	31, 33, 35
15:7	40, 74
15:11	33
15:13	150
15:13–16	33
15:15	51
16	2, 32
16:10–14	35
17	2, 33, 35, 50, 51, 52
17:1	40, 50
17:1–26	50
17:7	33, 40
17:7–8	50
17:8	40, 143
17:10–14	33
17:15–21	33
17:17	34
17:18–20	35
17:19	332
17:20	33, 50, 51, 52
17:21	33
17:22	46, 50
18	32, 119, 120
18–19	xiv, 14, 32, 119
18:1	119, 120
18:1–9	119
18:2	119, 120
18:3	119
18:4–5	120
18:6	119, 120

18:9	119
18:9–15	33, 119
18:10	32
18:10–15	119
18:12–15	34
18:14	33
18:16	119
18:16–22	120
18:17–19	119
18:17–21	119
18:20–21	35, 119
18:22	119
18:23–33	119
18:23–19:38	120
19	33, 118, 120
19:1–19	119
19:1–25	120
19:13	119, 120
19:18	119
19:19	119, 120
19:24–25	119, 120
19:29	32, 35
20	32, 36
20:1–18	31, 35, 118
21	2, 32, 53
21:1	33
21:1–7	21, 33, 50
21:2	34
21:2a	34
21:2–4	35
21:3	33
21:4	33, 50, 52
21:5	33
21:6–7	33, 34
21:8	34, 35
21:22–34	34, 35, 36, 53
22	35, 53
22:1–19	34, 35
22:15–18	35
22:17	44
22:19	35
22:23	40
23	31, 34, 35, 51
23:1	34, 51
23:1–2	34, 50
23:2a	34
23:3–18	34
23:11	42
23:17	34
23:17–18	34
23:18	34
23:19–20	34, 50
23:20	34

Ref	Pages	Ref	Pages	Ref	Pages
24	32, 34, 35, 38, 53, 56, 57, 58, 59, 60	26:12–33	34, 36	29:30	40, 41
		26:17–22	36	29:31	41
		26:23–25	67, 143	29:31–30:24	37, 41, 49, 68
24–29	56	26:29	53		
24:1–29:14	38	26:34–35	33, 36, 37, 50, 58	29:32	41
24:1–67	34, 35, 54			29:33	41
24:5–8	54	26:35	53	29:35	41
24:7	35	27	38, 44, 57, 58, 59	30	43
24:15	40			30–33	48
24:15–27	71	27:1–40	37	30:1–2	49
24:24	40	27:4	38, 48	30:2	41
24:25	35	27:40	53	30:4	49
24:30	35	27:41–45	55	30:6	41
24:39–41	54	27:42–45	58	30:15	41
24:40b	35	27:46	56	30:16	49
24:47	40	27:46–28:9	50, 58	30:17	41
24:50	40	28	2, 38, 39, 47, 48	30:18	41
24:59	46	28:1–5	58	30:20	41
24:61	35	28:1–9	58	30:21	45
24:62–67	35	28:2	40, 58	30:22	41
24:62b	35	28:3	39, 40, 46, 50	30:23	41
25–35	57	28:4	143	30:25–31:54	37
25–36	21	28:5	40, 57, 58	30:25–43	42, 49
25:6	40	28:6	40, 58	30:28	42
25:7	51	28:8	58	30:31	42
25:7–11	53	28:9	33, 52, 58	30:43	42
25:7–18	50, 51	28:10	56	31	42
25:8	51	28:10–12	39	31:2	43
25:9	34, 47, 52	28:10–33:20	46	31:3	42, 43
25:12	53	28:13	31, 39, 46	31:4–16	42
25:12–18	33, 51, 52	28:13–15	39	31:6–7	43
25:16	51	28:13–17	38	31:11–13	43
25:17	51	28:14	31, 39, 46	31:13	42
25:19	53	28:14b–15	39	31:15	43
25:19–20	57	28:15	37	31:18	42, 43, 51, 53
25:19–26	53	28:18	46	31:19	46, 55
25:19–34	35, 36, 37, 57	28:18–19	39	31:19b	43
25:20	40, 51, 52	28:19	46	31:24	43
25:21	37, 45, 53, 57	28:20–21a	39	31:29	43
25:21–34	57	28:21b	39	31:30b	43
25:22	36	28:22	39	31:32–35	43
25:22–23	37	29	34, 37, 60	31:37	43
25:23	36, 53	29–30	92	31:38–40	43
25:24	36	29:1	37, 40, 60	31:41	42, 55
25:26b	53, 57	29:1–14	38, 40, 60	31:42b	43
25:27	53	29:2–12	71	31:44b	43
25:28	57	29:5	40, 60	31:45–53	43
25:34	53, 56	29:10	60	31:46	43
26	36, 53, 58	29:12–13	60	31:48–50	43
26:1–11	32, 36, 118	29:14–15	45, 57	31:49	42
26:1–33	37	29:15	40	31:51–53	43
26:2	36	29:15–30	41	31:53	53
26:3–5	36	29:24b	41	31:54	43

Genesis (*continued*)
32   44
32–33   36, 45, 53
32:2b–3 (NRSV 32:1b–2) 43
32:5 (NRSV 32:4)   45
32:8 (NRSV 32:7)   37
32:10 (NRSV 32:9)   53
32:10–13
  (NRSV 32:9–12)   44
32:12 (NRSV 32:11)   44
32:13 (NRSV 32:12)   44
32:14a (NRSV 32:13a)   44
32:15–16
  (NRSV 32:14–15)   37, 45
32:22b (NRSV 32:21b)   44
32:29 (NRSV 32:28)   46
33   45
33:4   44
33:10   44
33:11   44
33:12–17   44
33:12–20   45
33:14   45, 111
33:15   45
33:16–17   37
33:17   56
33:18   43, 46
33:19   56
34   45, 50, 52
34–36   37, 39, 48, 52
34:13   59
34:15   52
34:30   46
35   37, 45, 47, 50,
                           52, 92
35:1   38, 46, 54, 56
35:1–8   46, 50
35:1–29   50
35:2   55
35:2–4   54, 56
35:4   46
35:5   46
35:6   46
35:7   46
35:9   46, 50
35:9–13   38
35:9–15   45, 46, 50
35:11   39, 40, 50
35:11–12   38, 39
35:12   38, 39, 40, 46
35:13   50
35:15   46
35:16–21   46

35:16–26   50
35:16–29   46
35:21   54, 56
35:22b–26   46
35:27   34, 53
35:27–29   47, 50
35:28   51
35:29   48, 51, 52
35:29b   45
36   36, 45, 50
36:1   53
36:1–8   47, 48
36:5   47
36:6   45, 48
36:6–8   45, 47, 48, 52
36:7   47, 52, 143
36:8   48
36:9   47, 53
36:29–30   48
37   63, 64, 66
37–50   100
37:2   53
37:5–8   64
37:5–11   64
37:9–11   64
37:21–22a   66
37:22b   65, 66
37:23   67
37:27   65
37:28a*   65
37:29–30   65
37:36   65
38   63
38:1   64
38:8   63
38:14   63
38:14–16   64
39   65
39:1   65
39:2   65
39:3   66
39:5   65, 66
39:11   111
39:20   66
39:21   65
39:23   66
40–41   64
40:1   66
40:2   65
40:3   65, 66
40:4   65
40:5   65, 66
40:7   65, 66

40:15   66
41   62
41:10   65
41:12   65
41:14   66
41:25   62
41:28   62
41:34–57   66
41:38   62
41:40   64
41:40–44   54, 62
41:46   63
41:48   54, 62
41:54   66
41:54–57   66
41:55   54, 62
41:57   54, 62
42   66
42:1–3   63
42:6–25   66
42:22   64, 66
42:22b   64
42:23   66
42:24   68
42:27–28   66
42:35   66
42:37   64, 66
43:14   50, 66
43:30   68
44   64
44:1–2   67
44:6–12   67
44:27–31   68
45:1–15   67
45:2   67
45:3–4   67
45:5b–8   67
45:15   67
45:16   67
45:22   67
45:25   67
45:25–26   67
46   92
46:1   53, 67
46:5   67
46:6–7   67
46:6b   67
46:8–27   67, 68
46:15   51, 67
46:28   67
47   62
47:8   51
47:9   51, 143

47:14	62	3:10	73, 84	7:3	77
47:14–15	68	3:11–15	71, 73	7:4	76, 84
47:16–17	54, 62, 68	3:12	72	7:5	77
47:19	54, 68	3:13	71, 72, 73	7:7	70
47:19–20	54, 62, 68	3:14	72, 72	7:9	110
47:21	54, 68	3:15	72, 73	7:10	110
47:21–25	62	3:16	73	7:12	110
48:1–7	50, 62	3:17	73	7:13	74
48:3	50	3:18	73	7:15	73
48:7	51	3:18–22	73	7:15b	75
49	41, 68	3:21–22	75, 76, 148	7:16	84
49:1a	50, 52	3:22	75	7:17	73
49:23	59	4:1	72	7:17b*	75
49:25	108	4:1–5	73	7:18	110
49:29	52	4:5	73	7:19	108
49:29–33	50, 52	4:9	108	7:20b	75
49:30	34	4:10–13	70	7:21	110
49:33	51	4:13–16	73	7:22	75
50:7–14	62	4:17	74	7:23	75
50:10	59	4:18–26	74	7:23–24	75
50:15	59	4:20	73, 81	7:26 (NRSV 8:1)	84
50:25	148	4:27	146	8:3 (NRSV 8:7)	75, 109
50:26	67	4:27–28	73	8:11 (NRSV 8:15)	75, 77
		4:27–31	74	8:16 (NRSV 8:20)	84
Exodus		4:29–31	72, 73	8:28 (NRSV 8:32)	77
1	92	5:1	73, 84	9:1	84
1–2	69	5:5–19	74	9:7	77
1:1–7	70	5:6	70	9:12	75
1:1–14	69	5:10	70	9:13	84
1:5–6	70	5:13	70	9:14–16	148
1:7	109	5:20–23	74	9:22	109
1:7–9	100	6	8, 69	9:22–23a	75
1:8–14	70	6:1	74	9:23	73
1:9	70	6:2	71, 74	9:24a*	75
1:12	70	6:2–3	72	9:25	109
1:14	71	6:2–8	74	9:25a	75
1:15–22	70	6:2–9	74	9:34	77
2	34	6:4	143	9:35a	75
2:1–10	70	6:4–5	74, 88	10:3	84
2:11–15a	70	6:6	74	10:12	109
2:11–25	70	6:7	148	10:12–13a	75
2:23–25	69, 71	6:8	74	10:13	73
2:24	88	6:13	74, 148	10:15	109, 111
3	8, 69, 73	6:13–20	74	10:15a*	75
3–4	71	6:14–25	70	10:15b	75
3:1	71	6:20	70	10:19	78
3:4	71	6:26	76	10:20	75
3:6	71, 73	6:26–27	74	10:21	59
3:7	70, 73, 76,	6:27	148	10:21–22	108
	83, 84	6:28–30	74	10:21–23	75
3:7–10	71	6:29	148	10:27	75
3:8	73	7	8	10:29	148
3:9–10	73	7:1	74	11:1	75

Exodus (*continued*)

11:1–3	75	15:26	82	20:1–23:33	86
11:3b	75	15:27	80	20:18–21	83, 86
11:4–5	75	16	2, 82	20:19	85
11:4–8	75	16:1	80	20:21	85
11:9–10	75	16:2–3	93	23:31	78
12:14	149	16:3	83	23:32	88
12:17	76, 149, 150	16:4–5	82	24:1	83, 85
12:28	76, 149, 150	16:7	90	24:1–2	85
12:29–32	75	16:10	90	24:1–11	85, 87
12:29–39	76	16:12	82, 93	24:3	84, 143
12:31	76	16:21–22	82	24:3–8	83, 85
12:35–36	75, 76, 148	16:28–31	82	24:6	85
12:36	75	16:30	111	24:7	84, 85
12:37a	76, 148	17:1	80	24:7–8	88
12:38	94	17:1–7	81	24:8	85
12:40–41a	76	17:1ab*	81	24:9–11	83, 85
12:40–51	76	17:3	81	24:10–11	85
12:41b	76	17:6	81	24:12–14	83
12:42–51	76	17:7	81	24:12–15a	83
12:51	76	17:8	81	24:14	83
13:17–14:31	76	17:8–16	81	24:15	83, 87
13:1–16	76	17:9	73, 81	24:16–17	90
13:21–22	93	17:9–13	81	25	89
14	29, 123, 124	17:10	152	25–30	88
14:1–4	76	17:12	152	25–31	87, 88, 91
14:2	78, 125	17:14–16	81	25–40	91, 92, 93
14:4	77	18	83	25:8	81, 86, 87
14:5	77	18:1–27	80	25:9	88
14:8	77	18:5	146	25:22	81, 87, 88, 90
14:16	108	18:5–11	81	25:40	88
14:17–18	77	18:13–27	81	26:33	108
14:20	108, 124	19–Num 10	25	29:42	88
14:21	78	19	2, 83, 86	29:43	88
14:29	108	19–24	8, 87, 105	30–31	88
14:30	78	19:1–2	83, 87, 143	30:6	88
14:31	82	19:1–2a	80	30:36	88
15:1–12	79	19:2	80, 83	31:16	88
15:1–18	24, 77, 79	19:3	70, 86	32–34	83, 87
15:5	108	19:3–6	84, 86	32:7–14	155
15:8	108	19:3–25	86	32:17	152
15:14–15	79	19:3–24:11	86	33:7	91
15:17	79	19:5	86, 88	33:7–11	94
15:19	79	19:5–6	84, 86	34	83, 87, 88
15:19–21	79	19:8	84, 85	34:10	107
15:20–21	79	19:12	86	34:10–28	83
15:22	78	19:12–13	86	34:21	111
15:22–26	81	19:16	86	35–40	88
15:22a	80	19:17	85, 86	40	7, 8
15:22a*	80, 81, 82	19:18	86	40:2	90
15:22ab*	80	19:19	86	40:17	90
15:24	81, 93	19:20	83, 85	40:34	87
15:25b–26	82, 150	19:20–24	86	40:34–35	90, 92
		20	23	40:36	90

40:36–38	87, 93	10:33–34	93	14:44b–45	96
40:38	24, 87	10:34	88	14:45	96
		10:35–36	93	15:1–41	94
Leviticus		11	80, 82, 93,	16:1–50	94
2:13	88		94, 96	16:13	150
2:17	90	11:1–3	94	16:19	90
8–9	87	11:4	94, 148	16:30	107
9:23	90	11:4–6	82	16:35	95
9:24	95	11:5	110	17:1–19:22	94
10:2	95	11:11	95	17:7 (NRSV 16:42)	90
11:36	108	11:12	95	20:1	91, 94
11:44	110	11:13	95	20:2–13	94
11:46	110	11:14	95	20:8	96
20:25	110	11:16	91, 94, 95	20:14–21	94
24:8	88	11:17	59	20:22	91, 94
25	93, 100	11:18	95	20:23–29	94
25:30	34	11:19–23	95	20:24	51
26	88	11:24	91, 94, 95	21:1–3	94
27:19	34	11:24–30	95	21:4	78, 91, 94
		11:26	91, 94	21:4–9	94
Numbers		11:31	95	21:5	150
1	92	11:31–33	94	21:10–20	91, 94
1–10	90, 91, 92, 93,	11:33	82, 94, 95	21:21–35	94
	94, 95, 105	11:35	91, 94	22:1	91, 94
1–24	7	12	94	22:4	111
1:1	90	12:16	91, 94	25–36	97
1:1–10:28	91	13	92	25:6–15	149
1:5–16	95	13:1–2a	92	26	92
2	92	13:3a	96	27:13	51
3:1	53	13:3b–17a	96	31:2	51
7	92	13:17b–33	96	33:1–49	91
9:15–23	93	13:26	91	33:10	78
9:15–10:34	9	13:33	132	33:11	78
9:22–23	93	14:1b	96	34	92
9:23	93	14:2	150	34:16–29	92
10	92	14:6	96		
10:11	93	14:7	42	**Deuteronomy**	
10:11–28	90	14:10	90, 96	1–3	96
10:12	87, 88, 91	14:11–25	96	1:9–18	95, 96
10:12–28	91, 95	14:21	90	1:19–45	96
10:13	93	14:25	78	1:31	95
10:13–28	91	14:26–35	96	1:40	78
10:14–16	90	14:27	96	2:1	78
10:14–28	88	14:30	96	4	96
10:17	88, 90	14:35	96	4:5–8	85
10:18–20	90	14:36	96	4:6–8	98
10:21	91	14:36–38	96	4:9	98
10:22–24	90	14:37	96	4:11	108
10:25–27	90	14:38	96	4:18	110
10:28	89	14:39	96	4:32	108
10:29–32	93	14:40	96	4:41	108
10:29–36	93	14:41–44a	96	5:3	86
10:33	88	14:44	93	5:5	86

Deuteronomy (*continued*)

5:11	85
5:23	108
7	45
7:6	84
8:7	108
10:8	93, 108
11:10	111
11:15	109
11:26–28	98
12–26	98
14:2	84
14:13	109
14:14	109
14:15	109
14:18	109
14:19	109
19:2	108
19:7	108
25:5–10	63
26	84
26:5	55, 56
26:16–18	98
26:16–19	84
26:17	84
26:18	84
26:18–19	84
28:29	59
29:21	108
29:29	98
30:6	98
30:11–14	98
30:15	98
30:19–20	98
31:9	93
31:25	93
31:26	93
32:2	108, 109, 110
32:33	110
32:50	58
33	92
33:13	108
34:1	77
34:7–9	77
34:8	59

Joshua

4:22	108
13–14	21
18–19	91
18:1	91
19:51	91
24:14	46
24:23	46
24:32	68

Judges

5:5	83
5:18	58
11:16	78
16:16	58

Ruth

4:18	53

1 Samuel

2:16	58
2:22	91
2:27–36	57
3:3	91
6:5	110
6:11	110
14:47	55
17–18	29
17:46	110
20:4	58
24	17

2 Samuel

5:1	57
8:12–14	55
11–20	106
16:5–8	xv
17	17
19:13–14 (NRSV 19:12–13)	57
19:35 (NRSV 19:34)	51

1 Kings

5:13 (NRSV 4:33)	110
6:1	150
7:47	42
8:4	91
8:9	83
8:53	108
9:26	78
11:14–17	55
14:21	14
15:1–2	14
15:9–10	14
15:15	14
15:33	14
17:1	71
19:8	83
21:2	111
22:42	14

2 Kings

8:17	14
8:20–22	53
8:26	14
10:4	42
11:18	110
11:21	14
14:2	14
14:21	14
15:2	14
15:33	14
16:2	14
16:10	110
18:2	14
19:26	108, 109, 111
21:1	14
21:19	14
22:1	14
23:31	14
23:36	14
24:8	14
24:18	14

1 Chronicles

1:29	53
29:28	51

2 Chronicles

1:19	39
5:10	83
20:25	59
36:16	59

Ezra

8:27	59

Nehemiah

9:13	83

Esther

2:17	61
9:22	59
10:3	61

Job

5:14	59
5:22	110
7:12	26, 110
9:13	26
12:10	109
12:25	59
13:3	40
16:9	59

Reference	Page	Reference	Page	Reference	Page
26:6–13	26, 98, 129	18:18	111	37:25	56
30:21	59	22:10	111	42:6	59
38:1–30	98	23:3	58	47:9	109, 110
38:4–38	26, 129	23:6	58	47:10	109, 110
				48	92, 93, 100

Psalms

Ecclesiastes

Daniel

Reference	Page	Reference	Page	Reference	Page
19:2 (NRSV 19:1)	108	6:3	51	2:48	61
37:2	111			5:29	61
39:7 (NRSV 39:6)	110			10:7	59

Isaiah

Reference	Page	Reference	Page	Reference	Page
55:3	59	13:14	110	10:16	110
55:4	59	15:6	111	12:3	108
58:5 (NRSV 58:4)	110	22:11	108		
66:6	108	27:1	110		

Hosea

Reference	Page	Reference	Page	Reference	Page
68:9 (NRSV 68:8)	83	37:27	111	1:9	72
68:18 (NRSV 68:17)	83	40:18	110	2:18	110
69:35 (NRSV 69:34)	110	50:2	110	12	21, 47, 50, 54, 55
73:20	110	51:9	110	12:1	59
74:12–17	26	51:9–10	26	12:13 (NRSV 12:11)	56
74:13	110	60:20	59		
74:16	109	63:11–12	21		

Amos

Jeremiah

Reference	Page	Reference	Page	Reference	Page
79:2	110			1:11	55
89:12	107	1:2–3	14	2:10	21
89:47	107	2:31	59	3:1	21
90:8	109	3:17	108	4:13	107
90:10	51	7:3	86	5:26	110
91:13	110	7:7	86	7:2	109
103:22	109	15:1	21	7:9	21
104	98, 129	25:1	14	9:7	21
104:5–30	26	25:3	14		
104:20	110	28:1	14		

Jonah

Reference	Page	Reference	Page	Reference	Page
104:25	110	28:3	39	1:9	108
104:30	107	32:1	14	1:13	108
105:29	110	33:26	21	2:10	108
105:30	109	36:1	14		
106:19	83	36:9	14		

Micah

Reference	Page	Reference	Page	Reference	Page
106:20	109	39:1–2	14	4:8	21
107:26	108	48:4	39	6:4	21
114:2	109	50:9	39		
119	85				

Ezekiel

Haggai

Reference	Page	Reference	Page	Reference	Page
135:6	108			1:1	14
136:8	109	7:20	110	1:15	14
136:9	109	8–11	92	2:10	14
137:7–9	48, 55	16:17	110		

Zechariah

Reference	Page	Reference	Page	Reference	Page
145:13	109	23:14	110	1:1	14
148:5	107	28:25	56	1:7	14
148:7	110	29:3	110	7:1	14
148:10	110	29:4	110	7:2	54
150:1	108	29:5	110		
		32:2	110		

Proverbs

Malachi

Reference	Page	Reference	Page	Reference	Page
8:22–31	26, 98, 129	32:4	110		
8:27	108	32:8	109	3:22	83
15:17	111	34:28	110	4:4	21

	Judith		**Sirach (Ecclesiasticus)**	
2:4	61	44:16	xv
11:21	61	49:16	xv
12:16	61		

Author Index

Alter, Robert, 63, 74, 157
Astruc, Jean, 2, 3, 4, 6, 16, 157
Auld, Graeme, 89, 157

Bacon, B. W., 79
Bartlett, J. R., 48, 157
Ben Zvi, Ehud, 20, 95, 157, 160, 161
Blenkinsopp, Joseph, 3, 26, 34, 87, 91, 157
Blum, Erhard, xi, 13, 26, 34, 35, 36, 37, 38, 39, 45, 56, 68, 71, 87, 157, 160, 162
Boadt, Lawrence, 20, 157
Boorer, Suzanne, 21, 157
Braulik, Georg, 15, 158
Brodie, Thomas L., 57, 157
Brueggemann, Walter, 33, 43, 50, 54, 132, 157
Budd, Philip J., 80, 97, 157

Campbell, Antony F., 2, 6, 15, 16, 21, 43, 48, 64, 67, 69, 76, 80, 88, 95, 97, 106, 123, 132, 142, 146, 148, 157, 158, 160
Carr, David M., 64, 158
Childs, Brevard S., 69, 70, 71, 72, 74, 75, 76, 77, 78, 79, 80, 81, 82, 83, 84, 85, 87, 88, 148, 150, 152, 158
Clanchy, M. T., 17, 158
Coats, George W., 62, 64, 90, 158, 159

Cross, Frank M., 22, 23, 161

Dalley, Stephanie, 17, 158
Dicou, Bert, 48, 158
Diebner, B., 57, 158
Durham, John I., 69, 70, 71, 76, 79, 80, 83, 85, 87, 88, 152, 158

Egnotovich, Stephanie, ix
Eichrodt, Walther, 92, 158
Einstein, Albert, vi
Ellis, Peter F., 19, 158
Emerton, J. A., 63

Feynman, Richard, 93, 100, 158
Frerichs, Ernest S., 7, 159
Fretheim, Terence E., 71, 76, 84, 85, 158
Friedman, Richard E., 1, 159
Frye, Northrop, vi, 4, 158

Gerstenberger, Erhard, 89, 100, 158
Gertz, J. C., 19, 20, 26, 33, 34, 62, 67, 69, 71, 76, 87, 90, 157, 158, 160, 161
Gese, Hartmut, 92, 158
Graf, Karl Heinrich, 4
Greene, Brian, 18, 158
Groß, Walter, 15, 158
Gunkel, Hermann, 16, 17, 20, 42, 62, 141, 158

Ha, John, 33, 159
Hahn, Herbert F., 3, 159
Hummel, Horace D., 3, 159
Hyatt, J. Philip, 5, 159

Ilgen, Karl David, 21

Johnstone, W., 80, 159
Josipovici, Gabriel, vi

Kitchen, Kenneth, 34, 159
Knierim, Rolf, xv, 80, 90, 159
Knight, Douglas A., 3, 159
Kohata, Fujiko, 69, 76, 159
Kolarcik, Michael, 67
Kratz, Reinhard, 1, 159
Kraus, Hans Joachim, 3, 21, 159
Krieger, Martin, 96, 159
Kuenen, Abraham, 82
Kugler, R. A., 89, 157, 159, 160
Kuhn, Thomas S., 18, 159

Lemaire, André, 18, 159
Levenson, Jon D., 1, 7, 159
Levin, Christoph, xiv, 19, 159
Levine, Baruch A., 7, 89, 91, 159
Lohfink, Norbert, 15, 21, 82, 84, 150,
    158, 159

Macchi, J.-D., 36, 44, 45, 57, 157, 159,
    161
Macholz, C., 34, 157
Marx, Alfred, 36, 159
Maxwell, James C., 96
Mayes, A. D. H., 63, 159
McEvenue, Sean, 15, 158
Meinhold, A., 61, 159
Miller, Patrick D., 106

Neusner, Jacob, 7, 159
Nicholson, Ernest W., 3, 85, 160
Niditch, Susan, 17, 18, 160
Noth, Martin, 21, 22, 29, 35, 36, 39, 42,
    43, 45, 48, 56, 66, 69, 70, 74, 76, 77,
    78, 79, 80, 81, 82, 83, 84, 86, 88, 89,
    90, 91, 95, 97, 108, 109, 123, 132,
    141, 146, 148, 152, 154, 155, 160,
    162

O'Brien, Mark A., 2, 21, 43, 64, 67, 69,
    76, 80, 88, 96, 97, 123, 132, 142, 146,
    148, 158, 160
Olson, Dennis, 90, 160
Otto, Eckhart, 87, 160

Perdue, Leo G., 18, 159
Pliny, Gaius, vi
Propp, William H. C., 71, 76, 160
Pury, Albert de, 47, 55, 160

Rad, Gerhard von, 19, 20, 56, 84, 120,
    160
Redford, Donald, 54, 61, 64, 66, 68, 160
Rendsburg, Gary, 57, 160
Rendtorff, Rolf, 4, 34, 43, 84, 89, 112,
    157, 159, 160
Ricoeur, Paul, 8, 160
Roberts, J. J. M., 106
Rofé, Alexander, 34, 53, 56, 57, 160
Rogerson, John, 3, 160
Römer, Thomas, 20, 21, 31, 33, 36, 56,
    87, 89, 97, 157, 159, 160, 161
Rothschild, Babette, vi
Rudolph, Wilhelm, 66

Sanders, James A., 17
Schama, Simon, 19, 160
Schmid, Hans Heinrich, 19, 160
Schmid, Konrad, 19, 44, 62, 67, 68, 72,
    158, 160, 161
Schmidt, Werner H., 68, 72, 161
Schmitt, Hans Christoph, 64, 161
Schult, H., 57, 158
Scullion, John, 33, 34, 161
Seebass, Horst, 29, 39, 41, 43, 45, 54, 56,
    91, 141, 161
Simon, Richard, 2, 3, 4, 161
Ska, Jean Louis, 20, 56, 57, 84, 161
Soggin, J. Alberto, 20, 56, 62, 161
Stegemann, E., 34, 157
Sweeney, Marvin A., 20, 95, 157, 160,
    161

Talmon, Shemaryahu, 23, 161
Thucydides, 113
Tucker, Gene M., 3, 159

Van Seters, John, 3, 19, 36, 56, 80, 161
Veijola, Timo, 34
Vervenne, M., 68, 69, 80, 84, 87, 159, 160, 161, 162

Weimar, Peter, 69, 73, 161
Wellhausen, Julius, xiv, 3, 4, 9, 12, 64, 77, 81, 82, 87, 112, 161, 162
Wénin, A., 31, 162
Westermann, Claus, 20, 21, 26, 33, 34, 41, 42, 43, 44, 45, 48, 63, 64, 66, 120, 132, 133, 141, 143, 162

Wevers, John W., 92, 162
Whybray, R. Norman, 3, 13, 162
Williamson, Hugh G. M., 1, 159
Wilson, Robert R., 14, 162
Winnett, F. V., 56, 162
Witte, Markus, 19, 26, 158, 162
Witter, Hennig Bernhard, 2
Wolff, Hans Walter, 55, 162
Wynn-Williams, Damian, 35, 38, 39, 162

Zimmerli, Walther, 92, 162

Subject Index

Aaron, 51, 69, 70, 71, 73, 74, 75, 94, 95, 96, 147, 149, 150, 154
Abel, 28, 130, 131
Abimelech, 32, 34, 36, 140
Abraham, xv, 2, 7, 21, 22, 30, 31–40, 43–60, 68, 71, 74, 103, 117–20, 128, 134–37, 140, 141
Abraham cycle, 7, 31–36, 47, 49, 50, 53, 134
Abraham, Isaac, and Jacob, 21, 30, 52, 56, 59, 60, 71, 74, 103
absence of P
  from Genesis 1–11, 11–12, 107–15
  from Genesis as a whole, 12–15, 115
Accordance 5.7, 9
Adam, xv, 28, 29, 111, 112, 130, 131
Adam: splendor of, xv
age(s), 14, 31, 51, 57, 60, 63, 89, 135, 139, 149
ages (and dates), 13, 14, 15
all the families of the earth, 38, 50, 101
all-holy God, 28, 124
Ammon, 48, 118
analysis, xiv, 4, 7, 11, 20, 63, 69, 72, 75, 79, 87, 88, 90, 96, 97, 107, 127, 132, 136, 141, 152
analyze, 17, 79, 110, 123, 133
ancestral traditions
  discordances present, 52–60

  overall, 30–60
  presented biblically, 30–52
ancient storyteller(s), 12, 17, 65, 67, 117
anti-Semitism, 3, 16
Ark Narrative, 106

Babel, 29, 30, 133
base for
  operations, 6, 8, 24
  storytellers, xiii, 17, 42
  users, xiii, xiv, 6, 11, 12
Beer-sheba, 36, 56, 67, 143
bellringers, 96
Benjamin (son of Jacob), 41, 48
Bethel, 31, 32, 37, 38, 39, 40, 42, 43, 45, 46, 47, 49, 52, 54, 56, 117, 118, 139, 140
biblical presentation in Gen 12–36, 30
Bilhah, 41, 49, 55, 140, 143
birthright, 36, 37, 44, 53, 139
boundaries and human living, 24, 28, 30, 84
brevity of text, 12, 15, 16, 17, 25, 124
burial of
  Abraham, 34, 47, 51, 53, 136
  Isaac, 47
  Jacob, 68, 143
  Sarah, 34, 51, 136

Cain, 28, 129, 130, 131
call of Moses, 7, 8, 74, 149, 153
Canaan, 32, 34, 42, 43, 46, 47, 48, 49,
    51, 55, 56, 62, 63, 67, 74, 79, 96,
    97, 118, 135, 136, 139, 141, 142,
    143, 150
canonical (and scriptural) status, 7, 16,
    17, 19, 61
cave near En-gedi, 17
challenge in Deuteronomy, 98, 99, 100
choice, 16, 17, 18, 59, 103, 104, 119
choose, xiii, 5, 12, 13, 16, 17, 42, 45, 79
Chronicles, 3, 14
circumcision, 33, 50, 51, 52, 136, 141,
    147
composers: music and performance, 6
condensed base text, 17
congregation (of the people), 80, 90, 94,
    96, 154
continuity, 2, 4, 20, 23, 25, 37, 90, 112,
    150
continuous sources. *See* sources:
    continuous
contradictory, 6, 16, 125
copying of manuscripts, 18, 19, 23
core insight, 17–18
covenant, 2, 29, 33, 43, 44, 50, 51, 71,
    74, 83, 84, 85, 86, 88, 93, 97, 124,
    136, 152
creation accounts, multiple, 2, 8, 26, 27,
    98, 110, 111, 112, 128, 129
crossing of the Sea, 29, 76, 77, 78, 108

Daniel, 61, 62, 110
dates (and ages), 11, 14, 15
David's supporters, xv, 106
Decalogue, 8, 83, 87, 152
deliverance at the Sea, 76, 77, 78, 79,
    123, 125, 146, 149
deliverance from Egypt, 76, 81, 100, 125,
    153
dense final text, 17
descendants (offspring, seed), 28, 31, 32,
    33, 36, 38, 39, 40, 47, 48, 50, 51,
    54, 63, 70, 99, 109, 111, 112, 132,
    135, 136, 137, 140, 141, 149
destiny of Israel, 30, 34, 100, 101, 105
detour around Edom, 94, 97, 154

Deuteronomistic History, 19, 23, 97, 98,
    106
Deuteronomy, 3, 7, 8, 21, 24, 85, 91, 97,
    98, 99, 100, 108, 111, 146, 148
Diaspora literature, xv, 60, 61, 62
Dinah, 41, 45, 52, 140
discordance in Gen 12–36, 30, 52
discordances, 30, 52, 59, 60
discordances about ancestors, 52–60
discordances, four areas
    late Joseph story, 53, 54
    late links between Isaac and Jacob, 52,
        53–54
    no Isaac cycle, 52, 53
    problems for a single family, 53, 54
divine name(s), 4, 5, 6, 13, 14, 19, 20,
    39, 41, 42, 81, 146
Documentary Hypothesis, 1, 2, 3, 5, 7, 18
documentary sources, xiii, 48, 64, 68
doubt and dissatisfaction, 2, 3
dramatists: actors and text, 6
dream experience, 39, 40
dream(s), 43, 54, 61, 64, 65, 66, 67, 139
duality, 2, 24, 33, 69, 77, 79, 97, 124, 133

E, xv, 3, 21, 42, 65, 69, 71, 74, 97, 148, 152
editors and users: skillful and intelligent,
    xiv, 4, 13, 18, 23, 70, 77
Edom, 36, 48, 53, 55, 56, 79, 91, 94, 96,
    97, 154
Egypt(ians), xiv, xv, 7, 24, 31, 32, 35, 54,
    55, 60–78, 81, 83, 84, 85, 90, 100,
    117, 118, 123, 124, 125, 136, 137,
    142, 143, 146, 147, 148, 149, 150,
    153
El Shaddai, etc., 15, 31, 33–40, 46, 47,
    48, 50–52, 59, 66, 74, 136, 140, 143
elohim, 1, 2, 4, 5, 6, 13, 20, 33, 38, 39,
    41, 42, 50, 71, 86, 131, 132, 139,
    146, 151
Elohist, xiii, 2, 3, 8, 19, 21, 41, 42, 75
enhancement(s), 9, 28, 31, 36, 37, 39,
    40, 42, 45, 64–67, 71–76, 79, 81,
    82, 83, 94, 95, 96, 131, 137, 139,
    143, 146–54
Enoch, xv, 131
enrichment(s), 9, 31, 32, 33, 34, 69
Ephraim, 51, 52, 68, 92, 143

Ephraim and Manasseh. *See* Ephraim;
　　Manasseh
Esau, 33, 35, 36, 37, 44, 45, 47–53,
　　55–59, 139, 140, 141
Esther, 61, 62
Eve, 130
exodus from Egypt, 71–76
Exodus Narrative (ExN), 8, 69, 71,
　　74–79, 82, 83, 84, 86, 93, 146, 147,
　　148, 150
Exodus passages
　　15　　　8, 24, 77, 79
　　19–24　　8, 86, 87, 105, 152
　　25–31　　87, 88, 91
　　32–34　　83, 87, 152
　　35–40　　87, 88, 91
expand, xiii, 9, 11, 12, 16, 17, 18, 24, 43,
　　60, 93, 96, 119
expand not expound, 16, 17
expansion(s), 12, 17, 18, 19, 25, 29, 39,
　　40, 42, 43, 67, 69, 73, 86, 88, 104,
　　132, 137, 140, 143, 150
explorers, 1, 2
expound, 16, 17
Ezra–Nehemiah, 14

faith claim, etc., 24, 27, 93, 99, 105, 106,
　　115, 123, 124, 125, 128
far-from-holy humankind, 27, 28
final text, xv, 6, 9, 16, 17, 35, 44, 60, 90,
　　104, 118, 121, 134
finding God rather than revealing God,
　　60, 106
flight and return (Jacob), 47, 55
flood, 2, 29, 111, 112, 113, 115, 124,
　　128, 131, 132
flood text, xiv, 11, 12, 15, 28, 29, 79,
　　107–15, 123, 124, 131, 132
foreign gods, 46, 54, 55, 56
fragment, 132, 151, 152
Fragmentary Hypothesis, xiii, 2
fragmentation, 2, 4, 8, 20, 23, 64, 96, 133
functions (of the text), 7, 14, 69

genealogy, etc., 11–15, 29, 30, 31, 41,
　　111, 112, 131, 132
Genesis One: as ideal, 7, 8, 24, 26, 27,
　　30, 97, 98, 99, 100, 115, 128, 129

Genesis passages
　　1–11　　xiv, 11, 12, 26, 30, 40, 100,
　　　　　　107, 111, 115, 128
　　1 (One)　7, 8, 11, 12, 24, 26–28, 30,
　　　　　　87, 97, 98, 99, 107–15,
　　　　　　128, 130
　　2–4　　　8, 28, 30
　　5–10　　　28–29
　　5:1–2　　　111–112
　　6–9　　　123–24
　　12–36　　21, 30–52, 52–60, 100
　　12–13　　xiv, 117
　　18–19　　xiv, 32, 119
　　24　　　32, 34, 38, 53, 54, 56–60
　　27　　　38, 58–59
　　34–36　　37, 39, 48, 52
　　37–50　　64, 100
　　46–50　　143
Gerar, 32, 35, 36, 136, 140
gift of
　　God's presence, 100
　　land, 31, 38, 39, 40, 56
　　law, 83, 85, 100, 105, 151, 152
　　Torah, 83
"glory of the LORD," 87, 90, 92, 96
God, 1, 4, 9, 13, 24, 26, 27, 28, 29,
　　31–40, 42–47, 49, 50, 54, 55, 56,
　　59, 60, 62, 64, 65, 66, 67, 69–88,
　　99, 100, 106, 111, 112, 113, 115,
　　117–20, 123–25, 128, 129, 130,
　　132, 133, 134, 136, 140, 146, 147,
　　148, 150, 151, 154, 155
Greek symbols, 9, 127
guidance, 78, 87, 93, 98, 100

Hamlet, 62
Haran, 38, 44, 54, 55, 56, 60, 135, 141
harden (heart), 69, 74, 75, 77, 147, 149
hearing preferred: Clanchy, 17
Hebron, 31, 34, 54, 56, 68, 118, 136,
　　140
hermeneutic(al) markers, 13, 20, 147
historical-critical, 5
history/historian(s)/historical, 3, 5, 8, 9,
　　10, 19, 33, 42, 49, 55, 59, 62, 63,
　　78, 83, 89, 91, 92, 93, 103, 104,
　　105, 129
holy nation, 84, 86

Hosea, 12, 21, 47, 54, 55
house in Bahurim, 17
household gods, 43, 55
humanity, stories of
    Babel, 29, 30
    Cain and Abel, 28, 130
    Flood, 28, 29, 123, 124, 128, 131, 148
    Garden (of Eden), 28, 29, 129, 130
    Lamech, 28, 129, 130, 131

ideal. *See* Genesis One: as ideal
identity and diversity, 15, 50, 56
inequality of human life, 28, 130
institutional infrastructure, 6
interweaving, 15, 78, 124
intimacy, 28, 31, 86
Isaac, 21, 22, 30, 32–40, 42, 43, 46–54,
    56–60, 71, 74, 103, 119, 135, 136,
    137, 139, 140, 141
Ishmael(ites), 32, 33, 34, 35, 47, 48, 50,
    51, 52, 53, 55, 58, 59, 65, 135, 136,
    140, 141, 142
itineraries
    pre-Sanctuary Narrative, 80, 81, 94, 105
    Sanctuary Narrative, 79, 80, 81, 94,
        145
itinerary, 60, 79, 80, 81, 91, 93, 94, 105,
    117, 154

J, xv, 3, 8, 16, 19, 20, 21, 26, 42, 64, 65,
    71, 76, 77, 78, 80, 81, 83, 86, 97,
    105, 107–10, 113, 152
Jabbok, 44, 47, 49, 139
Jacob, xv, 7, 21, 22, 30, 33, 35, 36–60,
    62, 63, 64, 66–71, 74, 103, 137,
    139, 140, 141, 143
Jacob cycle, 7, 35, 36–50, 53, 54, 55, 137
Jacob, variant versions of
    birthing and naming of sons, 37, 38
    gaining of wealth, 37, 42
    parting from Laban, 37, 42–43
    meeting with Esau, 37, 44–45
JE, 3, 19, 76, 77, 82
Jehovist, 3, 77
Jethro, 71, 80, 81, 147
Joseph, 41, 51, 54, 60–68, 70, 92, 148
Joseph story, xv, 7, 8, 49, 53, 60–65, 67,
    68, 143, 153

Joshua, 21, 22, 81, 96, 149, 152
Judah (son of Jacob), 41, 63, 64–68,
    143
Judah (tribe, nation), 14, 21, 90, 92
Judith, 61, 62

Laban, 37, 40, 42, 43, 44, 45, 48, 49, 55,
    57, 58, 60, 139, 140
land, 31–38, 40, 42, 43, 46, 47, 51, 54,
    56, 60, 62, 63, 66, 67, 68, 73, 74,
    76, 78, 90, 91, 94, 95, 96, 108, 113,
    118, 136, 139, 152, 154
Leah, 40, 41, 49, 52, 139
less-than-perfect world, etc., 29, 35, 112
Leviticus, 24, 86–90, 94, 95, 100, 108,
    109, 110
limits of modern scholar, 23
literacy, 18
literary industry, 18, 19, 23
Lot, 31, 32, 33, 35, 45, 48, 50, 52, 53,
    117, 118, 119, 120, 135, 136, 141

Macbeth, 62
Manasseh, 51, 52, 68, 90, 92, 143
manna, 82, 94, 148, 149
markers. *See* hermeneutic(al) markers
meal on the mountain, 83, 85, 152
meaning (to be recovered), 2, 7, 22, 25,
    41, 48, 49, 72, 91, 93, 100, 101,
    129, 132, 147
men's outer world, 42, 50
Midian, 70, 71, 72, 73, 146, 147, 150
Midianites, 65, 142
midwives, 69, 70, 150
mindless mutilation, 22
Moab, 48, 96, 118, 135
modern scholar(ship), 11, 12, 23, 78
Moses, xiv, xv, 2, 7, 8, 21, 22, 24, 51,
    69–82, 84–90, 93–97, 100, 124,
    125, 146, 147, 149, 150–55
Mount Seir. *See* Seir
music. *See* composers: music and
    performance

Nahor, 40, 60, 137
name of God, 13, 71–73
naming of Jacob's sons, 41
narrative thread, 8, 35, 37, 79, 140

nature of the text, 8, 16, 17, 100, 103, 104, 123

Noah, 28, 29, 111, 112, 131, 132

notes or texts: Niditch, 17

Numbers, xiv, 7, 24, 79, 87–93, 95, 97, 98, 105, 109, 127, 148

Numbers passages
1–10   90–95, 105
25–36   97
33   91

objectivity, myth of, 4, 23

option(s)/optional, 6, 7, 9, 11–18, 20, 24, 25, 29, 31, 35, 42, 43, 44, 45, 53, 63, 64, 65, 71, 79, 103, 104, 120, 121, 130, 132, 150, 151

options preserved, 7, 25

options and variants, 11, 12, 15, 16, 103, 104

originating myth, 105

P, 3, 4, 5, 6, 8, 11, 12, 13, 15, 16, 19, 26, 43, 45, 48, 76, 80, 81, 82, 97, 105, 107–15, 152

P/Priestly (document, editing)
general, xiii, 2, 3, 5, 21, 25
Genesis One, 11, 12, 107–11, 115
Genesis One and P flood, 11, 12, 110, 112–15
Genesis 1–11, xiv, 11, 12, 107–15
Genesis as a whole, 11, 12, 26, 115
Pentateuch, xiii, 4, 8, 15, 19

Paddan-aram, 43, 46, 51, 57, 139

paradigm, 1, 6, 9, 12, 15–19, 23, 24, 103, 104

Passover, 75, 76, 77, 79, 124, 146, 149, 150

pedantry, 3

Pentateuch
originating myth, 105
pondering present, 9, 103, 104, 105
remembering past, 9, 103, 104, 105

pentateuchal traditions: impact in OT, 21–22

performance of story, 5, 7, 11, 16, 17, 19

plague(s), 8, 68, 69, 73, 74, 75, 76, 79, 94, 96, 109, 124, 146, 147, 149

plausibility in narrative, 20, 42

political failure and theological thought, 99

pondering the present, 9, 103, 104, 105

possibility, xiii, 4, 5, 6, 12, 16, 18, 19, 22, 23, 24, 26, 27, 43, 45, 48, 60, 63, 66, 71, 72, 77, 79, 92, 93, 97, 98, 103, 112, 128, 142, 143

possible does not equal necessary, 4, 14, 20, 22, 54, 66, 75, 88

postexilic, 26, 34, 56, 57, 58, 84, 89, 100, 150

priestly attribution, 13–15

priestly circles, material, etc., xv, 5, 15, 80, 89, 92, 94, 96, 100

Priestly Code, 3

Priestly Document, etc. See under P/Priestly

priestly kingdom, 84, 86

Priestly Writer, 3, 8, 15, 111, 115

prolegomena, 9, 10

Prophetic Record, 106

quail, 82, 94, 95, 148, 154

quest for history, 5

Qumran, 19, 23

Rachel, 40, 41, 46, 49, 55, 60, 64, 139

radically new, xiii, xiv, 17–18

reader(s), xiii, 6, 9, 17, 20, 30, 34, 71, 72, 74, 124, 128

Rebekah, 8, 34, 37, 38, 49, 52, 53, 54, 56–60, 137, 139, 140

Rebekah material, 8, 38, 52, 59

reception in ancient Israel, xv

reconciliation, 37, 44, 45, 61, 64, 67, 68, 142

Red/Reed Sea text, xiv, 8, 24, 29, 76–80, 108, 123–25

relationship with God, 24, 28, 51, 69, 71, 74, 83–86, 98, 100, 112

remembering the past, 9, 103, 104, 105

repetitions, 4, 5, 12, 16, 19, 64, 82

report and story, the difference, 55, 63, 95, 96

Reuben (son of Jacob), 41, 64, 65, 66, 70, 140, 143, 149

royal counselors, 7

sanctuary, xv, 7, 8, 15, 24, 39, 79, 81, 85, 86, 87, 88, 91, 100, 101, 103, 105, 109, 111, 149
Sanctuary Narrative (SaN), 8, 69, 71, 74–84, 86, 87, 105, 147, 148, 149, 150, 153
Sarah, 31–35, 49, 51, 52, 56, 59, 118, 119, 120, 135, 136, 137
Saul's supporters, xv
Sea, deliverance at, xiv, 8, 24, 29, 76–80, 108, 123–25
Seir, 33, 44, 45, 47, 48, 50, 141
select, xiii, 3, 7, 9, 11, 12, 17, 18, 41, 118, 119
selection(s), xiii, 6, 12, 19, 24, 25, 104, 105, 113, 121
shared interests, 15, 96
Shechem, 31, 38, 39, 45, 46, 54, 56, 68, 117, 139, 140, 141
Shimei ben Gera, xv
short(ness), 6, 8, 11, 16, 17, 19
signals for storytelling: Sanders, 17
Sinai, xv, 4, 8, 21, 24, 78–87, 89, 91, 92, 93, 94, 97, 100, 105, 146, 149, 152
skeletons to flesh out: Dalley, 17
Sodom (and Gomorrah), 32, 35, 118, 119, 120, 135, 136
Song of Moses, 8, 24, 79
sources
    continuous, xiii, xv, 2, 5, 12, 13, 14, 16, 20, 24, 25, 31, 41, 52, 89, 149
    J, E, D, P, xv, 3
    pentateuchal, xiii, 4, 7, 9, 24, 26, 29, 41, 76, 90
spies, 94, 96, 154
Stories of David's Middle Years, 106
Stories of David's Rise, 106
story. See report and story, the difference
storyteller(s), xiii, 5, 6, 7, 12, 13, 16, 17, 18, 20, 23, 24, 33, 35, 36, 39, 42, 43, 45, 56, 65, 66, 67, 73, 81, 85, 96, 117, 118, 119, 120, 121, 124, 133, 141, 143, 147, 148, 149, 150, 158
storytelling, 2, 6, 17, 18, 24, 25, 26, 35, 42, 43, 64
studies in humanity, xv, 7, 8, 26, 100, 103

subjectivity, 23, 105
Succoth, 33, 38, 39, 45, 54, 56, 76, 139
Supplementary Hypothesis, xiii, 2

tabernacle, 87, 88, 89, 90, 92, 93
Tamar, 63, 143
telling of story, 7, 12, 17, 18, 44, 60, 65, 80, 81, 118, 132, 136
tent of meeting, 87, 88, 90, 91, 94, 95
text as base for
    operations, 6, 8, 24
    reflection, 2, 6, 17, 26, 35, 100, 136
    storytellers, xiii, 17, 42
    users, xiii, xiv, 6, 11, 12
"text-as-base-for-user," xiv, 12, 15, 17, 25, 26
theology/theologian(s)/theological, xiv, 5, 6, 7, 8, 10, 15, 19, 20, 28, 30, 33, 35, 57, 59, 60, 62, 66, 77, 79, 83, 93, 99, 100, 103, 105, 112, 113, 119, 123, 124
theophany, 39, 67, 83, 86, 89, 100, 151
Torah, 83, 85
tradition pool, 7, 128
traditional investigation, 11–15, 107–15
traditionalists, 1
treasured possession/people, 84, 86, 98

unconditional, 29, 84
unsystematic, 89, 90
user-base, xiv, 17, 25, 31, 53, 103, 104
users, xiii, xiv, 2, 4, 5, 6, 9, 11, 12, 13, 14, 16, 17, 18, 23, 24, 76, 77, 80, 104, 118, 120, 121, 147, 151

variant(s), xiii, xiv, 2, 6, 7, 11, 12, 13, 15, 16, 18, 20, 24, 27, 31, 35, 37, 39, 45, 53, 64, 78, 79, 86, 88, 103, 104, 123, 124, 130, 136, 154
version(s), xiii, xv, 5, 6, 7, 18, 23, 24, 29, 36, 37, 38, 39, 40, 43, 44, 53, 54, 64, 65, 72, 75, 76, 79, 80, 98, 106, 123, 124, 130, 132, 133, 136, 139, 142, 143
violence, 27, 28, 29, 55, 130
visionary construct(s), 91, 93, 100

water from rock, 81, 94, 96, 153

Wellhausen's views, xiv, 3, 4, 9, 12, 64,
    77
women's inner world, 41, 42, 50
world of
    men, 49
    tribes, 49
    women, 49
wrestling at the Jabbok, 44, 47, 139

Yahwist, xiii, xiv, xv, 3, 8, 19, 20, 41, 42,
    60, 82, 87
yhwh (YHWH), 1, 2, 4, 5, 6, 13, 20,
    38–43, 50, 55, 65, 71, 72, 73, 74,
    77, 81, 84, 86, 91, 93, 96, 119, 120,
    131, 132, 133, 138, 139, 151

Zilpah, 41, 50, 55, 143